Affirming Equity

A Framework for Teachers and Schools

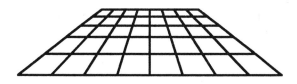

Fred Rodriguez
University of Kansas

KENDALL/HUNT PUBLISHING COMPANY
Dubuque, Iowa

CONTENTS

PREFACE   xiii

PART ONE   **Framing the Equity Perspective**   1

Chapter One   **A Framework for Equity**   3

The Children at the School House Door   4

Equity in Education: Lessons Learned   5

The Single-Group Approach   6

The Comparative-Group Approach   7

The Multicultural Approach   8

Equity in Education: A Working Definition   10

What Have We Learned?   13

Summary   15

Assigned Task   17

Discussion Questions   19

Individual or Group Work   25

Chapter Two   **A Call for Reform**   29

What Did We Learn in the 80s?   30

The Nature of the Reports   32

Why Is Systemic Reform Needed?   33

Problems with the Status Quo   37

The Reform Cycle of Excellence and Equity   37

A History of Inequity   38

Higher Standards and Equity   39

Equity and Reform   40

The Many Names of Reform   41

Questions and Lessons for Reform Efforts   42

Criteria for Progress   43

Summary   45

Discussion Questions   49

Small Group Work   53

Chapter Three   **Striving for Quality-with-Equity Schools**   **57**

The Effective-Schools Movement   58

The School as a Unit of Change   61

School Improvement   62

Analysis of Correlates   65

Planning Teams   67

Developing School Improvement Plans   68

An Outcomes-Based Approach   69

Quality-with-Equity   70

Current Trends   71

The Continuum of Equitable Competence for Schools   75

Summary   79

Discussion Questions   83

Small Group Work   89

Individual or Group Work   91

PART TWO	**Linking Equity to Teaching and Learning**	**97**
Chapter Four	**Classroom Issues and Their Impact on Learning**	**99**

Effective Teachers   99

Reform in Classroom Instruction   100

Teacher-Centered Instruction   100

Teacher Expectations   103

Classroom Interactions   105

Raising Expectations   106

TESA   107

Assessing Intelligence and Ability   107

The Power of Tradition   108

Grouping and Tracking Practices   109

Reforms in Teacher Education 116

A Growing Shortage of Ethnic Minority Teachers 118

Teacher Testing and Certification 119

The Holmes Group 121

Summary 122

Discussion Questions 127

Assigned Group Work 133

Individual or Small Group Work 135

Chapter Five **Diversity: An American Trademark 151**

Terminology 153

A Shift in our Diversity 155

The Children of the 21st Century 155

Ethnicity 156

Ethnic Minority Groups 157

A Nation of Immigrants 157

The Melting Pot 158

The Anglo-Conformity Theory 161

Cultural Pluralism 162

Addressing Diversity: A Five-Level Approach 167

Summary   171

Discussion Questions   175

Small Group Work   183

Individual or Group Work   185

Chapter Six   **A Generation in Jeopardy   189**

Growth of the At-Risk Population   190

At-Risk Students   192

Ethnicity   196

Past and Current Responses   197

Indicators for At-Risk Students   199

Current Responses to At-Risk Students   201

Compensatory Education   202

Assessing the Needs of At-Risk Students   206

Guidelines for Prevention Strategies   206

Guidelines for Identification Strategies   208

Summary   210

Discussion Questions   215

Individual and Group Work   219

Worksheets 1, 2, 3, 4   220

Chapter Seven   **A Host of Languages: Policies and Issues   225**

Historical Overview   226

Role of the Federal Government   228

Bilingual Education   231

Assessing the School's Perspective   234

Unresolved Issues in Bilingual Education   235

English as a Second Language   237

Legal Implications   238

Lau v. Nichols   239

State Involvement   240

The English-Only Movement   241

English-Plus   242

Summary   242

Discussion Questions   245

Individual or Group Work   253

Chapter Eight   **Instructional Materials: A Matter of Use   259**

Impact of Textbooks and Instructional Materials   260

Who Selects the Textbooks and Instructional Materials?   260

State Textbook-Adoption Policies   261

Adoption Policies and Equity   262

Reviewers   263

Is the Task Too Large and Too Difficult?   265

Funding   265

Publishers Respond   266

Local Strategies   269

Textbook Evaluation   270

A Sampling Technique for Equity   271

Technology   276

Strategies to Counter Biased Material   279

Summary   280

Discussion Questions   283

Small Group Work   287

Individual Work   305

PART III   **Affirming Equity: Strategies for Teachers and
                    Schools   311**

Chapter Nine   **Understanding Change: Redefining Staff Development   313**

A Matter of Priority   314

Effective Staff Development   314

The Problem of Isolation   317

Collaboration   318

Efficacy   319

Locus of Control   319

Understanding Change   322

Classroom and School Improvement   323

A Matter of Time   324

A Continuum of Staff Development   325

Results-Oriented Staff Development   327

Basic Beliefs or Assumptions on Staff Development   329

Summary   329

Discussion Questions   333

Individual and Small Group Work   339

Chapter Ten   **Moving Forward   345**

Developing a Capacity for Change   348

Developing a Strategic Plan   348

Formulating Strategic Goals   351

Assessing Where You Are   353

Developing the "Can-Do" Approach   354

Assessing Equity: An Individual Equity Action Plan   355

Levels of Equity Understanding   356

Assessing Equity: Classroom Applications   359

Assessing Equity: School-Wide Applications   360

Guiding Principles   361

Gauging Progress   363

Summary   364

Discussion Questions   367

Small Group Work   371

INDEX   385

FIGURES

1. Equity: A Multidimensional Concept   12
2. Shifts in Society   34
3. Differences Between Industrial Age and Information Age and the Relationship to Education   35
4. The Transition   36
5. Correlates of an Effective School   61
6. Outcomes-Based Approach   70
7. Change in Number of Course Units Required for High School Graduation   72
8. Increased Academic Requirements   73
9. The Continuum of Equitable Competence   75
10. Reforms in Teacher Education   116
11. The U.S. Teaching Force Ethnically   118
12. Ethnic Breakdown of Students and Teachers   119
13. State Required Testing for Initial Certification of Teachers   120
14. State Required Testing for Initial Certification of Teachers   120
15. Percent of Change in U.S. Population by Race and Ethnicity, 1989–1990   151
16. U.S. Total Population by Race and Ethnicity—1990   152
17. Percent of U.S. Population by Race and Ethnicity—1990   152
18. High School Graduation Rates   193
19. States Using Minimum Competency Testing   204
20. Evolutionary Pattern of Language Treatment in the U.S.   227
21. Number of Persons with Non-English Mother Tongues by State   229
22. State Textbook-Adoption Policies   261
23. State Textbook-Adoption Process   264
24. Rating the Level of Equity Input   306
25. Effective Staff Development   328
26. Results-Oriented Staff Development   328
27. Classroom Applications   359
28. Analyzing Your Department   361
29. School-Wide Applications   362

PREFACE

We appear to be at a moment in our history in which a series of very important policy decisions will have to be made concerning American education. The two major educational policy goals we face are: creating a quality system of education as well as a system of schooling that is equitable.

The mid-1990s are alive with the spirit of change in our system of education. The future of education will be affected by the recommendations of the various commissions, research studies and task forces cited throughout this text. To what extent systemic change takes place remains to be seen. It would appear that the tidal wave of recommendations will produce basic changes in how teachers are trained, how schools will position themselves for diversity and change, and how elementary and secondary schools will be organized to meet these demands for the 21st century.

It is all too easy when discussing equity in education to ignore the diversity of policies and practices within the concept and thereby to limit the scope of its development. Equity in education, as a general category, is all too often collapsed into one or the other of its constituent elements: for example, the special needs and programs for students from ethnic minority groups or the problems and possibilities of teaching in a multiracial classroom. One of the purposes of this text is to broaden the terms of reference so that the various elements that comprise equity can be individually distinguished and yet still be seen as part of a coordinated whole-school concept.

The buzz words of the '90s have been: quality and equity. What do these two terms mean? Are they mutually exclusive? Quite the contrary, they reinforce one another. Quality and equity are in conflict only if equal outcomes are expected. Quality means that some students will do better than others; equity means that each student will be given an equal chance. The crucial test of the reforms urged in this text will be whether improvements in American education become available for *all* students.

The topics and issues presented in this text are designed to stimulate discussion, create dialogue, and provide varying perspectives about the issues at stake in the current debate over quality-with-equity in our schools.

I raise the issues in this book not only with the hope of resolving them here, but also with the belief that it is necessary to place the various issues surrounding equity in a broader perspective. To treat equity as an administrative problem or as merely the re-shifting of curriculum priorities denies the relationships between equity and the other aspects of our educational system. The reform for equity improvement must be accompanied by significant changes in a variety of other areas within our schools.

Part I: Framing the Equity Perspective begins with Chapter One—**Developing a Framework for Equity**. This chapter provides a brief background on the use and misuse of the terminology related to providing an equitable education. The chapter describes three common approaches used by schools over the past several years and their subsequent successes and shortcomings. The chapter concludes with a working definition of equity and the premise upon which it is based. Chapter Two—**A Call for Reform** examines the current insights into the dilemma of reform and the magnitude of those movements. The chapter examines the nature of the reports, the call for reform, the many names of reform, and the need for systemic reform. Chapter Three—**Striving for Quality-with-Equity Schools** is designed to examine the movement toward effective schools; explore the process of school improvement; highlight current movements that are intended to address a more challenging and responsive system of education and to present a continuum of equity that schools can use to measure their progress.

Part II: Linking Equity to Teaching and Learning begins with Chapter Four—**Classroom Issues and Their Impact on Learning**. This chapter is designed to examine effective teaching, teacher expectations, learning styles of students and the role and responsibility of teacher education programs. Chapter Five—**Diversity: An American Trademark** is intended to help focus our direction and planning with regard to the ethnic diversity of its students. The chapter attempts to address three fundamental questions: What should be the role of the school in addressing ethnic diversity? How much diversity are we willing to allow in our society... in our schools? And, what is the future of diversity in this country? An examination of the melting pot, separatism and cultural pluralism also are discussed. Chapter Six—**A Generation in Jeopardy** is organized to focus on the growing number of students who are at-risk of failing within the education system. Who are they? What are their needs? How can the schools position themselves to be more responsive? Demographic information is provided to give a broad scope of the generation that is now in the schools across this country—a generation that is in jeopardy. Chapter Seven—**A Host of Languages: Policies and Issues** provides a variety of viewpoints on the educational needs of linguistically different students and the most popular methods used in addressing those special needs. Chapter Eight—**Instructional Materials: A Matter of Use** addresses the importance of instructional materials in education, identifies who selects textbooks and instructional materials, examines state adoption policies, identifies criteria for the selection of materials, and provides the opportunity to evaluate materials.

Part III: Affirming Equity: Strategies for Teachers and Schools begins with Chapter Nine—**Understanding Change: Redefining Staff Development**. The chapter's intent is to briefly examine the process that schools generally use in educating staff; identify those approaches that seem to more effective than others; understand the isolation of the teaching profession; outline what it means to collaborate as professionals; examines efficacy and its impact on school improvement; identifies characteristics of the change process; and identifies a continuum for changing current practice and priorities that can better position schools engaged in staff development initiatives. Chapter Ten—**Moving Forward** provides what a strategic plan would look like; highlights what areas are involved in the equity-improvement process; and introduces three levels of assessing equity within the system. The chapter is embedded with questions and strategies to assist teachers and schools in addressing equity.

This approach to equity is unique for two reasons. First, the book adds the needed conceptual clarity to what is meant by equity. Throughout the text, equity is defined, identified and incorporated as an integral part of a quality school. Equity is not treated as a singular issue that is to be considered and implemented if the need arises, rather it is presented as an imperative for becoming a quality school.

Second, the issues identified throughout the text are intended to: stimulate the reader; develop an interaction between the issues; and to provide the opportunity to generate written reactions and responses. The book offers no easy solutions to the problems facing education; rather it warns that what appears to be simple solutions often are only partial answers that may waste resources and frequently not adequately provide for students. What is needed is a fundamental change in the prevailing approach to educating students. No single formula for creating such educational settings is proposed here. Emphasis is on the development of the many links to equity which reflect the diversity and pluralism that characterizes our country. Each chapter concludes with discussion questions, individual group or small group activities. In addition, several chapters have case studies that amplify the concepts in the material covered. I have strived to articulate realistic notions of what constitutes equity and have suggested better ways to do the things that are necessary. Everything that should be known about equity has not been put into this book. No single book can address all the issues involving equity. This book intentionally covers only those issues most central to the task of improving all our schools to have a more equitable and quality system. This book does not, for example, address specific ethnic groups, the concept of culture, sex and gender, religion, age or disabilities. There are numerous publications that are available to you with these specific issues and information.

In short, this book attempts to assist you develop an equity perspective in your teaching and learning. As educators we are being held more accountable for providing *all* our students with the most meaningful and quality educational experience we can. The personal contributions you make can only lead to an improved social and educational system and an increasingly mature perspective for you, your colleagues and for all of your students.

I wish to acknowledge those individuals and institutions who were supportive and provided permission to include their excellent work. Shirley McCune and Gretchen Wilbur—McRel Sex Equity Center, Larry Cuban and David Tyack—Stanford University.

I have been a teacher for all but two years of my professional life. I have great faith in education and I have profited much from my involvement in all its phases. My experience in teaching has contributed enormously to my growth and fulfillment, not just as a teacher, but as a person as well. I am deeply grateful to this institution called a school and believe it to be the most significant profession. As a member of the education family, however, I am also keenly aware of its shortcomings, especially its slowness to respond to the current needs of society and youth and to the new perspectives offered by our diverse population. Perhaps this book may help to speed those needed adaptations. If so, I will be happy to have made some small contribution to the profession that has given so much to me.

F.R.

Part 1

Framing the Equity Perspective

A Framework for Equity

1

Introduction

Why some students succeed and some fail in school has been the subject of much research and debate during the last quarter of this century. During the first half of this century, equity, for the most part, meant making sure that each citizen had equal access to schooling. During the last quarter of this century and beyond, the primary interpretation of equity will be one of an equitable educational opportunity to benefit from a quality education. That is to say, it will not be enough to simply say a responsive system of education is one that makes educational services available in the established ways. The structure of the public schools was designed in a period when, at best, equal access was the goal. However, it has been discovered that equal access did not necessarily mean equal access to a quality education. The provision of equal access to a mediocre education is a goal unworthy of our schools.

Today our schools are unsuccessful with too many students. Why schools fall short of their mission to provide all students with an equitable and a high-quality education continues to dominate our thinking well into the '90s. Concerns are mounting that even the "best" schools, because of their comparatively high rankings and honors, largely escape the scrutiny that would reveal that they too are seriously deficient. Much more important today and in the future, will be the quality of those services schools provide and how they are delivered to a growing diverse student population.

A child without an adequate education is a child without a future. The future of all of us depends on our confidence that education can make a difference. Without a more equitable and high-quality educational system that addresses the needs of every learner, we will not secure this country's future. The future will belong to those who have the skills, those who know how to acquire new skills and those who can quickly adapt to a rapid social, economic and technical change.

The public's expectations exert tremendous influence on the schools. That list of expectations has been growing ever since colonial times, and it shows no sign of getting shorter. Consider your wishes for your own child and the children in your community. You want them to be healthy and emotionally strong, to feel confident, be ambitious, and have integrity. You want them to appreciate the aesthetic work of others and to be creative themselves. They must have the knowledge and commitment to be fully participating citizens. They must experience the richness and heritage of diverse cultures as they come to understand their own. You want children to understand and appreciate the skills they need to work and live harmoniously with neighbors and family. You want them to be sound, curious and critical thinkers. And of course, they must be competent in the basics, able to read, write, compute, and find information in a variety of resources. As Goodlad succinctly put it, "We want it all."

Chapter One—**A Framework for Equity** is intended to provide a brief background on the use and misuse of the terminology of the past twenty-five years with regard to equity in education. Why have so many good efforts gone astray? Why is the issue of equity still confronting our consciousness and our schools? The chapter describes three common approaches used by schools over the past several years and their subsequent successes and shortcomings. By providing a framework by what is meant by equity and the comprehensiveness of the concept, we may be better positioned to address our efforts in our schools and classrooms in a more systematic manner. The chapter concludes with discussion questions designed to focus on our perspective, our role and personal responsibility as educators to the concept of equity.

The Children at the School House Door

In the fall of 1993 3,600,000 youngsters entered school; 25 percent of these children live in poverty; 14 percent have teenage mothers; 16 percent were either physically or mentally handicapped, 15 percent spoke a language other than English, and 14 percent were children of unmarried parents.

Today, out of 80 million households in the nation, over 9 million are headed by a single female parent, 16 percent of whom are under age 25, 50 percent unemployed, 42 percent living in central cities. In fact, every day in America, 40 teenage girls give birth to their third child (Hodgkinson, 1993). Between one-fourth and one-third are latchkey children; and nearly 30 percent will not finish high school.

The 1950s family is gone. The family of today is different, maybe no better or no worse, but different. These children clearly reflect the forces at work in our society. That greater numbers will bring with them financial, racial, ethnic and socio-economic stress is becoming well known to educators. Less well understood is that if current trends persist, the proportion of children at-risk for school failure will grow with each passing year for the foreseeable future.

Today it is the nation's educational system that faces the challenge. Although at-risk children represent a minority of school enrollments, their impact on the system is great.

These very children, who many educators project to be 30 percent of the school population, will inherit the responsibility for sustaining and directing the social, political and economic institutions of the nation.

In the ideal sense, education in the United States is based on the values of democracy, freedom and equal access. In a break with the rigid systems of class and caste, on which education in most of the world was and still is founded, our educational system proposed to tear down these barriers and to provide all students with an equal education. Education was to be, as Hoarce Mann claimed, "the great equalizer." These were not to be charity schools for the poor, but rather free public schools for the sons and daughters of farmers, businessmen, professionals, and the rest. Mann intended common schools to teach the knowledge and habits citizens needed to function in a democracy. From the beginning, however, schools fell short of Mann's vision. Even so, we continue to pin our hopes on the public school. Americans see it as the ideal place in a democracy for all children to get a free and necessary education. Our schools have consistently failed to provide an equitable education for many students.

Equity in Education: Lessons Learned

If the concept of equity is to provide a sense of purpose and priority for American education, it must be clearly understood. The concept of equity in education has been historically plagued with ambiguity, generality and confusion. If we do not learn from our efforts of the past, we will continue these failed lessons in the future.

The 1960s and 1970s brought a new and dynamic challenge to American education. Equality of educational opportunity was the thrust in our schools. Much of that effort was focused on the "content" of equality of educational opportunities. That is, members of groups whose histories and cultures had been omitted from or stereotyped within the school curriculum began to request, sometimes demand, accurate, balanced and fair representation. First Blacks, then Hispanics, Native Americans and Asian Americans called for reform. Then came the new pluralism, with America's White ethnic groups appealing for educational inclusion of their roles and history. Cutting across all racial, ethnic and mainstream American groups were women, special populations, religious groups, and linguistically different groups who rightfully pointed out how their perspectives and contributions had also been omitted from the curriculum of our schools. Schools were in the business of attempting to diversify their curriculum in the name of equal educational opportunity.

These various approaches were attempts to either: (1) ensure equal educational opportunities, (2) address the special educational needs of a targeted population, (3) incorporate into the curriculum historical and educational experiences of a particular minority group or of all minority groups; as a way of including in the curricula a local or regional minority perspective (usually one major group), (4) serve as a compensatory approach in which the curriculum portrays "minority" groups as heroic or martyred, or (5) focus on international issues rather than on ethnic, racial, and other cultural groups in the United States. Whatever the merits of these efforts were, they were at best incomplete and are now viewed to be preferential, appeasing or evasive.

There are three approaches that were implemented for varying reasons and with varying degrees of success. They were the: (1) single-group approach, (2) comparative-group approach and (3) multicultural approach. By examining the rationale behind each of the three approaches; as well as the degree of success each had, we may be in a better position to understand how the concept of equity is similar and yet, different. More importantly, if we fail to learn from these lessons of the past, we are assured to repeat them in the future.

The Single-Group Approach

When the civil rights movement began in the mid-60s Blacks—in particular—demanded that schools and other social institutions respond more adequately to their needs and aspirations. They called for more Black educators for Black students, community input in their schools, specific courses of study about their culture and heritage, and the revision of textbooks that would more accurately reflect the history and culture of Black Americans. In time, other ethnic groups such as Mexican-Americans and American Indians, made similar demands on schools and colleges. Those institutions that responded, established courses on specific ethnic groups, which were characterized as monoethnic courses. An assumption was that only a member of an ethnic group could teach a course on that particular group, and a strong focus on White racism and how Whites have oppressed non-White minorities was evident. A pervasive assumption made during this single-group movement was that Black studies, for example, were needed only by Black students and that Asian-American studies were needed only by Asian-American students.

These single-group approaches focused on the specific richness and uniqueness of the particular culture. Single-group approaches typically included the historical and cultural knowledge of a particular group. Emphasis was on the individual as an ethnic member.

Banks (1991), one of the leading scholars on ethnic minority education, referred to these single-group approaches as ethnic studies. He defined ethnic studies as the scientific and humanistic study of the histories, cultures, and experiences of the ethnic groups within a society. Ethnic studies refers primarily to the objectives, concepts, methods and materials that make up the courses of study within schools, colleges and universities.

However, single-group approaches initiated in the past have declined in popularity. There are a number of possible explanations for this trend. Single-group approaches encountered the following stumbling blocks: (1) inadequate teacher preparation and commitment; (2) fragmented integration with school curriculum areas; (3) unresolved debate about content, grade levels, and student populations; (4) who would or should participate in such courses of study; (5) lack of community support; and (6) reliance and existence from temporary external support.

It is unfortunate that some educators often promoted separatism by advocating these approaches that were limited to the political power struggles of the groups involved. Although there is a place in education for comprehensive study of a single group, our educational system must address and teach all children of all people to include understanding that emphasizes equality of both ethnic minority and majority groups.

The Comparative-Group Approach

In the late '60s and early '70s, the early proponents of the single-group approach were joined by a group of scholars advocating a new ethnicity. They claimed that not only have ethnic minority groups not been completely assimilated and acculturated into the American culture, but neither have many other ethnic groups, particularly those descendants of Southern and Eastern European immigrants. These included such White ethnics as Polish Americans, Jewish Americans, Italian Americans, Greek Americans and Slovak Americans. As more and more ethnic groups began to demand the inclusion of their histories and cultures into the curriculum, schools began to offer the comparative-group approach which focused on several ethnic groups which viewed the experiences of ethnic groups from comparative experiences.

A basic assumption of the comparative-group approach was that ethnic groups had both similar and different experiences in the United States and that a comparative study of the groups could result in useful understanding between groups. This approach was based on the premise that it could: (1) help students view historical and contemporary events from a diverse ethnic perspective; (2) also help students develop a cross-cultural competency (the ability to function within a range of cultures); (3) provide students with cultural and ethnic alternatives; (4) also attempt to reduce ethnic and cultural separatism and enable students to understand their own cultures better; or (5) assist students to expand their understanding of what it means to be human, to accept the fact that ethnic minority groups are functional and valid, and to realize that a group can be evaluated only within a particular cultural context.

There is an infinite amount of information available about the great number of ethnic groups in the United States. It is unrealistic to assume that all levels of education can or should encompass all of it. Even if they could, the merits of this approach are questionable. There are many reasons to suspect that the mere memorization of ethnic facts is inadequate for teachers to understand the prominence of ethnicity; and the complex dynamics of cultural diversity in America; as well as their implications for education. These two approaches—single and comparative—were important beginnings, but in the long-term analysis have failed. There are several reasons: (1) they tended primarily to be curricular in scope; (2) they had little impact on school-wide policies and instructional practices; (3) they were usually offered as electives; (4) if offered, they were viewed as an "add-on" to the "regular curriculum" of the school; (5) they tended only to be initiated in schools where ethnic diversity existed; and (6) many were programs supported by temporary external funding sources, thus they never became an institutionalized part of the system. Once the funding support for these programs was no longer available, many of these programs ceased to exist.

Although we may all want our students to get along and be sensitive to and respect one another, these two approaches by themselves, without addressing the far more difficult issues of school-wide reform, simply continue to scratch the surface of educational shortcomings in our quest for an equitable system of education for all students.

The Multicultural Approach

An alternative concept for managing this ever-increasing body of information on ethnicity, pluralism and overall school practices and policies lead to the "program" of multicultural education. Educators became interested in an educational reform movement that would not only address the issues and concerns of ethnic groups, but the educational issues of other groups such as women, disabled populations, religious groups, linguistically different groups, socioeconomic status and age. This broader, encompassing movement became known as multicultural education.

The Intent of the Multicultural Approach

To endorse multicultural education was to endorse the principle that there is no one model American. To endorse multicultural education was to understand and appreciate the differences that exist among the nation's citizens. It is to see these differences as a positive force in the continuing development of a society which professes a wholesome respect for the intrinsic worth of every individual. The positive elements of a diverse society will be realized only if there is a healthy interaction among the diverse groups which comprise the nation's people. To accept multicultural education was to recognize that no group lives in a vacuum and that each group exists as part of an interrelated whole.

This multicultural approach was initiated and designed to be more multidimensional in its implementation—that is, far more comprehensive than the curricular thrust of the single or comparative group approaches were. However, the evidence since the mid 70s indicates that this never occurred. In fact, the multicultural approach has historically been interpreted and where implemented, as one dimensional: that is, a euphemism for "minority education."

The Reality of the Multicultural Approach

Progress was impeded, to a large degree, by the lack of a clear understanding of the goals and the necessary process of such an approach. The multicultural approach as a general category was all too often collapsed into one or another of these elements: (1) the special educational needs of students from ethnic minority backgrounds; or (2) the problems and possibilities of teaching in an ethnically diverse school or classroom. The multicultural approach became a popularized slogan, and the power and potential of the approach was lost to many. In the 1990s, when multicultural education is mentioned, many people first think of lessons in human relations, units about ethnic holidays, famous heroes or heroines, education in urban schools, or multicultural food festivals. Simply attempting to define the term multicultural was and still is one of the major stumbling blocks. The potential for substantive change in schools is diminished when multicultural education is interpreted and initiated as it has been for over the past twenty-five years.

Lessons Learned

What we have learned is that because of this narrow and limited viewpoint with the multicultural approach, over the past twenty-five years, evidence of very few pockets of success across the country are found.

The missing element in the three approaches has been that they have been approached and understood to mean that they were either "content" in scope or "a program" that needed to be implemented. The three approaches cited have not impacted the educational system in any long-term systemic manner. The multicultural approach, in particular, was not viewed as a concept that was multidimensional. The principle problem which emerges from an analysis of these three approaches is *not* one of content, but is one of interpretation and application to the total school process.

This gap between principle and practice has occurred despite the best intentions of literally thousands of individuals, schools, publishers, state departments of education, and accreditation agencies. The primary reason for the gap has been and continues to be the absence of a holistic view.

There is a widespread perception that these three approaches are for students of color, for urban schools, or for at risk students. This belief is based on the roots of the three approaches, which grew out of the Civil Rights and equal educational opportunity movements of the 60s and 70s. The primary objective of these three approaches were identified as addressing the needs of those students who historically had been most neglected or miseducated by the schools. In attempting to strike more of a balance, it was believed that attention should be paid to developing curriculum materials that reflected the reality of these students' history, culture and experience and that this curriculum should be destined particularly for schools populated primarily by children of diversity. These three approaches were historically necessary and are understandable today. However, the lessons of the past must be our framework for understanding the need to redirect our efforts and effectiveness with all students today who will soon be entering the 21st century.

Equity in Education: A Working Definition

We must understand that terms serve as ground rules for perceiving and understanding educational concepts. As we have learned, terms may have more than one meaning and thus may convey varying perceptions to different people. Single-group, comparative-group and the multicultural approaches were and continue to be common approaches for addressing specific concerns for a number of educators, scholars, organizations and agencies. In the 1990s, there is an increasing number of educational articles, journals, publications and policy statements with regard to multicultural education. However, much of this literature has taken the similar approach that was described in the 70s. We are positioning ourselves for repeated failure.

Today, the rationale for incorporating an equity perspective within all schools comes from many sources. Teachers and their professional organizations, parent groups, business and the private sector, state education agencies, colleges and universities, as well as public organizations, accreditation agencies, and foundations have all expressed the view that all Americans need to better understand, respect, appreciate and accept the diversity that exists in our society. A closer examination of these constituencies position indicates an understanding that is all too often narrow in focus.

As a teacher educator for the past seventeen years, I have had the primary role and responsibility for teaching the "multicultural education" courses. Through this personal experience, I have learned the term multicultural is often miscommunicated, certainly misinterpreted and eventually poorly designed and implemented by schools and teachers. With the history and continued confusion over the term multicultual, it is my belief that the term will continue to be plagued with uncertainty and misguided focus.

It is important for each of us to determine our own working definition of equity. Perhaps if we address equity from what it is *not*, only then can we begin to gain a clearer understanding of this inclusive educational concept.

Equity Is Not:

- ▶ a course or a subject area
- ▶ a miracle
- ▶ a unit of study on societal problems and concerns
- ▶ aimed at training teachers to work exclusively with ethnic minority student populations
- ▶ dependent upon the geographic setting of a school or the demographics of the student population
- ▶ a packaged program
- ▶ a program that is added to the current school offerings
- ▶ a quick-fix
- ▶ limited only to the delivery of a curriculum in a school setting
- ▶ an event
- ▶ treating all students the same
- ▶ limited to the distribution of resources

Defining Equity in Education

It is not my intent to have everyone accept and memorize the following definition of equity in education. Quite the contrary, I would hope that each individual at least understand the premise that the concept is founded on and then develop their own working definition of what equity means. Equity in education is defined as:

> The fair and equal treatment of all members of our society who are entitled to participate in and enjoy the benefits of an education. Equity in education is based on the premise that all students—regardless of race, color, national origin, sex, native language, age, social or economic status, family structure and lifestyle, religious preference or disability—have the right to an education of equal quality.

Equity by definition is expansive. Because it is about all people, it is also for all people. My framework for equity is thus a very broad and inclusive one. The concept of equity is multidimensional. (See Figure 1.)

Equity is at least three things: (1) a concept, (2) an educational reform movement, and (3) a process. It is concerned with the overall school policies and practices that our school systems endorse and reinforce—which may or may not be detrimental to the education some students receive. Equity is concerned with the outcomes of student achievement at all levels. As we have learned from the past, it is simply not enough to understand differences that may exist in our system. No educational philosophy or

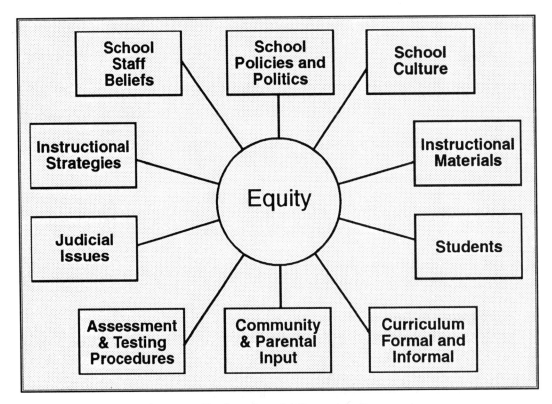

Figure 1. Equity: A multidimensional concept.

approach is worth pursuing unless is focuses on: (1) raising the achievement levels of all students, and (2) provides the opportunities for all students to become critical and productive members of a democratic society. What is required of all schools is the positive endorsement of such differences and a system responsive to those unique qualities that students happen to bring to our schools.

Equity is a more comprehensive term because it includes equal educational opportunities while at the same time demanding fairness and the real possibility of equality of outcomes for a broader range of students. Equity in education is the structuring of educational priorities, commitments, and the processes to reflect the reality of our diversity as a fact of life in the United States. Educational priorities must focus on developing and maintaining an awareness of our diversity as reflected by individuals, groups and communities. It requires commitment of educators to the basic concept of diversity as it is expressed through dimensional aspects of ethnicity, sex, language backgrounds, disabilities, religious beliefs, socioeconomic backgrounds and lifestyles. Equity in education recognizes that the maintenance of this diversity is crucial not only to a particular group's survival, but to the basic tenets that support the democratic ideal. Equity goes beyond providing the same resources and opportunities for all students. Equity must involve the interaction of students with teachers and other students, not merely the action of teachers and schools on students.

America is composed of many groups. The benefits of citizenship are distributed unevenly among many of these groups. Symptoms of inequity are easy to identify. For example, in or among the poor and many ethnic minority groups, as educators, we see: abnormally high drop-out rates, poor attendance at school, more at-risk youth, lower-track placements, special education placements, limited participation in the extra-curricular programs and overall a disproportionally lower representation in gifted programs. The list goes on, and almost all the national reports reinforce this uneven distribution. A broadly conceptualized equity perspective focusing on school reform represents a substantive way of changing the curriculum, the environment, the structure of the schools, the culture of the school, the policies, practices and instructional strategies so that all students will benefit.

No blueprint exists that will work for every school, nor should there be. The purpose here is not to suggest that equity is simplistic or a superficial set of activities, materials or approaches. On the contrary, a static "program in place" or a slick packaged program is in direct conflict with the framework of a comprehensive equity concept. If the purpose of education, however, is to prepare young people for productive and critical participation in a democratic and pluralistic society, the activities, strategies and approaches we use with them need to reflect these concerns. Schools, as currently structured, do little to prepare most students for this future. It is only by addressing all of the issues in a school in a systematic way that meaningful changes will be made.

What Have We Learned?

We learned from our past efforts that many educators interpreted equity to simply mean infusing regular school content with multicultural materials that reflect different customs, dress, food, cultures and other matters which fell under the label of multicultural appreciation. We have also learned that this has been a very limited perspective and that these efforts of the past contributed little to the solution of the fundamental problems of inequity in our schools today.

We also learned that there is a need to view equity from a broader dimension than single-group or comparative-group approaches. We learned that there is a need to distinguish equity from racism, sexism, elitism, ageism and exceptionalism, but simultaneously to understand the connections among those issues and equity.

Lessons Learned

▶   Articulating what we mean
▶   Program vs. concept
▶   Improvement is a process not an event
▶   Limited in focus
▶   No perceived need by some schools
▶   Failure to assess for academic gains
▶   Training and staff development methods
▶   Little transfer to classroom instruction

We learned that the equity concept strongly endorses the notion that all students—regardless of their backgrounds—should have an equal opportunity to learn in school. Therefore, all schools have a role and responsibility to the concept of equity. Equity is a concept, not a program. Our past efforts also failed to assess systematically whether the efforts made by many schools made any significant difference academically. We have also learned that success can be evident by how schools approach and implement training and staff development. Finally, a valuable lesson learned from the past is that there has been too little transfer to actual classroom instruction. By classroom instruction I mean the improvement of instructional skills, strategies, models, expectations, etc. versus textbooks and instructional materials.

Equity implies that some students, because of their characteristics, have a better chance to learn in schools as they are currently structured than do other students who do not belong to those groups or have different backgrounds. In the final analysis, we have also learned that equity is a moral and an ethical issue. Our student body is becoming more diverse than ever before. We have also come to learn and understand that our ability to understand these differences and to use them in constructive ways is still quite low.

From my experiences of working with schools, state agencies, professional organizations and higher education institutions, I firmly believe that if we don't take into consideration the lessons of the past, we will continue to fail in our collective efforts to ensure an equitable system of education for all students. Although educational leaders appear to agree that equity should be a part of the public schools policies and practices and an integral part of teacher training programs, the interest has yet to become reality.

Reluctance to incorporate equity appears to be five-fold: (1) many remain uncertain about what equity in education means, (2) many fail to see the link between equity and quality in our schools, (3) many are uncertain of how to proceed, (4) many fail to understand the comprehensive nature of equity, and (5) many are staff members of homogeneous public schools and colleges that operate as if equity is not needed in their particular setting. Many educators at such colleges and public schools continue to view equity from this persistent one-dimensional vision—ethnic minority populations. These educators seem to conclude that because the school has "only a few" if any ethnic minority students, the school doesn't have to address or worry about equity issues. If this rationale is taken to a logical conclusion, one would assume that students attending these schools are being prepared for a closed society where the same economic, political, social and cultural environment found in the school will always exist. Again, these attitudes, beliefs and behaviors are also a reflection of the continued misunderstanding and misinterpretation of the concept of equity.

We have spent a great deal of our time on the "content" of equity, that is, curriculum and materials. Equity in education is above all a process. First, it is ongoing and dynamic. No one ever stops learning and knowledge is never complete. Second, it is a process because it involves relationships among people. The sensitivity and understanding teachers show all of their students are often more important than the facts and figures they may know about the different groups. Third, and most important, equity is a process because it focuses on such intangibles as teacher's expectations, learning environments, students' learning styles, and other variables that are essential for schools to understand to be successful with all of their students.

What we have learned is that "process" is too often relegated to a secondary position, because "content" is easier to handle and has speedier results. For example, developing materials for a "multicultural fair" is far easier than eliminating the policy and practice of tracking in a school. Both are important, but the processes of equity are generally more complex, more politically volatile, or more threatening to vested interests. Changing a math series in a school is therefore easier than developing higher expectations for all students. The first involves changing one book for another; the other involves changing perceptions, behaviors, and knowledge, not an easy task. Equity must be accompanied by unlearning conventional wisdom as well as dismantling the policies and practices that disadvantage some students.

Summary

The framework for equity is based upon three principle beliefs about teaching and learning. Those beliefs are: (1) all students have the right to be treated fairly, (2) all students will learn when provided the proper learning opportunities, and (3) all students have the right to receive an equitable and quality education.

One may wonder, how can any educator argue with these three principles? Certainly, we would like to see all our current and future educators not only express these beliefs but more importantly, demonstrate these principles. However, these beliefs are not held by all educators. Repeatedly, in the forthcoming chapters we will see that the evidence is quite clear; either: (1) many educators don't believe in these principles, or (2) many educators do not understand the inequities they create in their schools and classrooms through their policies, practices and behaviors. This author happens to subscribe to the later rationale for many of the inequities that exist in our schools and classrooms today. From my experiences, most educators are sincerely interested in exploring ways to meet the educational needs of all of their students. The heart of most educators is in the right place, it is the structure, policies, practices, and the power of tradition that contribute to the inequities that are so vivid throughout our system of education.

Individual differences are a reality, and as we increase opportunities for personalizing learning within an institution called the school, we have to provide a structure which will respond to human diversity. We can say that equity, conceptualized as a broad-based school reform, can offer hope for change. By focusing on the major factors contributing to school failure, a broad conceptualization of equity permits educators to explore alternatives to a system that leads to failure for too many of its students. As history has indicated, the present structure has been geared to uniformity rather than diversity. During a period when high-quality in education is being emphasized, the institution must be updated to gear itself more effectively to individual learners and provide more personalized approaches to growth and development. Assuming that equity is the answer to school failure is simplistic at best, for it overlooks important social and educational issues that affect the daily lives of students. Educational failure is too complex an issue to be fixed by any single approach. However, if broadly conceptualized and implemented, equity can have a substantial impact on the educational experiences of most students. Therefore, the focus of equity will be on school reform, and on updating the school to make it more fully responsive to human variability. This, in essence, is equity in education.

 END NOTES

Banks, James A. *Teaching Strategies for Ethnic Studies.* 5th Edition. Boston: Allyn and Bacon, Inc., 1991.

Hodgkinson, Harold. *A Demographic Look at Tomorrow.* Institute for Educational Leadership, Inc., Center for Demographic Policy. Washington, DC, 1993.

 SUGGESTIONS FOR FURTHER READING

Banks, James A. and Banks, Cherry A. *Multicultural Education—Issues and Perspectives.* Allyn and Bacon, Boston: MA, 1989.

Banks, James A. *Teaching Strategies for Ethnic Studies.* 5th Edition. Allyn and Bacon, Boston: MA, 1991.

Bennett, Christine I. *Comprehensive Multicultural Education—Theory and Practice*. Allyn and Bacon, Boston: MA, 1986.

Grant, Carl A., and Christine E. Sleeter. *Turning on Leaning: Five Approaches to Multicultural Teaching*. Merrill Publishing Co, Columbus: OH, 1989.

Nieto, Sonia *Affirming Diversity—A Sociopolitical Context of Multicultural Education* Longman, New York: NY, 1992

 ## ASSIGNED TASK

1. Locate three educational journal articles from the past two years concerning multicultural or equity education. How are the authors of these articles using the terms? How do they differ from this author's interpretation?

2. Interview two practicing educators with regard to their viewpoints and understanding of equity at their building level.

Name: _____ Date: _____

✔ **DISCUSSION QUESTIONS**

1. What demographic information surprised you the most? Why?

_____

_____

_____

_____

_____

What significance does it have for education?

_____

_____

_____

_____

_____

2. What was the single-group approach? What was the rationale behind this approach? Was it successful? Why or Why not?

_____

_____

_____

_____

_____

_____

_____

3. What is the connection between the single and comparative group approaches?

_____

_____

_____

_____

_____

_____

4. According to the author, what was the missing element in the three common approaches cited in the chapter?

_____

_____

_____

_____

_____

_____

5. In reflecting upon your school experience, which of the three approaches was evident in your setting? Was it successful? Why or why not?

_____

_____

_____

_____

_____

_____

6. What is meant by the statement: Equity in education is a multidimensional concept. What is the difference between a program and a concept?

_____

_____

_____

_____

_____

_____

7. What are the lessons that must be learned from schools' and teachers' past efforts in attempting to address equity?

_____

_____

_____

_____

_____

_____

8. How would you modify the definition of equity provided in the chapter? Why?

_____

_____

_____

_____

_____

_____

Name: _____ Date: _____

INDIVIDUAL OR GROUP WORK

How would you respond to the following statements made by other educators? Be prepared to explain your response to each of the following statements.

1. "There just isn't the time to add all of these new ideas and curriculum content . . . besides, this is really an area for the social studies people to be concerned with."

Agree _____ Disagree _____

_____

_____

_____

_____

_____

_____

2. "I totally agree with equity in education, but I don't plan on teaching in a school with a large minority population, so I don't see that it involves me personally."

Agree _____ Disagree _____

_____

_____

_____

_____

_____

_____

3. "I am not so concerned with my students knowing 'equity stuff,' but whether he/she can read, write and compute. Let's get back to the basics—the 3 Rs and forget all of these frills and special interest group demands on education."

Agree _____ Disagree _____

_____

_____

_____

_____

_____

_____

4. "Differences, diversity, pluralism . . . why make such a big deal about it? We don't need to identify ourselves with our ethnicity, sex, or handicap. We're Americans!"

Agree _____ Disagree _____

---

5. "America is the land of opportunity. Everyone has an equal chance to 'make it' in this country, all you need is a little desire and initiative."

Agree _____ Disagree _____

---

6. "We did an equity program last year, we are working on 'whole language' this year."

Agree _____ Disagree _____

_____

_____

_____

_____

_____

_____

7. "This concept of equity education will promote a sense of 'separatism' in America, rather than uniting all of our citizens."

Agree _____ Disagree _____

_____

_____

_____

_____

_____

_____

A Call for Reform  2

Introduction

Reforming schools has been described as being as difficult as trying to change the wing structure of an airplane while in flight. Yet advocates of school reform argue that if we don't figure out how to do it successfully, we have little hope for reversing our nation's declining ability to prepare students for success in a rapidly changing world.

America's system of education has long been a model for the rest of the world. Its strength is drawn from hundreds of thousands of highly competent and dedicated teachers and administrators who put a tremendous amount of time and energy into their work. And its promise is evident in the precept that schooling must be and will be available to the entire population.

But despite past successes, the public's perception of American education has changed from pride to frustration. Why is this so? For one thing, there is a growing realization throughout the country that learning the same things that students learned 20 years ago isn't enough to prepare today's students for tomorrow's world.

Widespread concern has also resulted from the difficulty schools have in meeting the needs of an increasingly diverse student population. Social, moral, and political forces have created challenges that schools have never before had to address. How are schools to respond to the growing number of students whose native language in not English? And how are schools to deal with the social and economic issues that bring millions of students to school every day unready to learn because they suffer from poverty, drug abuse, or dysfunctional families?

The magnitude of these social issues is so enormous that many Americans worry that our education system in its current form may not be capable of responding adequately to the rapidly changing situation. The rules of the game have changed to the extent that the need to reform is evident.

Unfortunately, going beyond mere symbolism to true systemic reform is no easy matter. For better or worse, our education system has become a very stable institution that is highly resistant to change. Is there any way to overcome the inertia that threatens to destroy it? After more than a decade of trying, one thing is crystal clear—there are no quick fixes, or overnight solutions.

It may be helpful to think in terms of two different kinds of reform: 1) symbolic reform (involves changing something) and 2) systemic reform (replacing the whole thing). Systemic reform is comprehensive. It recognizes that a fundamental change in one aspect of a system requires fundamental changes in other aspects in order for it to be successful. For most educators, reform means some form of school improvement, such as the effective schools movement of the past decade. Yet for another, smaller group, reform means radical transformation, a systemic change in the structure of education itself. Do we really need such a radical change in our educational system?

Where does the concept of equity fit into this scenario? To begin with, *inequity,* perhaps more than any other single factor, has provided a major impetus for educational reform. In a single generation, disproportionate numbers of students are failing in large numbers within the educational system. Almost daily, in virtually every segment of our society the acknowledgment of this failure is being impacted. Certainly, the business community and the private sector are well aware of the dilemma of having so few students being successful in the educational system.

Chapter 2—**A Call for Reform** is intended to examine the current insights into the dilemma of reform and the magnitude of those reforms. The chapter includes: (1) the call for reform; (2) an examination of an antiquated system to meet the needs of the 21st Century, and (3) an analysis of equity within these reform efforts. Unless we view the bigger picture of reforming our schools and the relationship that equity has to those efforts, reforming our schools will unlikely be understood or achieved.

What Did We Learn in the 80s?

From the White House to the statehouse to the schoolhouse, there has been plenty of talk about school reform. Hundreds of organizations have embarked on diverse programs dealing with site-based management, school improvement plans, assessment, parental involvement, curriculum development, teacher collaboration, new student support services, schools of choice and so on. These initiatives reflect grave concerns for educational quality voiced increasingly by corporate and political leaders. The shortcomings of our schools has, of course, not gone unnoticed. Largely because of the political impact of *"A Nation at Risk,"* the 1980s was an era of feverish educational reform efforts. Legislators and boards of education in every state moved aggressively to tighten the course requirements for a high school diploma, raise teacher salaries, and set new standards for those entering the teaching profession. Everyone had new standardized tests—for teachers as well as students. Through these efforts, what have been our accomplishments? By most accounts, very little. The Policy Information Center of the Educational Testing Service (1990) issued a report summarizing the results of what it termed the "education reform decade" of the 1980s. The report looked at achievement test results ranging across all major curriculum areas, starting with reading, where it found no gains in average reading proficiency. The researchers identified some improvement in average math proficiency, but none at the higher levels of mathematics. Not surprisingly, American students were still performing low in science achievement. As for writing, the study concluded our students are poor writers, and they are not improving. They don't much like to write, and they like it less as they go through school. The only big increase, the study found, came in time in front of the television. Television watching increased substantially in the 1980s.

The reforms inspired by *A Nation at Risk* fell short of the aspirations and hope that accompanied the efforts. Many educators believed that those reforms contained no new ideas. After all, they called for more of the same: more core academic courses, more standardized tests, a longer school year, more money for teachers. By the end of the 1980s it was evident that the existing system of public education had been pushed to its limits and more of the same would not make any difference. As Fiske (1991) stated, "School reformers in the 1980s tried to squeeze more juice out of the orange. It took five years to realize that we were not dealing with an orange. We were holding a lemon."

Each new publication captured front-page attention, editorial comments and even significant time on the television networks. Public interest in the quality of education was clearly deep. The mood for change was strong. It even prompted several legislators to appropriate more money for education with the hope that it would produce higher quality.

The theme of the reports, taken as a group, was that the school curriculum had become soft, particularly for children with strong academic abilities; that standards were poorly defined and low; that the quality of teachers seemed to be declining; that teacher education programs were weak; and that schools were not meeting the needs of business and industry as well as they should have been. Most of the recommendations for improving schools were couched in general terms, but the reports converged on the remedy that a common curriculum for all children should be reinstated and that clear goals and expectations for pupils in the subjects of English, history, science, and mathematics be formulated.

The reforms of the 1980s were doomed from the outset because they asked American public schools to do something they were never designed to do, never did do, and never could do, (Fiske, 1991). Schools have been asked to prepare students—all students—for demanding, fast-changing jobs in the future with rigid structures and teaching methods designed for the factories of the early industrial age. Policymakers have been asking nineteenth-century institutions to educate people for the life in the twenty-first century.

The Nature of the Reports

It became very clear in the early 1990s that the American public was becoming increasingly concerned about the low quality of education our students were receiving. Educators, government agencies, the business community, and citizen groups launched research projects, commissions, and task forces to study schooling and to consider how to improve it. The following statements, drawn from a few of the studies, are presented to indicate both the nature of the problems that people were seeing in American education and the intensity of their concerns.

The nation's public schools are in trouble. By almost every measure—the commitment and competency of teachers, student test scores, truancy and dropout rates, crimes of violence—the performance of our schools falls far short of expectation. (*Making the Grade,* 1983).

Our Nation is at risk. Our once unchallenged preeminence in commerce, industry, science, and technological innovation is being overtaken by competitors throughout the world. . . . Education is only one of the many causes and dimensions of the problem, but it is the one that undergirds American prosperity, security, and civility. We report to the American people that while we can take justifiable pride in what our schools and colleges have historically accomplished and contributed to the United States and the well-being of its people, the educational foundations of our society are presently being eroded by a rising tide of mediocrity that threatens our very future as a Nation and a people. What was unimaginable a generation ago has begun to occur—others are matching and surpassing our educational attainments, (*Nation at Risk,* 1983).

Public education today faces. . .a crisis in confidence in which people have lost faith in the public schools' ability to educate its students; a crisis in performance in which students from public schools are graduating without basic or marketable skills necessary to pursue further education or a job; and a crisis in the concept of democracy in which officials are willing to write off a sizable portion of the student population as being uneducable and unentitled to educational opportunities, (Love, 1985).

While we have all been preoccupied with the twin deficits, budget and trade, a third deficit has developed that is more ominous in the long run—the deficit in highly motivated, well-trained people that will be required to provide a competitive world-class work force, (The Business Roundtable, 1989).

We do not believe the educational system needs repairing; we believe it must be rebuilt to match the drastic change needed in our economy if we are to prepare our children for productive lives in the 21st century, (Teachers for the 21st Century, Carnegie Forum, 1990).

We are a nation at risk. Today—not some time in the future—our nation must educate all of its children to be critical thinkers. This nation no longer can afford to "throw away" the 25 percent of our children who drop out of school each year; nor can it afford to write off two-thirds of those who graduate, but with such low skills that they are unable to function fully as citizens or workers, much less compete with students from other countries. The fact is that even our top 25 percent—those students we cite with pride—are not educated to today's world-class standards, (The Business Roundtable, 1991).

If we dream of the best for our children—at their schools, in their jobs, and throughout their lives—we must help them to aim higher. What was adequate in the past is no longer good enough, (The National Education Goals Report, 1991).

The nation's schools must be transformed into high-performance organizations in their own right. Despite a decade of reform efforts, we can demonstrate little improvement in student achievement. We are failing to develop the full academic abilities of most students and utterly failing the majority of poor, disadvantaged, and minority youngsters. By transforming the nation's schools into high-performance organizations, we mean schools relentlessly committed to producing skilled graduates as the rule, not the exception, (SCANS Report, 1991).

Why Is Systemic Reform Needed?

An education system fashioned specifically for the 19th and 20th century industrial revolution led by the United States is out of sync with the high-skilled workplace necessary to compete in the global economy of the 21st century. America cannot rely on the skills of those who enroll in postsecondary programs to provide the high intellectual standards characteristic of our competitors in the world market. True, about one-half of high school graduates attend postsecondary institutions. But by age 29, according to statistics from the U.S. Department of Education (1992), only 27 percent of our young people have acquired an undergraduate degree. In other words, if future generations are to have the academic/intellectual skills to be productive, they must learn them in our nation's elementary and secondary schools.

Couple these concerns with an increasingly diverse student population in the public schools and professional educators can only conclude that old premises about what and how to teach students must be reexamined.

Over the past three decades, our industrial society has been rapidly replaced by the Information Age. Marked by the presence of high technology and a global economy, this new era presents a great challenge to our traditional approaches to schooling. Therefore, the spirit of future schooling must reflect diversity rather than standardization, decentralization rather than centralization.

There is a fundamental difference between efforts to improve schooling by refining (symbolic) existing policies and practices and systemic reform—comprehensive reform. The former calls for simply doing better what is presently being done and reflects the attitude, "If it ain't broke, don't fix it." The latter calls for a major transformation of the structure and reflects the attitude, "It may not be broken, but is it really the best design to ensure the quality of learning necessary for young people who will be adults in the 21st century?"

As we have entered the information age, we find shifts are occurring or will likely soon occur in all of our societal system from communications and transportation to the family and workplace. (See Figure 2.) It is little wonder that we again find ourselves in need for a shift in education. Society is changing in sweeping ways that make our current educational systems obsolete. Thousands of schools across the country are designed like factories, organized like factories, and still function like factories. However well-intentioned and caring the teachers or administrators (and there are many), the system takes its toll on too many students.

Society	Agrarian	Industrial	Information
Transportation	Horse	Train	Plane & Car
Family	Extended family	Nuclear family	Single/Blended family
Business	Family	Bureaucracy	Team
Education	One-Room School-House	Current System	(Reform) ?

Figure 2. Shifts in society.

The need for a new shift in education is based on massive changes in both the conditions and educational needs of an information society. Therefore, we must examine those changes in order to figure out what the features of the new educational system should look like. Figure 3 shows many of the major differences between the industrial age and the emerging information age. These differences have important implications for the features of the new educational system: how it should be structured, what should be taught, and how it should be taught.

In the industrial age we needed minimally educated people who would be willing and able to put up with the tedious work on assembly lines. However, those assembly-line jobs are rapidly becoming an endangered species. Just as the percentage of the work force in agriculture dropped dramatically in the early stages of the industrial age, so the percentage in manufacturing has been declining dramatically over the past few decades. As Reich (1991) points out, even in manufacturing companies, a majority of the jobs today involve

Industrial Age	Information Age
Adversarial Relationships	Cooperative Relationships
Bureaucratic Organization	Team Organization
Autocratic Leadership	Shared Leadership
Centralized Control	Autonomy with Accountability
Autocracy	Democracy
Representative Democracy	Participative Democracy
Compliance	Initiative
One-Way Communication	Networking
Compartmentalization	Holism
(Division of Labor)	(Integration of Tasks)

Figure 3. Differences between industrial age and information age
and the relationship to education.

manipulating information rather than materials. Just as the industrial age represented a focus on our physical capabilities, so the information age represents a focus on our mental capabilities. This transition makes the need for more effective teaching and learning for all students paramount. (See Figure 4.)

To emphasize learning, the new reforms must no longer hold "time" constant and allow "achievement" to vary. It must hold "achievement" constant at a competency level and allow "time" to be the variable. There is no other way to accommodate the fact that different children learn at different rates and have different learning needs. But to have an outcomes-based rather than time-based system, we must in turn have a person-based progress rather than a group-based progress. This shift would require changing the role of the teacher to that of a coach or facilitator/manager, rather than that of dispenser of knowledge to groups of students.

Taken as a whole, these reforms from the Industrial Age model to the Information Age model represent significant reforms in a school's approach and philosophy. From the equity perspective, there is a growing body of research that supports the notion that these new directions also represent reforms that are more academically beneficial for a greater number of students. While some schools and communities have changed education in

The Existing State	The Future Image
a. Grade levels	a. Continuous progress
b. Covering the content	b. Outcomes-based learning
c. Norm-referenced testing	c. Individualized testing
d. Non-authentic assessment	d. Performance-based assessment
e. Group-based content delivery	e. Personal learning plans
f. Tracking and ability grouping	f. Cooperative learning
g. Fragmented learning time	g. Flexible scheduling, variable time block
h. Classrooms	h. Learning centers
i. Teacher as dispenser of knowledge	i. Teacher as coach or facilitator of learning
j. Teaching isolation in planning and instruction, limited planning time	j. Staff organized as teams for planning and instruction block of time for team/individual planning
k. Memorization of facts	k. Higher-level thinking, problem-solving, practical applications
l. Isolated reading, writing skills	l. Communication skills
m. Books as tools	m. Advanced technologies as tools
n. Classroom organized by age-grade	n. Multi-aged, non-graded
o. Promotion based on time spent in school	o. Promotion based on performance
p. Student as passive learner	p. Student as active participant

Figure 4. The transition.

fundamental ways, most of the 110,000 schools in the U.S. conform to the traditional model. For the most part, K-12 education has failed to make these transitions; too many schools continue to use the policies and practices of the industrial age to prepare our students for life in the information age. The challenge facing America's schools is one of moving from an outdated model for preparing young people to a more responsive system that will prepare them for the 21st century. During this transition, all schools must share an unrelenting acknowledgment and commitment to providing a more equitable system.

Problems with the Status Quo

The process of arranging schooling has become an end in itself and therefore a barrier to learning. Our education system has become a very stable institution that is highly resistant to change, for example, the system too often: (1) allows teachers and administrators to perpetuate the system rather than accept the responsibility for constructive change; (2) separates people from each other and from the real world and isolates disciplines and tasks, creating problems of communication, understanding and priorities; (3) ignores interdisciplinary opportunities, discourages caring and trust, hinders the development of common standards, and allows excessive specialization; (4) rewards covering and recalling of material, rote learning, grades, and GPAs; (5) promotes the "normal curve" approach to categorize students, discriminating against their potential and encouraging them to manipulate, play games with, or resist the system rather than master material, develop responsibility for their own learning, and build lifelong skills; (6) consumes the time needed for reflection on the use of material, solving problems individually and collectively, and relating material to the real world; (7) leads to excessive teacher activity and to student passivity, thereby exhausting and frustrating both groups while promoting mediocre performance; (8) grants freedom and opportunity to students but demands too little responsibility and self-discipline; (9) encourages, and may depend upon, an ethically neutral, valueless, depersonalized, do-your-own-thing, smorgasbord approach to education and to life; (10) limits the influence of teachers in decisions while it solicits renewal and reform from those distant from the classroom; (11) produces unhealthy cynicism among teachers, students, administrators, and at times, the public; (12) limits parental and community involvement in the education of young people; and (13) makes of education a routine instead of a stimulating activity.

The Reform Cycle of Excellence and Equity

The '50s to '90s Reform Cycle of Excellence and Equity outlined on the following page provides a capsule look at the evolutionary cycle we have experienced in education over the past forty years.

In the first phase, 1950s to mid '60s, we experienced a reform for excellence in our schools. This movement occurred after the Russians launched Sputnik in the late 1950s, when the media, the Congress, and the public concluded that America had fallen behind in the race for scientific and technical superiority in space because of inadequacies in the teaching of science, mathematics, and foreign languages. The target group for post-Sputnik school reformers was the gifted or the high-achieving students in our schools.

The second phase, mid-'60s to '70s, equality of educational opportunity (EEO) represented the greatest reform period in recent history. During this period, schools were

> **'50s to Mid-'60s**
>
> **Excellence**
>
> **Mid-'60s to '70s**
>
> **Equality of Educational Opportunity**
>
> **Mid-'80s—'90s and Beyond**
>
> **Quality with Equity**

being challenged to provide for a greater diversity of students and to offer a wider perspective within the school's curriculum and practices. Nontraditional students—ethnic minority students, exceptional populations, limited English proficient students, gender equity, and socioeconomic status were all challenged. Numerous statutes, laws, and court cases had a direct impact on the way schools were operating. This period of time represented the greatest change and challenge for schools because of society's demand for equality of educational opportunity within the systems of education in America.

Since then, one shortcoming after another briefly captured the public's interest, but it was not until 1983 that there was another full-blown sense of crisis in this country. The United States was labeled a "Nation at Risk." The difference between the '50s movement toward excellence and the '90s reform movement toward quality is that the '90s focus is now upon all students in all of our schools—not just a select group of high-ability students.

A History of Inequity

Perhaps, in the years following *Brown v. Board of Education* (1954)—(the Supreme Court decision which determined that separate schooling was not equal), we became complacent enough to believe that just wanting schools to make things right would be enough. We became disillusioned by the extraordinary difficulties well-intentioned school people face in trying to undo past inequities and current injustices. We concerned ourselves with what education really meant. Did we want students to have merely an equal chance at an education? Did we want to guarantee equitable educational resources for all students? Or did we want to ensure equal educational outcomes? Poorly conceptualized programs, mass confusion and overall misunderstanding to whatever brand of equity we proclaimed, it eluded us. Oakes stated, "Children in Head Start didn't catch up. Remedial and compensatory classes didn't seem to remediate or compensate. Children making long bus rides seemed to gain nothing but long bus rides. Millions were spent; achievement gaps between the haves and the have-nots remained." What went wrong? Could the failure of these students to learn be attributed to a deeply rooted linguistic or cultural deficiency? Or, as unthinkable as it was, could there be an unalterable genetic difference?

We were financially generous during the 1960s and '70s, but then the dollars got tight, and we were exhausted. In the attempt to correct inequities, we concluded, schools had neglected to do what they were supposed to do, teach academics. Equality moved out; academic excellence became the center of the nation's attention and commitment in the mid-1980s through the early 1990s. In looking over the past two decades, there are two important points to make with regard to equity and quality. First, in our search for the solution to the "problems" of educational inequity, our focus was almost exclusively on the characteristics of the students themselves. We looked for sources of their educational failures in their homes, their neighborhoods, their language, their culture and in their genes. In all of our searching, we almost entirely overlooked the real possibility that what happens within the schools they attend may contribute to inequitable opportunities and outcomes. We neglected to examine the content and processes of schooling itself for ways they may contribute to school failure. In our quest for higher standards and superior academic performance, we seem to have forgotten that schools cannot be excellent as long as there are groups of students who are not well served by them.

Higher Standards and Equity

Quality broadly defined may mean several things. At the level of the individual learner, it means performing on the boundary of individual ability in ways that test and push back personal limits, in school and in the workplace. Quality may be characterized as a school that sets high expectations and goals for all learners, then tries in every way possible to help students reach them. Quality may be characterized as a society that has adopted these policies, for it will then be prepared through the education and skill of its people to respond to the challenge of a rapidly changing world.

Quality has became equated with higher academic standards, tougher requirements for graduation and college admission, elimination of the frills in the curriculum, limiting options for students and generally working harder in school. Nearly all states raised graduation requirements from 1980 to 1990. Yet the changes still fell short of the recommendations in *A Nation at Risk*. By 1990, 37 states had met *Nation's* call for four years of required English, but only ten met standards in math, and four in science.

As standards are raised questions arise about the impact on the already low-achieving and at-risk students. Also, these higher standards raised questions on the effects of the dropout problem. A lot has happened in the past decade, but not much has changed. Thirty-one states and the District of Columbia toughened graduation requirements. Yet, 83% of American students complete high school, changing little since 1973. There has been relatively little improvement in white graduation rates, which were 81.4% in 1970, rose to 82.6% in 1979 and fell to 81.7% in 1991. African Americans experienced the fastest rising graduation rates of all ethnic groups—59.5% in 1970, 67.1% in 1979 and 75.1% in 1991. Hispanic graduation rates were 51.9% in 1970, peaked at 60.1% in 1984 and fell to 52.1% in 1991, (U.S. Department of Education, 1992).

What will happen to students who can not or will not meet these more rigorous standards and requirements? There are those who argue that to question whether all students can attain these new standards is being anti-academic; they say, it is only a matter of setting high expectations to be achieved. They argue that rather than frustrating students, these higher standards will serve as an incentive and motivation for higher achievement. As Boyer (1992) stated, "America's failing schools were bypassed by traditional reforms because they just weren't related to the nature of their problems. To add more to graduation requirements when you are dealing with students who are hungry or emotionally stressed out or feel unsafe, and say 'take another unit of math,' is almost laughable in terms of where the solution should be." Simply raising standards will not equate with improved academic performances. As we have learned from our past efforts, as long as schools continue to rely on traditional policies and practices, overall improvement will be minimal. Too many of the current practices and policies in our schools are failing to improve the academic performance of many of our students. The standards-raising movement has failed to take into account the nature of the relationship between educators and their students and the extent to which students are engaged in the learning process—in other words, the teaching and learning aspect of schooling. We have learned in the past decade that simply requiring more courses or units of instruction has not resulted in any significant academic improvement.

Equity and Reform

To the extent that students' educational opportunities are determined by ethnicity, social class, gender, or cultural background, the system violates the democratic principle of equity. The "effective schools" movement began with a clear focus on the issue of equity, as does much of the rhetoric about reforming schools. On the other hand, in most schools, vast inequities persist and aspects of reforming can exacerbate inequities by neglecting to address the issues directly. Administrators and teachers are profoundly concerned about how to respond more constructively to students of increasingly diverse backgrounds, interests, prior knowledge and styles of learning. Research on learning has dramatized the negative effects of schools' failure to adapt instruction to students' special needs. National reports on the changing demography of the student body are plentiful. However, policies for reform have given little attention to organizational mechanisms that might respond more equitably to escalating pluralism. By continually focusing on the experience of students of color, women, those from low-income families, and those of limited proficiency in English, and by highlighting consequences of equity to reform efforts, we can keep this concept visible and identify promising approaches for enhancing equity.

The Many Names of Reform

Reform has entered the dialogue of practitioners, policymakers and researchers with a burst of power, but also ambiguity. It represents a concern for fundamental changes in the way schools are organized, but the precise nature of those changes and the priority given to new reforms are in dispute. As we recall, one of the major stumbling blocks in understanding the concept of equity, was part and parcel to the use of the term. The same can be said for the term reform. The list that follows offers a brief description of some of the oft-mentioned and oft-used reform ideas or school techniques that came to be popular in the early '90s.

School (site)-based management: Shifting decision-making authority and responsibility away from the central office to professionals at the school who better understand the needs of students. Administrators, teachers, parents and other community members are given more control over what happens in schools. Decisions usually include budgets, curriculum and personnel.

Higher-order thinking skills: Teaching students to apply basic logic to concrete situations and objects.

Charter schools: Allowing teachers, parents and students to choose how to structure certain public schools. The independently operated public schools normally have a contract with a school district and usually guarantee certain academic achievements.

Outcomes-based: A movement that says students success shouldn't be measured by the amount of time students spend in a seat, but by whether they actually learn what they are taught. Students should be able to demonstrate their learning.

School choice: The movement to allow parents to pick the schools their children attend rather than have that choice dictated by districts according to where they happen to live.

National Education Goals: In the late 1980s, then President Bush and the nation's governors set six goals for the year 2000. By the year 2000: (1) all children will come to school ready to learn; (2) the high school graduation rate will increase to at least 90%; (3) American students will leave grades 4, 8, and 12 having demonstrated competency in challenging subject matter including English, mathematics, science, history and geography; (4) U.S. students will be first in the world in science and mathematics achievement; (5) every school in America will be free of drugs and violence and will offer a disciplined environment conducive to learning; (6) every adult American will be literate and will possess the knowledge and skills necessary to compete in a global economy and exercise the rights and responsibilities of citizenship.

Effective Schools: An effective school is one that can demonstrate the joint presence of quality (acceptably high levels of achievement) and equity (no differences in the distribution of that achievement among the major subsets of the student population). Achievement of these criteria must be demonstrated in outcome terms reflective of the school's teaching and learning mission.

Total Quality Management: This is the approach that large corporations have implemented in the refinement of their companies, which is currently being applied to schools in various forms. The belief is that quality is a comprehensive approach to the organization and the description of work processes. It also examines the way people treat each other in an organization. It is a process that allows an organization to improve constantly everything with which they are involved.

As educators have grappled with the notion of school reform, many have remarked that such initiatives as cited above are nothing new. At the same time, many schools and districts have developed approaches for revamping one of the areas mentioned above. But examples of districts that have attempted to reform all areas simultaneously are rare. They have not been put together in a strategy for reforming the entire system. For many educators, reforming schools has come to be seen as the addition of certain programs, rather than a comprehensive strategy affecting the entire system. For example, many districts and schools equate reform with site-based management or shared-decision making. These isolated initiatives carry the danger of being seen as ends in themselves, rather than as pieces in an overall strategy to raise student success.

Perhaps the trickiest part of reforming schools will be to completely reshape a system that has been measured thus far by compliance with bureaucratic mandates into one focused on the bottom line—evidence of authentic student achievement.

Questions and Lessons for Reform Efforts

Through past efforts our conventional wisdom would be to begin by asking: what things are we doing now that need to be improved so that five years from now we can show evidence that we are doing them better? Good planning in the '90s will ask: given our best current information about demographic, economic and organizational factors shaping our society and the world, how should we reform our schools to enable our youth to engage themselves more successfully? And a second question might be: what do we know about human learning that might reinforce a need to reform our schools? The former seeks to refine what is. The latter seeks to envision what is possible.

As schools wrestle with reform, many lessons will be learned in the process: (1) reform does not need to be built on deficit perspectives, (2) standardized reforms have little place in education, (3) meaningful professional and structural reform is impossible without regulatory relief, (4) if teachers and administrators are to resist expectations for immediate results, they need a protected atmosphere in which to develop and test new, complex authority relationships and school practices, (5) the flexible use of resources and site accountability are necessary work conditions for professionals, (6) reform efforts that ignore the need to redesign teachers' and administrators' roles will do little to unleash the expertise of educators or improve school efforts, and (7) to produce deep and meaningful reform, time must be provided during normal operating hours for educators to work collaboratively and effectively as accountable professionals.

Criteria for Progress

The following statements are only illustrative examples of areas to consider when looking at systemic reform in schools. Equity is the cornerstone of all questions.

From the students' perspective:

▶ is learning time more equally distributed among whole class instruction, small group work, and individual study, rather than dominated by whole class instruction?
▶ do students spend most of their time in heterogeneous groups?
▶ do learning and assessment tasks emphasize student production rather than reproduction of knowledge?
▶ do learning tasks aim for depth of understanding rather than broad exposure?
▶ do learning tasks emphasize "multiple intelligence's" and multiple cultures?
▶ are academic disciplines integrated in the curriculum?
▶ is time for school learning flexibly organized rather than in periods of standard length?
▶ do students participate in community-based learning?
▶ do students relate to adult mentors, either teachers or persons outside the school, in a long-term programmatic way?
▶ is student work assisted by extensive use of computer technology?
▶ do students serve as and have access to peer tutors?
▶ do students have substantial influence in planning, conducting and evaluating their work?

From the teachers' perspective:

▶ do teachers function in differentiated roles such as mentoring of novices, directing curriculum development, and supervising peers?

▶ do staff function in extended roles with students that involve advising and mentoring?

▶ do staff help to design on-going, on-the-job staff development based on local needs assessment?

▶ do staff participate in collegial planning, curriculum development and peer observation-reflection, with time scheduled for this during the school day?

▶ do teachers instruct in teams?

▶ do teachers exercise control over curriculum and school policy?

▶ are there specific organizational incentives for teachers to experiment and to develop new programs and curriculum that respond more effectively to student diversity?

▶ do teachers work with students in flexible time periods?

▶ do teachers work with students as much in small groups and individual study as in whole class instruction?

▶ do teachers work closely with parents and human service professionals to meet student needs?

▶ do teachers receive financial rewards based on student outcomes or evaluation of teaching performance?

Questions pertaining to the **leadership, management and governance** issues within a reforming school may ask:

▶ does the school exercise control over budget, staffing and curriculum?

▶ has the school been divided into schools within schools, divisions or houses?

▶ is the school run by a council in which teachers and/or parents have control over budget, staffing and curriculum?

▶ does the school make program decisions based on systematic analysis of student performance data disaggregated by student subgroups (e.g. ethnicity, gender, socioeconomic status)?

▶ does the district provide special incentives for the principal to participate in reform?

▶ do students enroll in the school by choice rather than residential agreement?

As we are witnessing, schools are becoming more and more community service agencies. To that extent, several questions with the reform of our schools and the **relationship with the community** may be:

▶ does the school have a systematic program for parent involvement in the academic life of students that goes beyond the normal activities of PTO, parent's night, and attendance at extracurricular events?

▶ does the school have formal mechanisms for coordinating with community agencies offering services dealing with child care, drug and alcohol abuse, family disruption, homelessness, sexual abuse, teen pregnancy, crime and delinquency, economic welfare assistance and parental employment and training?

▶ does the school participate in an external mentoring program, which follows students for several years?

▶ does the school have formal arrangements with local employers to place students in career-ladder jobs during the school year, summer and following high school graduation?

▶ does the school have formal arrangements with institutions of higher education to assist with staff development and curriculum design.

▶ does the school have formal arrangements with institutions of higher education to assist students to continue their schooling?

▶ does the school offer adult education programs and recreational opportunities for the community at large?

Again, these questions are illustrative examples, not an exhaustive list to check-off. A close examination of these questions, will reveal that the concept of equity is linked to each area. Striving for equity and striving for systemic reform is a process. The critical question concerning the areas illustrated above is: what documented evidence does a school have to verify that the areas are addressed and being implemented successfully?

Summary

In recent years many of the same American companies that gave birth to the old industrial model have been abandoning it. Corporations such as Ford, Xerox, and Motorola have recognized that, given the complexity of new production processes and the need to introduce new products more frequently, they must abandon the old structures. They have decentralized and trimmed their management structures and reorganized their workplaces around teams of workers, each given a responsibility for organizing and carrying out their assignments, whether they are assembling lawn mowers or processing insurance claims. They have adopted more flexible work schedules and developed new standards of quality control. To pull this off, they have poured billions of dollars into educational programs aimed at equipping workers to learn new skills, solve problems, and take a more active role in promoting the economic and other goals of the enterprise.

It is now time for schools to do the same. It is no longer possible to run a quality system of public education under the old values of centralized authority, standardization, and bureaucratic accountability any more than it is possible to run any large institution effectively in this fashion. Moreover, the "product" that schools must turn out is changing, and the traditional structures are ill suited to meeting the new demands. The educators of the twenty-first century can no longer be content with graduates trained to take in and recycle information handed out by teachers and other authority figures. Today's students must be taught to think for themselves and to generate new information.

This systemic reform of American schools is well underway in a number of small pockets throughout this country. Teachers, administrators, parents and political leaders are questioning the old way of doing things. Although full-fledged reform efforts do not yet exist, every one of the ingredients for creating them—new ways of managing school systems, running schools, organizing classrooms, using time, assessing results and so forth—exists somewhere in the country. Somewhere, some school or group of teachers within a school is turning every one of the elements of the factory-model school on its head. Most of these efforts are working in isolation, and by themselves none of their new ideas is powerful enough to transform America's schools.

The future is ahead, not behind. Some who call for school reform look to the past for guidance. There was, they argue, a time when our schools were better. Not true! There are more good schools today than at any time in the past. If there are also more bad schools, it is because there are more schools trying to educate students who, in the good old days, would have been working in factories and sweatshops.

Those who are serious about school reform must first understand that America's schools are not less effective than they once were. American's schools are clearly better at doing what they were expected to do in the past. The problem is that schools today are expected to take on tasks that they have never been held responsible for before. And, even more fundamental, the present school structure grew out of a set of assumptions about the purpose of schooling that is inconsistent with emerging social and economic realities. Those who would reform schools must therefore consider the purposes schools have been designed to serve, as well as the purposes schools could be designed to serve. It is, after all, the past that has given our schools their structure—and the way we envision the future will shape the new structures we try to create.

The crucial test of the reforms urged will be whether improvements in American education become available for all students. How does a school system determine if it is a quality school? How does a school system determine if it is equitable? Certainly, these are questions that address the relationship between quality and equity. What would such a school look like?

An excellent school is a work of art. It orchestrates the varying interests and abilities of its students, parents and community in concerted efforts toward educational quality. It enlists the creative abilities of all personnel to identify goals and to fashion programs that fit the needs of its particular clientele. It is accountable to the state for such basic outcomes as literacy in language and numbers, but it is free to innovate new materials and methods—and yet it must especially define and seek much broader dimensions of educational development. Above all, it is unique, responsive to personalities and values the needs and abilities that are never fully duplicated in any other school. Such schools would serve all of our students well.

The progress toward reforming, in fact, is slow, sometimes tedious, often frustrating. But it makes education an exciting place to be, and that in itself represents a substantial change in a school.

 ## END NOTES

Boyer, Ernest L. "Results Below Expectations—Analyzing the Lack of True Gains." *USA Today,* March 17, 1993.

Brown v. Board of Education, 347 U.S. 483 (1954)

Carnegie Forum on Education and the Economy, *A Nation Prepared: Teachers for the 21st Century.* New York: NY, 1990.

Education Policy. *Making the Grade.* The Twentieth Century Fund, New York: NY, 1983.

Fiske, Edward B. *Smart Schools, Smart Kids.* Simon & Schuster, New York: NY, 1991.

Love, Ruth B. "Proceedings of the Second Conference of the University/Urban Schools National Task Force." Washington, D.C., 1985.

National Commission on Excellence in Education. *A Nation at Risk: The Imperative for Educational Reform.* U.S. Government Printing Office, Washington, D.C., 1983. Also in ERIC—ED 226 006.

National Education Goals Report. *Building a Nation of Learners.* Washington, D.C., 1991.

Reich, R.B. *The Works of Nations.* New York: Alfred A. Knopf, 1991.

Report of the Twentieth Century Fund Task Force on Federal Elementary and Secondary The Secretary's Commission on Achieving Necessary Skills (SCANS). *What Work Requires of Schools—A SCANS Report for America 2000.* U.S. Department of Labor. June, 1991.

The Business Roundtable Participation Guide: A Primer for Business on Education. Developed by the National Alliance of Business. 2nd Edition, New York: NY, April 1991.

The Policy Information Center of Educational Testing Service, Princeton: NJ, 1991.

U.S. Department of Education, National Center for Education Statistics, Washington, D.C., 1992.

SUGGESTIONS FOR FURTHER READING

Barth, Roland. *Improving Schools from Within.* Jossey-Bass Publishers, San Francisco: CA, 1990

Fiske, Edward B. *Smart Schools, Smart Kids.* Simon & Schuster, New York, NY 1991

Goodlad, John I. *Teachers for Our Nation's Schools.* Jossey-Bass Publishers, San Francisco: CA, 1991.

Goodlad, John I. *A Place Called School: Prospects for the Future.* McGraw Hill Publishing Co., New York: 1983.

Oakes, Jeannie. *Keeping Track—How Schools Structure Inequality.* Yale University Press, New Haven: CT, 1985.

Sarason, Seymour B. *The Predictable Failure of Educational Reform.* Jossey-Bass Publishers, 1991

Schlechty, Phillip. *Schools for the 21st Century.* Jossey-Bass Publishers, San Francisco: CA, 1991

Sizer, Theodore. *Horace's Compromise—The Dilemma of the American High School.* Houghton Mifflin Publishing Co., Boston: MA, 1984.

Sizer, Theodore. *Hoarace's School—Redesigning the American High School.* Houghton Mifflin Publishing Co., Boston: MA, 1992

Name _____ Date _____

DISCUSSION QUESTIONS

1. What is the difference between the '50s movement for excellence and the '90s reform movement?

_____

_____

_____

_____

_____

_____

2. What are two types of reform movements? Which do you think most schools are engaged in? Why?

_____

_____

_____

_____

_____

3. Do you agree that the shifts in society should require a reform in our schools? Why or why not?

_____

_____

_____

_____

_____

4. How would systemic reforms address the needs of a growing diverse student population more effectively? Provide examples.

_____

_____

_____

_____

_____

5. Is there a common thread of concern among the various national reports and commissions cited in this chapter. What are they?

_____

_____

_____

_____

_____

6. What does the term "quality" mean to you? Does it mean higher standards? Why or why not?

_____

_____

_____

_____

_____

7. How would you determine if a school is one of "high quality"? Explain.

_____

_____

_____

_____

_____

8. How would you determine if a school is "equitable"? Explain.

_____

_____

_____

_____

_____

9. Is it possible to have an educational system that is quality with equity? Explain.

_____

_____

_____

_____

_____

10. How do you respond to the statement, "If there are shortcomings in learning, they are not necessarily shortcomings in the student as it may be shortcomings in the school." Explain your position.

_____

_____

_____

_____

_____

_____

_____

_____

_____

_____

SMALL GROUP WORK

There are some powerful reasons why schools find it difficult to change. If the structures and conditions aren't identified and applied, the probability of wasted resources and failed change is almost assured.

These are the organizational structures and personal behavioral conditions that either support or inhibit change. A useful method to identify the structures and conditions that support or inhibit reform in a school is to identify the "beliefs" that reflect the way people in the organization know effective change takes place. Below is a list of statements that reflect beliefs about the structures and conditions effecting change.

Your Task

▶   Each member of your group (independently) should read each statement and identify the ten statements they believe contribute to effective change. (They don't necessarily have to be in rank order.)

▶   Each person will share one priority statement from their list and continue from member to member until each member has shared all their priority statements that do not duplicate what has already been shared. (Record the statements—by number—on newsprint as they are stated.)

▶   Your group must prioritize the list of statements just generated using a consensus process (Rank order).

▶   Each group will present their rankings and a brief rationale for the decisions.

"We Believe Statements About Change"

Individual Rank: **Group Rank:**

_____ 1. We believe you create effective change by empowering teachers so that _____ they can change the system from the bottom-up and by allowing them to make the most critical teaching/learning decisions.

_____ 2. We believe that change can occur when the school culture is changed _____ from one that is bureaucratic and rigid to one that is adaptive and innovative.

_____ 3. We believe you do not expect all or even most people or groups to _____ change. The complexity of change is such that it is impossible to bring about widespread reform in any large social system.

_____ 4. Implementation is a necessary but not a sufficient step toward sus- _____ tained improvement.

_____ 5. Practices, in order to effect change, must be used on a large enough _____ scale to alter entire patterns of learning and teaching.

_____ 6. Lasting learning for teachers is most likely to occur within a supportive _____ environment that encourages practice, idea sharing and peer observation.

_____ 7. Conflict and disagreement are not only inevitable but fundamental to _____ successful change.

_____ 8. Effective change takes time. Unrealistic or undefined time lines fail to _____ recognize that implementation occurs developmentally. Expect significant change to take a minimum of two or three years.

_____ 9. If you attempt more, you will get more. Small is not beautiful when it _____ comes to school improvement.

_____10. We believe the key to the problem of resistance to change is to _____ understand that what people resist is usually not technical change but social change-the change in their human relationships that generally accompanies change.

Individual Rank: **Group Rank:**

_____ 11. We believe that change is difficult, if not impossible, if the culture of _____ the organization doesn't support improvement and foster cooperative behavior.

_____ 12. We believe you must expect things not to turn out exactly as planned. _____ The change will have unforeseen consequences, regardless of how carefully you plan.

_____ 13. We believe it is the responsibility of the leader to subject the staff to as _____ much change as he/she thinks either of them can tolerate.

_____ 14. We believe the primary role of the leader is to establish, activate and _____ nurture a focus on vision, purpose and outcomes of the school.

_____ 15. We believe that administrators and teachers live in different worlds. _____ Effective change requires bridging between administrative initiative, pressure and support, on the one hand, and teacher's effort, mastery and commitment on the other.

_____ 16. We believe the principal is not the key to school improvement. The _____ principal is important but so are many other people.

_____ 17. We believe forceful leadership is the factor that contributes most _____ directly and surely to major effective change.

_____ 18. We believe that participation in decision making by all affected is _____ critical to planned change. It increases motivation and promotes ownership of the planned change.

_____ 19. We believe that with any change, things will have a tendency to get _____ worse before they get better.

Striving for Quality- with-Equity Schools  3

"We can, whenever and wherever we choose, successfully teach all children whose schooling is of interest to us. We already know more than we need to do that. Whether or not we do it must finally depend on how we feel about the fact that we haven't so far."
—Ron Edmonds

Introduction

An educational system fashioned specifically for the 19th and 20th century industrial revolution led by the United States is out of sync with the high-skilled workplace necessary to compete in a global economy of the 21st century. Reforming schools so that all students have an equitable opportunity to a quality education requires a new vision of education and professionals who are willing to advocate for and participate in change.

As we have learned, striving for an equitable system is a process, not an event. Even though there has been some progress in providing all students with a more equitable educational opportunity for education, much more is needed.

When we consider the fact that *every day* in the U.S...

► 17,051 women get pregnant
► 2,795 of them are teenagers
► 1,295 teenagers give birth
► 689 babies are born to women who have had inadequate prenatal care
► 67 babies die before one month of age
► 105 babies die before their first birthday
► 27 children die from poverty
► 3 children die from child abuse
► 10 children die from guns
► 6 teenagers commit suicide

- ▶ 135,000 children bring guns to school
- ▶ 1,512 teenagers drop out of school
- ▶ 1,849 children are abused or neglected
- ▶ 3,288 children run away from home
- ▶ 1,629 children are in adult jails
- ▶ 2,556 children are born to unmarried women
- ▶ 2,989 children see their parents divorced
- ▶ 34,286 people lose jobs
- ▶ 100,000 children are homeless (Oski, 1992).

Schools cannot ignore these societal realities. Are schools solely to blame? Certainly not. Not only are there a greater number of diverse students entering our schools, but a host of other variables must be factored into the equation. For example, family backgrounds, health care issues, neighborhoods, crime, the judicial system, poverty, homelessness, abuse/neglect, drugs, unemployment, and underemployment. Certainly these changes in our society are reflected in the challenges and opportunities facing our schools. How does the school position itself to be more responsive and effective to these societal changes? Can schools do this alone? No. Consequently, developing an appropriate environment for equity has implications for every facet of the school setting. First, the future of equity depends on the ability of all who are, or will be involved, in the improvement of our schools. A coordinated effort between state and local boards of education, administrators, teacher training programs, classroom teachers and the community at large must be orchestrated. If and when this support system is in place, the likelihood of equity as an integral part of our schools will be imminent; because then educators like ourselves will have the necessary support systems to ensure successful implementation.

Chapter 3, **Quality-with-Equity Schools** is designed to: (1) examine the movement towards effective schools, (2) explore the process of school improvement, (3) highlight current movements that are intended to address a more challenging and responsive system of education, and (4) present a continuum of equity that schools can use to measure their progress.

The Effective Schools Movement

The history of the effective schools movement began in 1966, with the publication of *Equality of Educational Opportunity* (popularly known as the Coleman report) by James Coleman et al. The report by Coleman concluded for educators and policymakers that variations in school quality affected a child's achievement considerably less than did a child's socioeconomic background. In other words, the study concluded that educational achievement was related more to a student's family background than to the characteristics of the school. The Coleman study (1969) concluded:

> "Schools bring little influence to bear on a child's achievement that is independent of his background and general social context. . . . This very lack of an independent effect means that the inequality imposed on children by their home, neighborhood and peer environment are carried along to become the inequalities with which they confront adult life at the end of school. For equality of educational opportunity must imply a strong effect of schools that is independent of the child's immediate social environment, and that strong independence is not present in American schools."

The landmark study left educators and policymakers deeply concerned. As a result, the most important point to filter through the media was that schools don't make a difference. If student achievement is determined largely by family background and scarcely at all by teachers, books and facilities, the reasoning went, then improving the school is unlikely to have much effect on student achievement. In the 1990s, unfortunately, public acceptance of the Coleman hypothesis still constitutes a real barrier to the advancement of equity and to the general improvement of student achievement through schooling.

Fortunately, several researchers did not accept the Coleman theory. Their strategy was to go into the real world of public schools and see if they could identify individual schools that represented clear exceptions to Coleman's theory. The initial findings from these studies became the foundation for the research base of the effective schools movement.

Mounting evidence indicated that school structure and organization had a powerful effect on what a child learned. Ironically, Coleman was the researcher whose work most conveyed this finding in the United States. Coleman's research group concluded that the conditions of educational success were discipline (physical and intellectual), high expectations and standards (for both teachers and students), and a safe and orderly environment. According to their research, these conditions were more likely to be found in private and Catholic schools than in public schools, a conclusion that stimulated great debate and in the process actually diverted attention from the broader lessons. However, they acknowledged that schools can and do make a difference in the education of all students. Coleman and his colleagues identified what conditions must exist for a school to be effective. Lazotte (1990) offered the following definition of an effective school.

> An effective school is one that can demonstrate the joint presence of quality (acceptably high levels of achievement) and equity (no differences in the distribution of that achievement among the major subsets of the student population).

A good school, however, the kind of school that Perkey and Smith (1983) discuss, goes beyond this definition. In a good school, students perform well in a number of areas. They exhibit social responsibility and ethical behavior, acquire vocational skills and good work habits, and develop higher-order thinking skills (such as problem solving, creative thinking or critical thinking). More importantly, a good school is an equitable school, one that meets the needs of all students, whether they are at the top or at the bottom of the ability scale.

Effective schools case study research has proven Coleman and his colleagues wrong in one sense. The literature clearly demonstrates, in numerous settings, that some schools are able to attain remarkably high levels of pupil mastery of basic school skills, even though these schools are serving large proportions of economically poor and disadvantaged students, ethnic minority and majority students.

How Do Effective Schools Differ?

How do effective schools differ from not so effective schools? School leaders, teachers, and local boards of education began to take a more active interest in the effective schools research in the '80s as the descriptions of the schools made their way into the literature and language of the educational community. During the late '80s researchers sought to answer the following general question: In what ways do effective schools differ from their less effective counterparts?

The research methodology consisted of three steps. First, effective schools, based on measured outcomes, were identified and paired with schools that were similar in all respects except for the more favorable student outcome profile. Second, field researchers spent time in the paired schools, they conducted interviews, observations, and surveys designed to develop as rich a description of the life of these schools as possible. Finally, the data were analyzed with the following question in mind: What are the distinctive characteristics of the effective schools that seem to set them apart from their less effective counterparts?

Several characteristics (correlates) of effective schools have been formulated. The following list is not be used as a template, but to be used as a guide to understanding the scope of effective schools. (See Figure 5.)

The effective schools movement is framed by three central assumptions: (1) schools can be identified that are unusually effective in teaching poor and ethnic minority children basic skills as measured by standardized tests; (2) these successful schools exhibit characteristics that are correlated with their success and that lie well within the domain of educators to manipulate; (3) the characteristics of successful schools provide a basis for improving schools not deemed to be successful. Implicit in this last assumption is a belief that the school is the appropriate place to focus educational reform efforts.

School site management

Leadership (Principal)

Staff stability

Curriculum articulation and organization

School-wide staff development

Parental and community involvement and support

School-wide recognition of academic success

Maximized learning time

District support

Collaborative planning and collegial relationship

Sense of community

Clear goals and high expectations

Order and discipline

Figure 5. Correlates of an effective school.

The School as the Unit of Change

The effective school can and generally does stand alone, even among its counterparts in the same local school district. The major implication is that the institutional and organizational mechanisms that exist with effectiveness can be attained by individual schools, one school at a time. This means that effective schooling is within the grasp of the teachers and administrators who make up the teaching community of the single school. In the late '80s it became clear that more schools could organize themselves to achieve these results. The important question became: How could the knowledge about these effective schools become the basis for planned change initiatives for even more schools?

One School at a Time

In the late '80s when schools began in earnest to realize that the effective schools movement could be described by a relatively short list of correlates, some educators began to explore the possibilities for their schools. However, as we have discovered the notion of an equitable system is a process, not an event. The effective schools movement provided a vision for a more desirable school, but gave little insight as to how to best make the journey. As a result several problems resulted. First, many central offices and local boards of education attempted to mandate that their local schools become more effective. This directive led many practitioners to conclude that this was another top-down model for school improvement. Second, many building principals were given the impression that they carried the responsibility of creating an effective school. So for many schools, there was only one player in the process, the building principal. Needless to say this generated a lot of anxiety and resistance, for principals where they have a history of not being trained to be change agents but efficient managers of a school. Their training, and most educators as well, were concerned with processes, rather than on results. And finally, many teachers began to see the effective schools process as an administrative tool that too often implied that teachers were not already doing their best. For too many teachers, creating an effective school meant more work. Some of the lessons learned from the effective schools movement have been the acknowledgment that:

▶ All schools can do better.
▶ We can control the conditions of the school.
▶ We have good schools by design, not chance.
▶ We need to address the results of the school—not the activities of the school.
▶ Teachers and other school members must be an integral part of the process.
▶ The school should not be a contributing factor to a students failure.
▶ Improvement of education is with the school as a unit of change.
▶ School improvement, like any change, is best approached as a process, not an event.

Effective schools research emphasizes that if school improvement is going to occur, it will take place one school at a time.

School Improvement

Two lessons have been learned in the effective schools movement. First, researchers do not have all of the answers, but a growing number of educators do know that there are clearly established strategies of planned change that do work better than others. Second, the process of school improvement takes time, involvement and commitment. In fact, many reformers indicate a time period of five to seven years before they will witness systemic school improvement. For many educators, this timeline factor can be discouraging. When schools attempt to gloss over any of one of the essential elements, the results will soon be diminished. Clearly, when schools follow the process of school improvement, they will have a better school. However, when the processes are not implemented properly, they will fail to produce better schools for more students.

Growth in school improvement activity during the past several years has been remarkable. Literally hundreds of schools launched their effective school improvement plans. Some schools did it with assistance from outside consultants, some chose to proceed on their own. Some followed the guidelines of the lessons we had learned, even without knowing the research per se; and others chose to try to implement change and ignore what the research on successful change had reported. As a result of this diversity of approaches, we can say that the effective schools movement worked for some and not for others. Fortunately, results from a growing number of schools can claim that they have the results to prove that more of their students are learning, and learning at a higher level.

The Focus of School Improvement

The schools that have demonstrated success have implemented a process and they have generally proceeded to first examine and strengthen the following areas:

1. **Instructional Focus**   establishing a clear and focused school mission. There is a clearly stated academic mission which is articulated throughout the school. The staff shares an understanding and a commitment to the instructional goals, priorities, assessment procedures, and accountability of this mission. The mission is literally the keystone upon which the entire plan is built. Typically written in four sections, it provides the primary focus of the organization. The mission statement must emphasize the uniqueness, the distinctiveness, the singleness of the organization. Essentially, it represents the commitment of the organization's resources to one purpose.

- *Product*   Competent graduates who can succeed at their next level of endeavor, who believe in the worth and dignity of themselves and others, and who pursue lifelong learning in an ever-changing, richly diverse society.
- *Process*   By providing an environment conducive to learning and a well-balanced curriculum, delivered by a highly qualified staff responsible for learning, with an uncompromising commitment to quality.
- *Purpose*   To be the preferred source of education for all eligible students by guaranteeing competent graduates.
- *Motto*   Building a foundation of quality-with-equity. Putting it all together may appear as:

Building a Foundation of Quality-with-Equity

_____ School District will be a preferred source of education for all eligible students by guaranteeing competent graduates who can succeed at their next level of endeavor, who believe in the worth and dignity of themselves and others, and who pursue lifelong learning in an ever-changing, richly diverse society. This will be done by providing an environment conducive to learning and a well-balanced curriculum, delivered by a highly qualified staff responsible for learning, with an uncompromising commitment to quality-with-equity.

There has recently been some confusion as to the *mission* vs. *vision* of a school or organization. Simply, a vision is what the school will look like when the mission is accomplished. On the other hand, a mission provides a focus for the school.

2. **Measurement**   frequent monitoring of student progress. Information on student academic progress is obtained frequently and feedback is provided to the teacher and student regularly. Multiple assessment methods such as teacher-made tests, samples of student work, mastery skills checklists, portfolios, criterion-referenced tests, and norm-referenced tests are used. The results of testing are used to improve an individual student's performance, to improve the instructional program, and facilitate curriculum improvement.

3. **Learning Climate**   safe and orderly environment. There is an orderly, purposeful atmosphere which is free from the threat of physical harm. However, the atmosphere is not oppressive and is conducive to teaching and learning. It evolves from a commonly agreed upon school purpose and is characterized as positive and businesslike. Safety for all is a primary concern.

4. **High Expectations**   the school exhibits a climate of expectations in which the staff demonstrates a belief that *all* students can attain mastery of basic skills and the staff has the capability to help all students attain this mastery.

5. **Instructional Leadership**   the principal acts as the instructional leader who effectively communicates the mission of the school to the parents, staff, and students. The principal also understands and gives direction, emphasis, and support to the school's instructional program.

6. **Parent/Community Involvement**   home/school partnership. Parents understand and support the basic mission of the school and are given the opportunity to participate in helping the school achieve this mission. They are aware of the importance of their role in bringing the mission to fruition.

The school must be able to address what they are currently doing and what could they be doing with each of the six areas.

Accountability

The age of accountability has come to school systems. Educators are no longer believed as they were twenty years ago. School personnel must collect data to establish baseline information, implement prescriptive change and follow this with data collection to validate change. A critical question would be, what documented forms of evidence would you accept under each of the six areas cited above?

Analysis of Correlates

School: _____

Correlate: _____
(List the correlate identified for improvement)

Problem Area: _____

Data Collection Categories: List the factual data you would accept as evidence of this weakness and for validation of improvement.

Disaggregation Categories: List the categories for disaggregation that would best identify the subgroup of students or staff members most responsible for the area of concern.

Strengths: List the school's strengths in this area. Strengths are those attributes that may be built upon to enable the school to achieve its mission. Schools that achieve quality-with-equity do so by capitalizing on their strengths—doing what they do best. (Examples: qualified, talented staff, collaborative planning effort, parental confidence in the quality of their children's education, high average daily attendance, success of graduates).

Major Weaknesses: Specifically state the major cause of the area(s) of concern. The weaknesses are those inadequacies that impede the organization's ability to achieve its mission. These must be overcome if the school is going to be successful in its endeavors toward quality-with-equity. (Examples: no uniform grading policy, sub-groups of students not performing well academically, no formalized system of accountability in place, resistance to change by some, academic recognition is less than athletic recognition, no consistency in discipline.)

Establishing a Timeline

Goal (Year 1):   Specifically state your desired change for the coming year.

The goals are practical, specific parts of the mission. They express, in measurable terms (time, money, quality, quantity) the results the school will achieve as it fulfills its mission. Specifically stated, they must have broad, school-wide implications; and, they are aspirations, expressions of the desired, measurable end results, not projections. The time limit for reaching goals may be up to five years. (Examples: to graduate 100% of our students beginning with the 1995-96 eighth grade class. To increase the percentage of students achieving in the top two quartiles on norm referenced tests by 2% annually.)

Objectives (3-5 years):   State your desired long-term change in this area.

Objectives in this process are used to refer to the means used to achieve the goals in the school and its major parts. The objectives are the "what" and the "how" of the plan. They are the broadly stated means of gathering resources to achieve the school's goals. Objectives should represent "this year's" goals. (Example: To develop and implement a comprehensive program to meet the emerging social needs of our students. To develop and implement a comprehensive process for the assessment of quality-with-equity in the school. To develop and implement processes that strengthen the partnership between home, school and community.)

_____   _____
School   Year

Goal: _____

_____

Rationale: _____

_____

Expected Outcomes (List)

Monitoring (List)

Documentation:_____

Planning Teams

Two types of leadership teams can be created—building and district. Each building must establish a "building improvement team (BIT)." Often districts have "district improvement teams (DITs)." According to the research, the building is the strategic unit of change in the school improvement process. The major work of school improvement is accomplished by the building improvement team. The building team has the task of developing a building plan which is compatible with the overall goals of the district and devising strategies for improving student outcomes in their building. The building team develops or revises their plan on an annual basis.

Building leadership teams are the critical variable in school improvement. Successful change develops from commitment, not authority. This commitment must be developed and maintained over time and is a natural outgrowth of involvement. Educators will have a tendency to support what they create. The BIT is the catalyst, the critical unit for change, and must assure the rest of the staff representative input on BIT decisions.

Membership should represent all staff members in the building. For example, in an elementary school, it may include the principal, representatives of each grade level, and one special service representative, student(s), and parent(s). In a secondary school, it may include representatives of at least the major departments, special services, and the principal, custodial/clerical, student(s) and parent(s). The BIT should be large enough to be representative, yet small enough to be functional.

The purpose of the District Improvement Team (DIT) is to support the individual schools. This is different from most traditional hierarchical central office operations. Traditionally, the central office tells schools what they need, and then tells them how to meet those needs. The DIT listens to what each school needs and then responds to BIT requests for support. The DIT has responsibility for communication between schools and support of improvement in each school. However, ultimately, improvement must happen within each school under the direction of the BIT.

Beyond communication, the DIT has the responsibility for district planning, staff and curriculum development and assessment of student progress. The DIT members should ensure district consistency in staff evaluation and develop a student data management system for data collection and disaggregation. The DIT should include a member from each BIT, (elementary, middle or high school), teacher's associations, principals, non-instructional staff, Board of Education, and parent(s). The superintendent must serve on the DIT, but should not chair it.

The Nature of Collaborative Work

One of the strengths of the school improvement process is its collaborative nature. Some of the characteristics of collaborative work both on an individual and organizational level are highlighted.

- ▶ Some type of organizational structure is needed to collaborate.
- ▶ Time for collaboration needs to be allotted.
- ▶ Initially, activities propel the collaboration, not goals.
- ▶ People often underestimate the amount of energy it takes to work with other people.
- ▶ Ambiguity and flexibility better describe collaborations than certainty and rigidity.
- ▶ Conflict in collaborative work is inevitable.
- ▶ Shared experiences over time build mutual trust, respect, risk taking and commitment.

Developing School Improvement Plans

School improvement plans should include annual goals. School improvement plans should be limited to a manageable amount of activity—generally, three objectives or less. The one factor that has bogged schools down in the process, is the mistake of taking on more than one can reasonably be expected to accomplish. When in doubt, less is better. School improvement plans should be brief. School improvement objectives should be observable, measurable, and doable, and should identify who will do what by when. School improvement plans should list chronically the activities necessary, who is responsible, who is involved, and a target date for accomplishing the objectives. The following is an example:

ACTION PLAN

Action plans insure that the objectives are implemented. They allow specific assignments of task/s to individuals within the organization. They provide a means for measuring both individual and organizational performance, and an effective system of accountability.

Activity	Who's Responsible	Who's Involved	Target Date	Date Accomplished

Task Forces

Once needs have been identified, goals and objectives are set, prioritized, and agreed upon, the BIT is ready to plan improvement activities. A "task force" can be identified to deal with the action plan and accomplish each goal. As always, too many task forces will overload the system and lead to discouragement and failure. Each site should limit its activities to one to three goals for the year. Task force members should only include volunteers who are willing to undertake a particular challenge. Members should maintain systematic communication with the BIT.

Monitoring Progress

Progress should be monitored by the Building Improvement Team. There should be measurable positive change in perceptions of the school. Hard data, in disaggregated form, should be compared annually. The school improvement plan should be monitored during the year by the BIT for progress on each objective, and results should be reported to all stakeholders.

An Outcomes-Based Approach

An Outcomes-based approach is founded on three basic premises: (1) All students can learn and succeed (but not on the same day in the same way); (2) Success breeds success; and, (3) Schools control the conditions of success,(Spady,1988). Outcomes-based models, whether operating under the label Mastery Learning, Outcome-based instruction (OBI), Outcomes-Driven Development Model (ODDM), Outcomes-Based Education (OBE), Quality Performance Accreditation (QPA), or something else are growing at an astounding rate throughout the United States.

What is most essential for our students to know, be able to do, and be like in order to be successful once they've graduated? This question is the driving force behind the efforts of literally thousands of schools across the country. The intent of the Outcomes-Based approach is for schools to be able to document in a systematic manner what is being learned by each student in the system. The focus is on student outcomes (the end-product of the instructional process), rather than the process that a school follows. An outcomes-based approach requires schools to engage in establishing specific learner outcomes for all students in their school. Figure 6 shows a simplified example of an outcomes-based approach.

The common phrase associated with this alignment is for schools to "Design Down" and "Deliver Up." Similar to the effective schools movement, an outcomes-based approach requires schools to document where the school is achieving specific learning goals. A key feature of OBE is the principle of expanded opportunity. Expanded

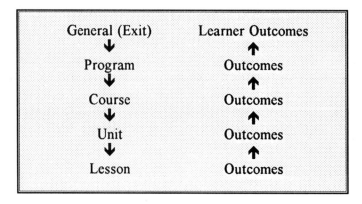

Figure 6. Outcomes Based Approach.

opportunity may be more easily understood as a second-chance system. According to Fitzpatrick (1991), failure is often considered an indicator of one's low ability, thus narrowing the scope of future options. The more final a failure is considered to be, the lower the probability of finding future options open. Consequently, real equal opportunity calls for a possibility of a second chance. The principle of expanded opportunity implies that schools must deliberately give students more than one routine chance to learn what they want them to learn before making them accountable for it. The essence of the second chance idea is that failure should not be considered final, should not be seen as a clear indicator of one's potential ability, determining the future to a great degree, but should be looked upon as a temporary setback which may be overcome. In other words, opportunity ends when students receive a permanent grade. The common denominator is a principle that failure is not absolute and another try is worth the effort.

If a school implements an outcomes-based approach based on these beliefs, that school will be better positioned to be able to address the needs of a wider range of students. It has the potential to be a system that is more equitable in learner outcomes for a greater number of students.

Quality-with-Equity

The outcomes approach defines quality programs as those in which student performance meets or exceeds expectations. Can a school claim to be a quality school if there are within it under-performing students—students who have not been achieving at the level of their capabilities, or students who have failed in the past and no longer respond to challenges, or ethnic minority students who believe that no one has an interest in their learning problems? Educators who believe in quality-with-equity reject the idea that students from certain socioeconomic classes do not have the ability to learn effectively or that it is acceptable for any students to perform below their capabilities, regardless of the level of those capabilities.

To make the first step toward quality-with-equity requires a critical mass of educators who believe all students can learn and who believe that it is worth the teacher's effort to provide the instruction which will make that happen. Currently, not all educators believe that all students can learn effectively and not all educators who believe all students can learn are willing to expend the effort required. In the quality school, principals and teachers believe that all students can learn and that all teachers can learn to teach all kinds of students. Responding to the following questions will indicate the school's commitment in providing a school characterized by quality-with-equity:

Are students who come to the school with educational disadvantages being challenged? Are educationally advantaged students achieving at the level of their capabilities? Is there evidence that teachers have high expectations for every student? Are resources being provided to assist students in overcoming whatever educational deficits they may have brought to the school? What are the documented evidences that educationally advantaged and disadvantaged students in this school are being challenged?

The outcomes process is relatively new. The process compliments the concept of quality-with-equity. An outcomes approach, when designed correctly, will require schools to document their results with *all* students. Those students who have historically underachieved in our schools stand a far greater chance to be better served in an outcomes-based approach. Why would that be true? First, it focuses the school on the outcomes of significance for academic achievement, not on the processes of schooling itself. Secondly, if there are students who are not achieving the stated outcomes of the school, the school must find ways to make certain that they accomplish the outcomes the school professionals believe they should have before they move on. This approach should "catch" more students who are underachieving and those who are currently slipping between the cracks.

Current Trends

What are some of the current policies and practices that are being implemented by schools that attempt to address the growing concern for improving quality, but at the same time to be more equitable? Since the mid-'80s, nearly two-thirds of the states have increased their high school graduation requirements. (See Figure 7—Change in Number of Course Units Required for High School Graduation.) Will these increased academic requirements affect all students the same way? Will these increased requirements be more equitably advantageous? If it is the consensus of many of the national reports and studies—that there are significant numbers of students in our schools that are not being well served—what will be the result of raising these requirements?

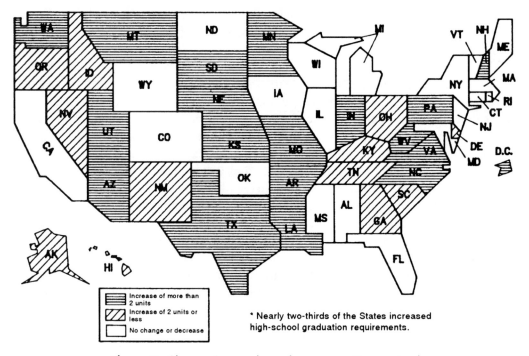

Figure 7. Change in number of course units required
for high school graduation.

If stricter academic requirements do what they were intended to do, no doubt some of the effects will be positive. On an individual basis, some students' lives may be enriched by the added exposure and challenge. More students may pursue rigorous, and more challenging courses. Some will be better prepared for postsecondary work, may require less remediation there, and can acquire more credit for advanced placement courses. Stronger backgrounds in academic subjects may make it possible for college students to specialize in their studies earlier.

There remains, however, the possibility that these added requirements may prove counterproductive for substantial numbers of students, and thus ultimately for society. To explore this issue, it may be useful to divide entrants of high school into four categories. (See Figure 8.)

The first category corresponds roughly to the 31 percent of academically successful students who eventually enter four-year colleges. Category two reflects the fact that 18 percent of high school students enter two-year college programs after high school. The

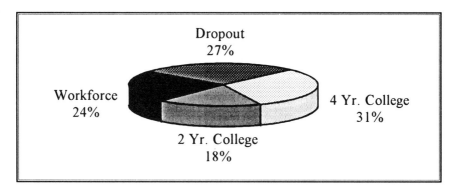

Figure 8. Increased academic requirements.

third category is the approximately 24 percent of students who are currently destined for—or typically interested in—further education; but they are likely to enter the work force immediately upon graduation. The last category of students are those most likely to fail and dropout of school prior to graduation; they now do so at a national rate of 27 percent.

Barring the possibility that course content will be diluted to accommodate students with less academic aptitude, new requirements will probably change life very little for the first category of students. College entrance requirements and expectations have always governed programs of study for college-bound students, and college requirements generally demand as much or more than the mandates require. Moreover, since these top performers have always expended great effort in school, impressive quantitative increments in their achievement are unlikely. The greatest difference for these students will perhaps be slightly different academic distribution and fewer available electives.

The second category is the group that might be affected most positively by new requirements. These young people have sufficient perseverance and academic orientation to have postsecondary aspirations, but their achievement falls below that of the most academically talented. Whether increased requirements will actually discourage their efforts remains an unsettled issue. In the early '90s, the two-year institutions are experiencing a tremendous growth in their enrollments. Whether this trend is attributed to the increased requirements is not clear. More likely, it would be the increased costs of a four-year institution, the need to work, possibly remaining at home to cut costs, a vocational training interest, or unsure of an academic pursuit at the time.

Although current national averages suggest that most of the third category of students graduate from high school, large percentages of these students are in vocational tracks. If the removal of such alternatives results in extensive withdrawals among this category, the aggregate impact of the new requirements will reduce rather than increase academic learning for many students. Simultaneously, this category of students will be denied access to courses that promote their retention in school and employability. Students in the fourth category are currently not being well served by the traditional academic program; thus they are dropping out. Imposing increased course requirements in these studies (with stronger focus on drill and repetition) is likely to lead to lower success rates for this group. Some educators believe that many of these borderline students may drop out of school earlier and in greater numbers.

Increased Requirements and Equity.

Many believe that the increased academic requirements may hit equity broadside. The present strong negative correlation between school success and diversity among students already challenges the capacity of our schools to compensate for certain social groups. For example, current reports of Hispanic drop-out rates reach as high as 35 percent nationwide. Overall, African-American drop-out rates are 21 percent—twice the rate for Whites. The drop-out rates among the lower socioeconomic students are also significantly higher than those among other students. If more third- and fourth-category students respond to increased requirements by abandoning their pursuit of a diploma, society's have-nots will be the ones most negatively affected by the new requirements. Concern is therefore growing that if increased requirements push drop-out rates still higher, education, already unable to forestall the formation of a "permanent underclass," may unwittingly make a bad situation worse. (Brandt, 1985)

The national commitment to quality and higher standards places a serious responsibility on all of us to weigh any proposal very carefully if it seems likely to disengage more people from the functioning society. I am not suggesting that we should be anti-academic or anti-higher standards, but I am suggesting that we need to seriously examine the **logic** and possible **consequences** of such reforms.

Let me provide an analogy. For a number of years the high jump bar has been set at four feet. We had some students who were able to make that height, but we also had students who were unable to meet that challenge. Now, we have raised the bar to four feet six inches. Common sense would tell us that we will more than likely have greater numbers of students who will not be able to meet this new height. To carry the analogy farther, if one does not provide additional coaching/or practice time for those particular students, the logic of raising the bar is questionable. Simply to raise the standards, and not address the needs for a growing number of students in our schools, will only enhance the likelihood of more students not being successful.

The Continuum of Equitable Competence for Schools

The word competence is used because it implies having the capacity to function effectively. An equitably competent school system—at all levels—acknowledges and incorporates the importance of the multidimensional aspects of equity.

Certainly this description of equitable competence seems idealistic. How can a school accomplish all of these things? How can a school achieve the higher expectations, new attitudes and policies? Equitable competence may be viewed as a vision that schools can strive for. Accordingly, becoming equitably competent is a developmental process. No matter how proficient a school may become, there will always be room for growth and improvement. It is a process in which the school can measure its progress according to the school's mission and vision and specific goals and objectives for school improvement. As the goals and objectives are defined the school will be guided toward a more progressively equitable system. First, it is important for a school to internally assess its level of equitable competence.

To better understand where a school is in the process of becoming more equitably competent, it may be useful to think of the possible ways of responding to school improvement. Imagine a continuum which ranges from Inequality to Advanced Equitable Competence. There are a variety of possibilities between these two extremes. (See Figure 9—The Continuum of Equitable Competence.)

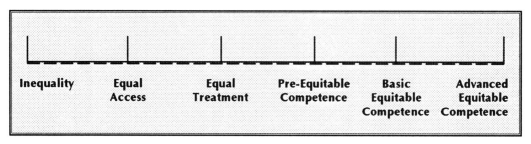

Figure 9. The continuum of equitable competence.

Inequality

The most negative end of the continuum is represented by attitudes, policies, and practices which are destructive to certain groups of students, consequently to the individuals within that group. The most extreme example of this orientation are schools which actively participate in the systematic attempt to treat groups differently. An historical example, would be the *Plessy v. Ferguson* (1986) Supreme Court decision—which stated the doctrine of "separate but equal." While we currently may not see as many overt examples of this extreme in our schools, nonetheless they exist in several pockets throughout the country. But for most schools this point on the continuum provides a reference point for understanding the various possible responses to equitable competency. A school which adheres to this extreme assumes that one race is superior and should eradicate "lesser" groups because of their perceived subhuman position. Bigotry coupled with vast power differentials allows the dominant group to disenfranchise, control, exploit or systematically destroy the targeted population. Today, there are schools, because of the lack of resources and facilities, that are inherently unequal and extremely disadvantaged as to the opportunities those students, staff and faculty will have in achieving a quality-with-equity system.

Equal Access

The next position on the continuum is one at which the school does not intentionally seek to be negative, but lacks the capacity to help targeted populations. The system remains extremely biased, believes in the superiority of the majority group and assumes a paternal posture towards "lesser" groups. These schools may disproportionately apply resources, discriminate against people of color, and provide segregated policies and practices within the schools offerings. The schools may reinforce racial, ethnic, or socioeconomic beliefs which maintain or reinforce stereotypical views about certain groups. Such schools are often characterized by ignorance and an unrealistic fear of people who happen to be different than the majority. The underlying philosophy of these schools is the expressed belief "that our doors are open to all students and they have equal access to our programs and staff." What these schools fail to recognize and change is that once inside the schoolhouse, students are not provided an equitable opportunity because of existing policies and practices that exist within. Simply endorsing the philosophy of equal access does not ensure equity in learning. Several schools have found themselves in the position of defending the equal access philosophy as being synonymous with equity. Typically, these arguments center around a variety of situations. For example, arguments for equal access have been based on the characteristics of forced busing policies, mandated court orders, hiring policies and practices, lack of effort to involve certain segments of the community in the school, and generally lower levels of academic achievement of a significant number of their students.

Equal Treatment

At the midpoint of the continuum this school has an expressed philosophy of being unbiased. They function with the belief that diversity makes no difference and that we are all the same. These schools expound on the strong belief that we don't treat students differently, we treat all students the same. These schools are based on the philosophy equal treatment is not a discriminatory practice. These schools are characterized by the belief that traditional approaches used by the majority are universally applicable; in other words, if the school worked as it should, all people—regardless of background—would be served with equal effectiveness. This view reflects a well-intended liberal philosophy; however, the consequences of such a belief are to make the school so ethnocentric as to render them useless to all but the most assimilated, and makes the erroneous assumption that all students have the same needs when they arrive at the schoolhouse door.

Such schools ignore the cultural strengths of the school, encourage assimilation and blame the students for their problems. People from diverse backgrounds are viewed from the cultural deprivation model which asserts that problems are the result of inadequate resources in the home or they lack the inherent ability to be successful. Outcomes are usually measured by how closely these students approximate a middle class nonminority student. These schools may participate occasionally in special projects with targeted populations when monies are specifically available or with the intent of "helping" the disadvantaged population. Unfortunately, such projects are often conducted without proper guidance and are the first casualties when funds run out. Equal treatment schools suffer from a deficit of information and often lack the avenues through which they can obtain the needed information. While these schools often view themselves as unbiased and responsive to nonmajority needs, their ethnocentrism is reflected in attitude, policy and practice.

Pre-Equitable Competence

As a school moves toward the positive end of the scale they reach a position referred to as pre-equitable competence. This stage on the continuum implies movement. This pre-equitable school realizes its weaknesses in serving certain students and attempts to improve some aspect(s) of their programs to a specific population. Such schools try pilot programs, make efforts to hire a diverse staff, begin to explore how to reach targeted populations more effectively, initiate staff development on diversity, enter into needs assessments concerning targeted populations, and actively recruit from diverse populations to serve on building improvement teams and advisory committees.

Pre-equitable schools are characterized by the desire to deliver a quality education and a commitment to civil rights. These schools are more responsive to non-majority populations, by asking, "what can we do?" One danger at this level is a false sense of accomplishment or of failure that prevents the school from moving forward along the continuum. A school may believe that the accomplishment of one goal or activity fulfills their obligation to the expressed needs of a targeted community or may undertake an activity that fails and are therefore reluctant to try again. These schools may appear to be responsive to diversity by organizing and conducting a one-day multicultural fair, but lack any on-going effort in a systematic manner. These schools have a tendency to believe that the process of an equitable system is an event, not a continual process. These schools have a history of jumping on the latest bandwagon fad, and riding it for awhile. Then this school abandons the effort, and proceeds to conduct business as usual until the next phenomenon comes along. Any real change in the system over the past several years is not evident. Most of the professionals in these schools express great cynicism to any real change that could or will ever to happen in their school. These schools have a tendency to resemble a sail boat that occasionally has its sails up and moving, but too often the sails are down and it seems to float along aimlessly with its mission of avoiding the rocks.

The pre-equitable school, however, is one that may be receptive to long-lasting reform with the necessary information on what the change process entails and how to proceed.

Basic Equitable Competence

Basic equitable competent schools are characterized by acceptance and respect for difference, continuing self-assessment regarding diversity, careful attention to the dynamics of difference, continuous expansion of cultural knowledge and resources, and a variety of adaptations to models in order to better meet the needs of all students. These schools are continually refining school policies and practices that are not achieving the intended results. These schools have established organizational structures that are responsive to the diversity of their students, staff and communities. The basic equitable school has an established criteria in hiring policies that reflect the mission and vision of the school and district. These schools have a tendency to secure outside funding sources to maintain many of their programs or strategies to meet the needs of specific targeted populations. The equity efforts exhibited by these schools are usually found with a relatively small number of faculty and staff and are not school-wide. There is evidence that central administration encourages individual schools to design, implement and document pilot programs that address instructional strategies or organizational structures. These schools have an on-going professional development program in place. They have established school improvement plans that prioritize the area(s) to focus their attention on a given timeline. These schools are beginning to base instruction on data-driven information. This school has a data base of all of its students, and it has moved from aggregate data to disaggregation of data. The basic equitable school provides several provisions for students who are academically under-achieving.

Advanced Equitable Competence

The most positive end of the scale is advanced equitable competence or a quality-with-equity school. This point on the continuum is characterized by holding diversity in high esteem. The advanced equitable school seeks to add to the knowledge base of equitable competence by conducting its own research, establishing pilot projects, and disseminating the results of demonstration projects. The advanced equitable school may hire or designate staff to coordinate equity issues in the school/district. Such schools advocate and can demonstrate quality-with-equity throughout the school system. These schools have established partnerships with the business community, private sector and institutions of higher education. Many of the programs are financed and supported by the local budget and not by outside temporary sources. From an instructional point, there are advisor-based systems in place, team-teaching is common, interdisciplinary approaches are every day occurrences, staff development is specifically focused and followed by a mentoring or coaching model. The staff in these schools are conducting and disseminating their own research findings on the practices or strategies they have implemented. These schools have a tendency always to never be fully satisfied with their efforts, they are constantly asking, how do we improve what we are doing? Can we do it better? If so, how? These schools are not satisfied with any student achieving below their ability.

In conclusion, the degree of equitable competence a school achieves is not dependent on any one factor. Attitudes, policies, and practice are three major arenas where development can and must occur if a school is to move toward advanced equitable competence. Attitudes change to become less ethnocentric and biased. Policies change to become more flexible and culturally impartial. Practices become more congruent with the background of the student from one year to the next. Positive movement along the continuum results from an aggregate of factors at various levels of a school's structure. Every level of the school (school board, policymakers, administrators, teachers and students), can and must participate in the process. At each level the principles of valuing difference, self-assessment, understanding dynamics, building cultural knowledge and adapting practices can be applied. As each level makes progress in implementing the principles, and as attitudes, policies and practices change, the school becomes more equitably competent.

Summary

The goal of educational reform today is quality. Some educators believe that the new emphasis may not mesh with equity concerns; and some observers believe it may be detrimental to those who cannot meet the latest requirements.

A recent report by a coalition of child advocacy groups warned that at-risk children have largely been ignored in the rush for educational reform. Policymakers at all different levels talk of bringing excellence to schools and tend to ignore the fact that hundreds of thousands of youngsters are not receiving even the minimal educational opportunities guaranteed under law. Nationally, recommendations include continued attention to the rights of the disadvantaged, more democratic governance of the schools, the establishment of comprehensive early childhood education and day care programs, and the enactment of more equitable and adequate systems for financing schools. Finn (1981) suggested that the new equity agenda (one that includes both quality and equity concerns), raises four separate issues: the differential impact of higher standards and tougher requirements; differential access to new curricula and better teaching; differential access to master teachers; and differential access to computers. These issues are very specific to individual sites. Great variation is easily possible within the same school district. Measuring these elements, and taking steps to ensure equity is likely to prove more challenging than the equity initiatives of the past twenty-five years.

Whether these recent national, state and local efforts will be a passing phenomenon or a genuine transformation of elementary and secondary education remains to be seen. The results will depend largely on the actions of state policymakers in the next few years. Precisely, what the states should do to maintain the impetus of reform is unclear. Defining a common set of tasks for all states is impossible. What California should do (and can do) is far different from the agenda in Mississippi. Indeed, if there were a single set of solutions equally applicable to the fifty states, the federal government would probably have pursued it.

As we have seen, some observers are concerned that today's preoccupation with quality will run counter to the nation's interest in equity. Such concern, although well motivated, is misplaced. Quality and equity are not mutually exclusive; to the contrary, they reinforce one another. Quality and equity are in conflict only if equal outcomes are expected. Quality means that some students will do better than others; equity means that each will be given an equal chance. A school that fears quality because it means unequal outcomes may be sure of one thing: That school will be neither one of quality or one of equity.

 ## END NOTES

Brandt, Ron (Ed.). *With Consequences for All*. The ASCD Task Force on High School Graduation Requirements, Washington, D.C., 1985.

Coleman, James S. *The Concept of Equality of Educational Opportunity*. Harvard University Press, Cambridge: MA, 1969.

Edmonds, Ronald. *A Discussion of the Literature and Issues Related to Effective Schools.* Paper presented for the National Conference on Urban Education, St. Louis, MO, 1978.

Finn, Chester E. "A Call for Quality Education." *Life Magazine*, March, 1981, pp. 68-77.

Fitzpatrick, Kathleen. "Restructuring to Achieve Outcomes of Significance for All Students." *Educational Leadership,* May, 1991.

Lazotte, Lawrence *Unusually Effective Schools: A Review and Analysis of Research and Practice.* National Center for Effective Schools Research and Development. Madison, Wisconsin, 1990.

Oski, Frank. *John Hopkins Magazine.* Presentation to the Maryland's Veterans, May, 1992. John Hopkins Children's Center.

Plessy v. Ferguson 163 U.S. 537 (1986).

Purkey, S.C., & Smith, M. S. "Effective Schools—A Review." *Elementary School Journal*, 1983, pp. 427-452.

Spady, Bill. "Organizing for Results: The basic authentic restructuring and reform." *Educational Leadership*, V. 46, No.2, 1988.

 ## SUGGESTIONS FOR FURTHER READING

Barth, Roland. *Improving Schools from Within.* Jossey-Bass Publishers, San Francisco: CA, 1990.

Fiske, Edward B. *Smart Schools, Smart Kids.* Simon & Schuster, New York: NY, 1991.

Glasser, William. *The Quality School.* Harper and Row, Publishers, New York: NY, 1990.

Goodlad, John I. *Teachers for Our Nation's Schools.* Jossey-Bass Publishers, San Francisco: CA, 1991.

Liberman, Ann. *Building a Professional Culture in Schools.* Teachers College Press, Teachers College, Columbia University, New York: NY, 1988.

Oakes, Jeannie & Lipton, Martin. *Making the Best of Schools.* Yale University Press, New Haven: CT, 1990.

Sarason, Seymour B. *The Predictable Failure of Educational Reform.* Jossey-Bass Publishers, San Francisco: CA, 1991.

Schlechty, Phillip. *Schools for the 21st Century.* Jossey-Bass Publishers, San Francisco: CA, 1991.

Name _____ **Date** _____

✔ **DISCUSSION QUESTIONS**

---

1. Purkey and Smith identified several characteristics of good schools. Select five characteristics you believe to be most important for a school to incorporate. (Rank order *your* five selections). Provide a brief rationale for your selection and ranking:

Number 1: _____

Number 2: _____

Number 3: _____

Number 4: _____

Number 5: _____

Rationale for your selections:

_____

_____

_____

_____

_____

_____

_____

_____

How do the five characteristics you have chosen *complement* or *conflict* with the equity perspective? Explain.

_____

_____

_____

_____

_____

_____

2. How would you define an effective school? How is an effective school different?

_____

_____

_____

_____

_____

_____

3. Identify the correlates for an effective school. Also, outline the process that a school should consider when establishing a school improvement plan.

_____

_____

_____

_____

_____

_____

_____

_____

_____

4. What is the outcomes-based approach? Briefly explain the concept.

_____

_____

_____

_____

_____

_____

5. Identify the six phases on the continuum for equity competence for schools.
In your opinion, where do you believe most schools are on the continuum today?
Explain.

_____

_____

_____

_____

_____

_____

_____

_____

_____

6. Nearly two-thirds of the states increased high school graduation requirements since the mid-'80s. Will these increased academic requirements affect all students the same way? Explain.

_____

_____

_____

_____

_____

_____

Do you agree or disagree with the concern raised by some of the educators that these new standards may be counterproductive for a significant number of students? Explain.

_____

_____

_____

_____

_____

_____

_____

_____

7. What is meant by the statement, "one school at a time?" Explain.

_____

_____

_____

_____

_____

_____

_____

8. Do you believe schools are spending too much time meeting the needs of "low-achieving" students at the expense of "high-achieving students"? Explain your position.

_____

_____

_____

_____

_____

_____

_____

SMALL GROUP WORK

If you were a member of a team that was asked to spend some time in a school (say two days) to determine if that school was an effective school—what would you want to know about that school or what would you look for?

Your group can identify which level to visit (elementary, middle or secondary). Identify a recorder to list all areas mentioned in your group and a presenter (who will verbally share with the other groups).

INDIVIDUAL OR GROUP WORK

Individually read the following case study of Emerson. Then in small groups discuss the case study with your group members. You should address each of the questions at the end of the case study.

A Loss of Excellence

A Case Study of Emerson Elementary*

Emerson school is a classic, old two-story building of brown brick and many paned windows decorated with snowflakes, flowers, valentines or pilgrims depending on the season. It is surrounded by asphalt and bushes dying from too many pounding feet. It is a small space for 285 children and 13 teachers. The gym is the auditorium is the music room is the meeting place. The principal likes to tell new parents that, "we all have to get along here because we live in each other's pocket."

It is a city school, it has a racially and ethnically diverse population of children. It has, however, been accused of being the only middle-class school left in the city.

The inside of the school as well as the outside is reminiscent of the schools of the '50s—long, dark, linoleum hallways with small boxed classrooms in a row on each side. But inside the classrooms there is great variety. Some are designed with quiet and order in mind, with desks still arranged in straight lines facing the teacher in the front next to the chalkboard. Others are a jumble of noisy business, with small groupings of desks and rug areas. The school is known for its eclectic styles of teaching.

There is one small teacher's room, and although it holds the only coffee pot in the school, many prefer to avoid the cliques and gossip about the students and other staff found

---

* (This case study was adapted from The Institute for School Improvement—Dr. Roland Barth, Harvard University, Summer 1991.)

there. An unexpected face in the doorway often causes dead silence to fall upon the room. It is not a place where there is talk of educational issues or constructive talk of problems.

Faculty meetings too, reflect the feelings of separateness and discomfort of many. Most come to the ½ hour meeting once a month with their coats on, ready to dash the moment the principal completes the list of nuts and bolts on the agenda. Most of the classrooms empty within 15 minutes of the final bell each day.

The staff is a mixture of young and senior teachers. Several of the staff were initially delighted to have the opportunity to get into this school, several others feared its reputation and would have chosen a school with lower expectations if there were openings. Some of the staff came from schools that were very traditional, while others came from more progressive schools.

The principal believes in protecting her teachers and giving them freedom in their classrooms to do what they want. "The principal allows us to be that way for good or bad. She would let me whether I was successful or not. It's her style of letting people alone." She rarely enters a classroom except to cover a break time when an aide was unavailable. She also believes too much was expected of teachers. When parents or teachers would ask about having a holiday assembly, a workshop on writing, team meetings, anything, her response was always the same. "We are a small school. Our teachers have to do everything already, so they can't possibly be expected to do more." Staff development is a city-wide workshop once a month during early release days.

As chairperson of the hiring committee and parent in this school, it came to my attention that three of the school's finest teachers were thinking of leaving. Carol had already accepted a position in another system for developing curriculum for gifted children. Shirley was applying to schools for principal positions, and John was thinking of returning to his previous job of science specialist. I was extremely concerned about the loss and wanted to understand their motivations for moving on. Because Carol had already begun working in her new position part time after school, she was unavailable to discuss her decision in depth. She did say that she needed a change which would allow her to use more of her talents, and that she wanted more opportunities for collaboration with other teachers. John and Shirley were eager to share their thoughts with someone.

John had been a classroom teacher in the school for only a year, in a 1-2 combination grade. He has tenure and his credentials are very strong in the sciences. Emerson had managed to hire him for a classroom position after all tenured teachers had been placed the previous fall. He had loved his year working with the children. "The enthusiasm of this age group is probably the single most important thing for my satisfaction." But he had been left alone in the classroom for his whole first year, and he was feeling unappreciated, unsupported, and very tired. The summer before beginning his new job, he had gone to England to study in a British Primary School, and he was anxious to begin using some of what he had learned. He talked with the hiring committee about his ideas on how to use math manipulatives, drama to teach social studies, his projects, and field trips. Long after other teachers had left each day, John was still working in his classroom. He had hoped to be sharing ideas and projects with other teachers, and as a new teacher he longed for feedback on how he was doing. His disappointment became evident in his conversation. " I don't understand the social dynamics of this school. I have probably had only 10 conversations about education with my colleagues all year. If we had more congenial relationships, I would have looked forward more to coming to work." When the central science department asked for him to come back, he was reluctantly considering the offer.

Shirley, the teacher next door to John was a 2-3 combination grade teacher who had been in the system for 15 years and in this class for five years. She was held in highest regard by both parents and teachers. Although she would prefer to stay in the classroom, she was looking at principal positions in other systems. Teaching for her was becoming routine, and she felt a need for more stimulation and challenge. "It's hard for me to imagine anyone coming up with something I haven't tried. There are only 6000 ways to cut a cake." She felt that she had achieved a significant level of expertise, and now she wanted to find ways of sharing it with others. Sharing would give her an opportunity for growth and new usefulness. She had tried "influencing" other teachers in the school indirectly through exhibitions of her class projects on bulletin boards in the halls. "Other teachers see what I am doing a safe way and become interested in it, and emulate it because it seems interesting to them. A lot of stuff I see going on makes me smile and feel good. The teachers are imitating me from what they've seen in the halls." But because she did not want to create tension and competitions, she did not share her expertise in more direct ways. "I want to influence without competition, be able to maintain peer relationships, have people feel safe and comfortable." She saw the position of principal as the only possible way of directly influencing teachers.

She was surprised to learn that John was also thinking of leaving. "I thought he was humming along." She saw him as conscientious, enthusiastic, and thoughtful, and saw him becoming a superb classroom teacher.

I was saddened and frustrated to hear their reasons for leaving the classroom. The loss of such commitment and excellence seemed so unnecessary. As I left the building that afternoon, I wondered if this type of workplace would be satisfying to any teacher with high expectations.

1. Given the description of Emerson, what are your initial reactions about this school?

_____

_____

_____

_____

_____

_____

2. Is there anything that can be done to hold on to teachers like Carol, Shirley and John in the future?

_____

_____

_____

_____

_____

3. How might one go about creating a congenial atmosphere where sharing of ideas, requesting feedback, asking for help, are acceptable and routine? Please be specific about the steps you would take.

_____

_____

_____

_____

_____

_____

_____

_____

4. What are your thoughts about why Shirley felt she had to be so cautious about how she shared her expertise with others? (It's not necessarily like this in other jobs...or is it?)

_____

_____

_____

_____

_____

_____

5. Is this a common occurrence in schools today? If so, why does this happen.

_____

_____

_____

_____

_____

_____

6. How should Emerson begin to turn itself around? Explain.

_____

_____

_____

_____

_____

_____

_____

Part 2

Linking Equity to Teaching and Learning

Classroom Issues and Their Impact on Learning

4

Introduction

Most observers agree that any efforts to reform the schools must pay careful attention to the teaching force. One of the common themes found in the current reports advocating reform has been the need for attracting and preparing future teachers to be more responsive and successful with the growing diversity of students.

Chapter 4—**Classrooms and Equity** is designed to examine: (1) effective teaching, (2) teacher expectations, (3) learning styles of students, and (4) the role and responsibility of teacher education programs.

Effective Teachers

An effective teacher is very difficult to define because the term effective is so value-laden. What appears to be effective teaching to one person may be considered poor teaching by another, because each one values different outcomes or methods. One teacher may run the classroom in a very organized, highly structured manner, emphasizing the intellectual content of the academic disciplines. Another may conduct the class in a less-structured environment, allowing the students much more freedom to choose subject matter and activities that interest them personally. Because of one's value system, an observer may identify the first teacher as an "effective" teacher, while he/she may criticize the second teacher for running "too loose a ship." Another observer may come to the opposite conclusion with respect to which teacher is better, again, because of a different set of values.

While it may remain difficult to agree on what an effective teacher is, effective teaching can be demonstrated. The effective teacher is one who is able to bring about intended learning outcomes. The nature of the learning is still most important, but two different teachers, as in the example above, may strive for and achieve very different outcomes and both be judged effective. The two critical dimensions of effective teaching are intent and achievement.

While effective teachers are defined as teachers who can demonstrate the ability to bring about intended learning outcomes, what enables them to achieve desired results with students? Have you ever stopped to think about what, if anything, makes teachers different from other well-educated adults? Why should you be the teacher instead of the person off of the street? What should effective, professional teachers know, believe, or be able to do that distinguishes them from other people?

It might be difficult to reach a consensus on exactly what knowledge and skills are unique to the teaching profession, but most educators would agree that special skills and knowledge are necessary and do exist. Certainly teachers must be familiar with children and their developmental stages. They must know something about events and happenings outside the classroom and school. They must possess enough command of the subject they are going to teach to be able to differentiate what is important and central from what is incidental and peripheral. They must have a philosophy of education to help guide them in their role as teachers. They must know how human beings learn and how to create environments which facilitate learning. Effective teaching, in essence, is the ability to communicate what one knows in a way others can understand them.

Reform in Classroom Instruction

For as long as anyone can recall, we have judged the quality of schools by what goes into them rather than by what comes out of them. A good school, we said, is one with ample facilities and resources, low student/teacher ratios, well-stocked library shelves, a variety of specialists, and numerous programs and activities. By the same token, we grant diplomas to students who accumulate enough Carnegie units to graduate. The rationale was based on the belief that what students study and for how long would stand as a rough barometer for what they actually learn. But educators know better now. The challenge for educators will be the outcomes that students leave our grade levels, buildings and districts with that will matter. The movement to outcomes-based approaches will in many respects force schools to address the needs of students who are not currently successful in the school. If the approach is based on designated outcomes, many of those students will be identified through the system and different approaches will be imperative. The outcomes focus has the potential to assist schools in striving for a more equitable system of education.

Teacher-Centered Instruction

Most teachers teach in much the same way they were taught—in an essentially didactic, teacher-centered mode. Recently, there are more and more classroom teachers trying different approaches and strategies, but for the majority of classrooms in this country, the teacher-centered approach is still the most common. Often this mode is dictated by the subject matter, which is outside the students' intuitive experience; the teacher knows the material and presents it to students, whose role is to absorb it. It is important to examine the strengths and weaknesses of this practice, for it has implications for the way students experience learning and for the way they perceive school.

In most classes, it is the teacher who determines the plan, the pace, and the specific activities for the day. This is as it should be, since presumably the teacher knows the subject, knows from experience what is within the interest and ability of the class, and knows how to present material so that students can assimilate it. To encourage student learning, the easiest and most common method of developing motivation is to use grades, and the easiest format for presenting material is the lecture. In a lecture, the teacher tells the class what he/she thinks is important, although he/she may modify the telling by asking questions that call for specific answers.

This process has many benefits. In the first place, it is a very efficient method of conveying information and making sure that material is retained, at least over a short span of time. A teacher can emphasize what needs to be emphasized, make difficult concepts understandable, and present summaries of what years of experience have shown to be important. Moreover, this teacher-centered, didactic model conforms with the community's expectations about what education should be. Most parents had the same kind of experience in school and feel comfortable when this is what their children are receiving. The system provides positive reinforcement of those values between school and family.

By mastering a given body of information, students may feel that they've learned and achieved, and teachers may feel they have accomplished something tangible and measurable. There are clear expectations, narrow boundaries between what is acceptable and what is not acceptable. Beyond this, the challenge of mastery gives a sense of seriousness of purpose and accomplishment. The process teaches students to deal with pressure and stress and to live up to others' expectations of them. If the teacher is able to set challenges that go beyond what students have done previously but not beyond their reach, students can stretch their minds to learn and grow. Teacher-centered instruction sometimes has the effect of forcing students to think about topics they find fascinating but would never have approached on their own. In the best situations, a teacher's passion and enthusiasm and way of seeing the world becomes those of his/her students.

Yet, there are serious liabilities in this way of teaching and the liabilities help to account for some of the problems schools face today. Perhaps above all, the process encourages incredible passivity. In most classes one sits and listens. Some concentration is necessary, but no matter how interesting the teacher, after a number of hours of sitting and listening, boredom almost inevitably follows. Possibly, what becomes boring is not what the teacher is saying, but the very act of sitting and listening for hours in a row. It is difficult for teachers to feel how passive the student's role is, for the role of the teacher is the essence of activity. For example, the minds of classroom teachers are constantly going . . . figuring out how to best present an idea, thinking about whom to call on, whom to draw out, whom to keep quiet, how to get students involved, how to make a point more clear, how to respond, when to be funny and when to be serious. Students experience little of this, as everything is done for them. This inactivity partially explains why students sometimes fail to grasp material even after going over it several times, for in teaching ideas, one must process the ideas and work with them to really understand them. But when only listening to ideas, only a minimal degree of concentration is required.

As Adler (1982) observed, "there is little joy in most of the learning that students are now compelled to do. Too much of it is make-believe, in which neither teacher nor pupil can take a lively interest." Without some joy in learning—a joy that arises from hard work well done and from the participation of one's mind in a common task—basic schooling cannot initiate the young into the life of learning, let alone give them the skill and incentive to engage in it further. Adler's conclusion is that all genuine learning is active, not passive. It involves the use of the mind, not just the memory. It is a process of discovery in which the student is the main agent, not the teacher.

Goodlad (1991) found that barely 5 percent of instructional time in the schools is spent on direct questioning and less than 1 percent is devoted to open questioning that calls for higher-level student skills beyond memory. The teaching observed in his study was characteristically telling or questioning students, reading textbooks, completing workbooks and worksheets, and giving quizzes. This pattern became increasingly dominant with the progression upward from primary to secondary classes.

We are almost embarrassed that so much about good teaching is so familiar, but at the same time, we are encouraged by this realization. There remain some old-fashioned yet enduring qualities in human relationships that still work—command of the material to be taught, contagious enthusiasm for the work to be done, optimism about the potential of the students, and human sensitivity, that is, integrity and warmth as a human being. As Boyer (1983) expressed, "when we think of a great teacher, most often we remember a person whose technical skills were matched by the qualities we associate with a good and trusted friend."

Why Are We Doing This?

Our class methods also promote the feeling that students have little control over or responsibility for their own education. Central to understanding this lack of responsibility is the fact that the agenda for the class is the teacher's; it is the teacher who is convinced that the subject matter is worth knowing and that the specific activities planned are the best ways of obtaining this knowledge. Students are often not convinced of this, and sometimes do not see why they have to know or do what the teacher asks. Students are products of a society which no longer automatically assumes that the teacher knows best. Without the legitimacy that assumption gives, teachers face a serious motivational task wherein they must convince students that what we think is worth knowing, is worth learning. How can we address this critical issue? Not to simplify a difficult task, what would happen if after the teacher has given the assignment or students have just completed an assignment—if the teacher asked the following question: (1) Can you tell me why in the world we are doing it? Or, for the completed assignment: (2) Can you tell me why in the world did we do this? As classroom teachers we must be able to give our students a decent and convincing answer to the question, "Why are we doing this?" The bottom line is the more relevant the lesson(s); the greater the motivation will be among students.

There is a tendency among some students and parents to believe that poor student performance is caused by poor teaching rather than poor learning. The critical question is not what does the teacher do? It's what does the teacher get the students to do? To encourage responsibility, and to encourage students to take a more active role in their own education, teachers need more accurate, on-going information from students. With the teacher doing most of the work, there is a danger of losing students, not knowing whether they're lost, bored, tuned out, or confused.

Beyond this, our class methods often promote the idea that learning is taking down copious notes and that knowledge is passing it back on a test. We discourage students from trusting their own observations or insights and from asking questions. Too often we discourage students from listening to each other, for "knowledge is what the teacher tells you." Real intellectual curiosity or pursuing any subject beyond requirements tends to be discouraged because there is so much that must be mastered that there is little time for anything else. Many students don't really learn how to learn, how to follow up a question they're curious about, or why they should want to learn, except to get good grades for college and to please their parent(s). So, for many students, there are two choices: do everything that's expected, or "opt out" completely and do the very minimum. We forget that young people, like most adults, do just enough to get by.

Teacher Expectations

What are the expectations that classroom teachers have toward students? Don't classroom teachers treat all students the same? Most educators are convinced that teacher expectations are a very critical dimension in the teaching process. Expectations have a direct effect on a teacher's behavior; they determine how teacher's view themselves and interact with others. Much research has focused on teacher's interactions with their students, specifically on their expectations. The term "self-fulfilling prophecy" means that students perform in ways in which teachers expect. Their performance is based on the subtle and sometimes not so subtle messages from teachers about their worth, intelligence and capability. For example, to label a student "slow," can be damaging simply because there are a few teachers who would stereotype on the basis of the word "slow." A slow student is an individual who has a learning difficulty as the result of low intelligence. This student is one of 14% of the school population who has an IQ between 70 and 85. Learning for this student is difficult particularly when all students are treated the same way, i.e., taught the same way and given the same assignments. To label or classify students has become a common practice and approach for a variety of reasons. The logic is that labeling allows for differentiation of treatment. The tragedy is that some teachers are so unprofessional that a label becomes the stigma. There are teachers who expect a slow student to do poorly and because they expect it the student tends to fulfill the prophecy. Another point that may help to dispel preconceived notions is the realization that a test score is the least the student knows—never the most. We need to instill in our teaching force that we must handle the information about our students in such a way that promotes understanding rather than makes excuses.

The Self-Fulfilling Prophecy

The classic study by Rosenthal and Jacobson (1968) provided the impetus for further research on the subject. In their study, several classes of children were given a nonverbal intelligence test, which was said to measure the potential for intellectual growth. A random number of students were selected by the researchers as "intellectual bloomers," and their names were given to the teachers. Although their test scores had nothing to do with their actual potential, the teachers were told to be on the alert for signs of intellectual growth. Overall, these children, particularly in the lower grades, showed considerably greater gains in IQ during the school year than did the other students. They were also rated by their teachers as being more interesting, curious, and happy and thought to be more likely to succeed later in life. Needless to say, this research caused a sensation in the educational community. Prior to this study, a students' failure in school could be blamed solely on family circumstances. Since this study, the influence of the teachers' attitudes, beliefs and behaviors had to be considered. These findings had major implications for the education of those students most seriously disadvantaged by schooling, that is, for students from culturally diverse backgrounds and lower-socioeconomic backgrounds.

Consistently, the issue of high teacher expectations is repeated throughout the national reports and literature for effective schools. Most teachers occasionally harbor attitudes or feelings toward students that are detrimental to their teaching effectiveness. To suggest that these findings implicate the classroom teacher as solely responsible for students failing academically is misguided. There are many variables that are out of the control of the classroom teacher. However, to place blame elsewhere and not look at the expectations of classroom teachers is equally misguided.

Classroom Interactions

What have we learned from the research? One of the more common interactions in most classrooms is the question posed by the teacher and the answer generated by the student. Is there equal opportunity to answer? No, say researchers—most teachers call more on their perceived "high" achievers to recite/perform than on those they think less able. There are several reasons for this. Teacher's don't want to embarrass a student they suspect doesn't know the answer. They want their classes to hear correct and thoughtful replies. And high-quality student performances obviously reward teachers more.

Research has clearly demonstrated that positive teacher expectations improve behavior and increase achievement. These research findings clearly demonstrate that teachers have greater expectations for, pay more attention to, and give higher grades to students who come from higher socioeconomic classes and students who happen to be White.

Teachers are also more likely to perceive ethnic minority students and students from lower socioeconomic classes as low achievers. Teachers tend to behave differently toward students who have been labeled low achievers. The result—these students are not provided with an equal opportunity to participate in the classroom instruction and experience. No one rises to low expectations. Research clearly indicates that teachers:

▶ Interact more with perceived high achievers and ignore and interrupt perceived low achievers more frequently.
▶ Ask more and higher-level questions of perceived higher achievers and provide perceived low achievers with questions that require simple recall.
▶ Follow up with probing questions for perceived high achievers and call on someone else if the perceived low achiever is unable to provide a prompt, accurate response.
▶ Provide a longer wait time for perceived high achievers to respond to a question and cut off response time for perceived low achievers who hesitate.
▶ Praise perceived high achievers more often and criticize perceived low achievers more frequently.
▶ Provide supportive communications for perceived high achievers and engage in dominating behaviors with perceived low achievers.

▶ Provide perceived high achievers with detailed feedback and give less frequent, less accurate and less precise feedback to perceived low achievers.

▶ Demand more work and effort from perceived high achievers and accept less from perceived low achievers.

▶ Are physically closer to perceived high achievers than with perceived low achievers.

▶ Provide more personal compliments and show greater interest in perceived high achievers than with perceived low achievers.

Raising Expectations

Obviously, when there is a match between teaching style (strategy) and the student's learning teaching style (strength) than higher achievement is more likely to occur. However, changing one's teaching style may not always be possible therefore one should supplement instruction by providing the student various forms of techniques that will relate to his/her particular learning style. What policies or practices could classroom teachers consider to combat the inequitable interactions that take place in the classroom? The following are illustrative examples of areas that should be considered.

▶ All students should be held accountable to the same standards for participation in classroom discussions.

▶ Teachers should maintain a uniform standard of behavior for all students.

▶ All written and verbal evaluations should be related to academic skills and the particular abilities being assessed.

▶ Teachers should group students in a manner that avoids segregated instructional or classroom activities.

▶ Teachers should make a special effort to avoid the use of stereotypes in assessment of and reaction to pupil behavior and achievement.

▶ Teacher's instructional strategies should relate to the individual learning styles of the students.

▶ If certain students are less active in classroom discussions and activities, the classroom teacher should make special efforts to include those students.

▶ Teachers should provide clear and specific information about student work, indicating what is right and what is wrong, suggesting that students can improve.

What forms of documentation should a classroom teacher have in order to verify that these policies exist?

TESA

Teacher Expectations and Student Achievement (TESA) is a staff development program for teachers of all subjects and all grade levels, including higher education. The program focuses on the need to provide both perceived low and high performing students with equal learning opportunities in the classroom. The program highlights 15 classroom interactions associated with effective teaching. The program has two principle objectives: (1) to insure that following training (six months), participating teachers will direct the positive behaviors specified in the interaction model toward students they perceive as low achievers more frequently than prior to training, and as frequently as they direct those behaviors toward students perceived as high achievers. (2) To demonstrate measurable and statistically significant gains in classroom performance for all students, both those perceived to be "low" achievers and those perceived to be "high" achievers. As a trainer, I have come to realize the impact that this staff development program can have on classroom instruction. If the program is planned, delivered and evaluated as suggested, schools can make a difference in the interaction patterns between the teachers and students.

Strong likes and dislikes of particular students, biases toward or against particular ethnic minority groups, low learning expectations for lower socioeconomic students and biases toward or against certain kinds of student behavior, all can reduce teaching effectiveness. Self-awareness of such attitudes toward individual pupils or classes of students is necessary if teachers are to cope with their own honest feelings and beliefs. The TESA staff development program highlights these concerns in a professional and meaningful manner.

Assessing Intelligence and Ability

Insufficient understanding of intelligence and unfair distinctions based on the misuse of tests result in mislabeling, misclassifying and miseducating many students. Too often, educators are overly concerned with classifying students and, as a result, rarely use high-quality, informative assessments to shape instruction at the school and to guide policy decisions.

Popular views of intelligence and ability, as well as perceptions about the distribution of talent in the general population, influence educational practice. What seems fair and reasonable at the moment—tests showing how students compare with others on global characteristics—such as mathematics and verbal aptitude—turn out systematically to limit some students' access to knowledge. For the most part, tests of intelligence, ability and achievement simply rank students, separating and segregating them and sorting them for future social participation. Such tests are used to select some students for enriched educational opportunities and slate others for low-level participation. Forecasting failure for some students severely limits their subsequent opportunity in school and later life.

Once the tests identify and legitimize students' differences, students are provided with different school experiences. In contrast, current research in cognitive psychology challenges traditional forms and uses of mental measurement (Education Commission of the States, 1988). The best evidence from this work reveals an abundance of cognitive processes that go unmeasured, that children learn to be intelligent, and that it is possible for schools to nurture mental growth and produce significant gains in the intellectual development of individual learners.

A regrettable side-effect of the widespread misunderstanding of testing and its uses is the current reliance on standardized, norm-referenced tests for judging school quality. It is simplistic to think that students' scores on a set of multiple-choice test items provide very much useful information about the quality of their school experiences. Certainly these test scores reveal something about what students have learned, but because much of the variance in scores can be accounted for by a wide variety of cultural factors, they say little about overall school quality. Unfortunately, not only the accomplishment of students, but also the goodness of schools, school districts, states and the nation as a whole are being judged by narrow bands of scores on standardized tests. While tests have the potential to provide useful information, they can also distract policymakers from the real business before them—supporting necessary changes in how schooling is conducted.

The Power of Tradition

What policies and practices lead to these alarming differences in the opportunities students have in the schools and classrooms they attend? One such practice and policy that is contributing to this differential opportunity is that of "tracking."

What exactly is tracking? To address this question, we need to examine the distinction between ability grouping and curriculum differentiation. Proponents of ability grouping stress flexible subject-area assignment. By this they mean that students are assigned to learning groups on the basis of their background and achievement in a subject area at any given moment, and that skills and knowledge are evaluated at relatively frequent intervals. Students showing gains can be shifted readily into another group. They might also be in different ability groups in different subjects, according to their own rate of growth in each subject. This practice suggests a common curriculum shared by all students, with only the mix of student abilities being varied. It also assumes that, within that curriculum, all groups are taught the same material.

In fact, it seems that group placement becomes self-perpetuating, that students are often grouped at the same level in all subjects, and that even a shared curriculum may be taught differently to different groups. Quite often, different ability groups are assigned to different courses of study, resulting in simultaneous grouping by curriculum and ability. Although ability grouping and curriculum grouping may appear different to educators, in fact they share several social similarities: (1) students are placed with those defined as similar to themselves and are segregated from those deemed different; (2) group placement is done on the basis of criteria such as ability or postgraduate plans that are unequally esteemed. Thus group membership immediately ranks students in a status hierarchy, formally stating that some students are better than others.

Grouping and Tracking Practices

Oakes (1985) defines tracking as "the process whereby students are divided into categories so that they can be assigned in groups to various kinds of classes." Testing individual aptitudes is the foundation for school practices that identify individual differences in order to determine which students get what instruction. Tracking practices begin with the assumptions that differences among students diminish instructional effectiveness, and that students can be assigned fairly and accurately to intellectually homogeneous groups for instruction. This systematic separation of students begins early in their education and forecloses opportunities for enriched coursework for many students. By the secondary level, tracking placements sort students for school opportunities and subsequent social roles.

Low-Level Placements

Research indicates that students assigned to low-ability classes are often taught differently, are less socially valued, and are provided limited knowledge and skills. Emphasis is predominately on rote learning, workbooks, kits and easy material. Regardless of ability or motivation, these students' academic mobility is constrained. They stand little chance for an improved school placement because those in low-track classes are usually denied access to the knowledge necessary to participate in more rigorous and interesting work.

Moreover, teachers in low-ability classes tend to be overly concerned with getting students to be punctual, to sit quietly and follow directions. They are often seen as less concerned and more punitive. Discipline, class routines and student socializing cut into the classwork of low-ability groups, further eroding these students' opportunities for an education of value.

High-Level Placements

By contrast, teachers in high-ability classes more often encourage critical thinking and independent questioning. They are more enthusiastic, better organized and make lessons clearer. Students in these advanced groups typically spend more time on learning activities and homework. Nearly all students can indeed benefit from enriched learning opportunities and high-quality experiences in literature, languages, science and mathematics. But sorting practices regularly exclude students from classes with high-quality instruction.

Tracking the myths and misinformation that support these grouping practices constitute a severe barrier to equity. The quality of the curriculum and instruction for the high-ability group and the resources that support advance-track students also work well for lower-ability students. While many studies describe students' progress in mixed-ability groups, those not in the top groups or tracks suffer clear and consistent disadvantages from their academic placements. Tracking often seems to retard the educational progress of students identified as average or low. Assignment to low tracks can lower student aspiration and self-esteem and negatively affect attitudes toward school. Sadly, those children who need more time to learn appear to receive less. Those who have the most difficulty succeeding in school have fewer of the best teachers. Those who stand to benefit from classroom with rich resources nearly always get the least (Oakes & Lipton, 1990)

Virtually all studies that address the assignment of students of different academic abilities to different tracks cite severe problems with the practice. Boyer (1983) discussed the effect on students' self-image and motivation, noting that tracking has a "devastating impact on how teachers think about the students and how students think about themselves."

Goodlad (1983) identified problems more tangible than self-image. In upper tracks, he consistently found more use of effective teaching practices more clarity, organization, and enthusiasm—and more focus on higher-level cognitive processes, such as drawing inferences, synthesizing, and making judgments. In classes that are more heterogeneous in terms of abilities, the studies agree that the teaching is more like upper-track than lower-track classes.

Another disadvantage that students in lower-track classes encounter is being in a classroom where the tone is set by a group of students who are, for the most part, unmotivated and who have low academic self-esteem. Students placed in lower tracks turn out to have higher dropout rates, more school misconduct, and higher delinquency. Track placement apparently affects students' plans for the future over and beyond their aptitudes and grades. A compounding problem is that ethnic minority and low socioeconomic students are disproportionately represented in the lower tracks. Goodlad sums up the situation with this observation: "Instead of creating circumstances that minimize and compensate for initial disadvantages in learning, teachers unwittingly create conditions that increase the difficulty of eliminating disadvantage."

Despite what we know about the effects of tracking, the practice continues. The essential question that remains is why? Why do we continue a practice that clearly runs counter to what we say we ultimately want in education? Lacking any academic rationale, it may lie in the "power of tradition." In other words, we have done it this way for so long, that it has become common practice and policy. There are four assumptions upon which the practice of tracking rests. The research clearly has demonstrated that these assumptions are not supported by the findings.

(1) Students learn better in groups of those who are academically similar. (2) Slower students develop more positive attitudes about themselves and school when they are not in day-to-day classroom contact with those who are much brighter. (3) Track placements are part of a meritocratic system with assignments earned by students and accorded through fair and accurate means. (4) Teaching is easier when students are grouped homogeneously, and teaching is better when there are no slower students to lower the common denominator.

Oake's research in 297 classrooms suggests that these common assumptions are false. If teachers accept her evidence, they should work to eliminate tracking from schools. However, emerging evidence suggests that educators have not been quick to do so. Finley (1984) found that support for the tracking system in the school came from teachers who competed with each other for high-status students.

How Did We Arrive at Tracking?

At the turn of the century, when just over ten percent of America's youth attended high schools and approximately two-thirds of these students were preparing for college, a relatively common curriculum devoid of tracking was provided. In a sense, what probably would be today's upper and perhaps middle tracks already were self-selected simply by attendance at secondary schools. A marked increase in high school attendance since then and, consequently, greater diversity in student populations changed all of this. The growth in testing not only provided measures of achievement differences among students but also a seemingly scientific basis for sorting them. Tracking became widely practiced by educators as a device for endeavoring to reduce the range of differences in a class and therefore the difficulty and complexity of the teaching task. The practice has been reinforced from outside the school by those who believe that able students are held back by slower ones when all work together in the same class.

For many people, tracking appears to be such a rational, common-sense solution to a puzzling problem that arguments against it are often ridiculed. The concept has particular appeal for parents who believe their children to be above average in ability and therefore are candidates for the more advanced classes. With advancing seniority, many teachers hope to be selected to teach the upper-track students, who are believed to be more eager to learn and less unruly.

The research findings raise serious questions about the educational benefits claimed for tracking and suggest some negative side effects. But these findings rarely are brought forward beyond the research literature to address tracking policies and practices. If we are to seriously examine equity and establish more effective instructional practices; the practice of sorting, labeling and tracking students must be addressed.

Methods of Selection

For ability grouping to operate as intended, the methods of selection would need to be highly valid, objective, and reliable. The evidence is generally discouraging in this regard. When ability is controlled, disproportionate numbers of middle-class students are found in the higher tracks, with a similar disproportion of lower-class students in the lower tracks (Oakes, 1985, Boyer, 1983).

The conclusion—ability grouping is practiced in the official belief that it helps the school meet the needs of individual learners. The mass of evidence suggests that it improves the achievement of few students and lowers that of many; that it damages student's self-esteem; that selection methods tend to be inaccurate and biased; that once initial grouping decisions are made, they tend to assign a stigma that is unalterable and self-fulfilling; and that it is based on erroneous assumptions regarding the validity and stability of intelligence measures and the concept of general aptitude.

One of the goals of our society is to promote the growth of each child through schooling to his/her full academic and social potential. Students come to school with the hope that it can help them gain the academic and occupational skills that will enable them to become somebody and be successful in life. Although this hope is compatible with the espoused goal of the school, in our unequal economic system, not everyone can be equally successful. The school, by sorting, classifying, tracking and labeling students, plays a part in casting students for different occupational roles in the economic system. Questions should be raised as to whether the schools should sort young people into different kinds of roles for future employment, and if so, on what basis should the sorting be done?

The recent work of a number of educators indicates that schools perpetuate social class inequity by assigning students to different positions on the basis of family background. Schools, they say, serve as an instrument of society for allocating students to different levels of status and for making decisions about their life chances. In essence, the school classifies students as good learners, average learners, and poor learners; and these classifications influence the opportunities available to them.

Students can be grouped in two ways: in terms of their abilities and in terms of the curriculum. When ability grouping is used, students are supposedly placed into groups based upon three factors: 1) their prior achievement in the subject area, 2) their mastery of the skills needed to learn the subject, and 3) their learning ability. When curriculum grouping is used, students are divided into areas on the basis of their educational and occupational aspirations so that each can receive instruction in preparation for a specific kind of future. Conant (1967) wrote that the purpose of curriculum grouping is to offer "opportunities for those who wish to step from high school right into a job, on the one hand, and to also offer opportunities for those who propose to start . . . college."

Tracking may be formal or informal. For example, in some schools students are officially classified into specific tracks. In other schools there is no official classification, but counselors and teachers know which classes are more challenging and which are easier and assign students accordingly. It is the rare school that doesn't have some mechanism for sorting students. Ability grouping within a single classroom may be fixed for the year or may vary from subject to subject and from month to month. No matter how formal or informal the system may be, the essential characteristics of tracking are similar.

Are There Alternatives to Tracking?

Clearly, one of the most effective ways to reduce the number of students who will ultimately need remedial services is to provide the best possible classroom instruction in the first place. Therefore, an essential element of an overall strategy to serve "low-achieving" students is to use classroom instructional methods that have a proven ability to increase student achievement. Slavin (1988) found nearly all the successful approaches for classroom change were either continuous progress models or certain forms of cooperative learning.

Continuous Progress Programs

In continuous progress models, students proceed at their own pace through a sequence of well-defined instructional objectives. However, they are taught in small groups composed of students at similar skill levels (but often from different homerooms or even different grades/multi-aged grouping). For example, a teacher might teach a unit on decimals to third, fourth and fifth graders who have all arrived at the same point in the skills sequence. Students are frequently assessed and regrouped based on these assessments.

Multiage Grouping

Multiage grouping is one way schools can organize around students and their learning, rather than around grade cut-offs and curriculum scope and sequence. In multiage grouping, students of different chronological ages are intentionally assigned to the same classroom. Every classroom teacher knows that students in any given class will be "all over the map" developmentally, with range abilities often spanning several grades. Multiage grouping recognizes these things as facts of life and organizes around them, rather than acting as though all students are the same and developing "remediation" or special programs for those who are the exception.

In multiage classrooms, students work in groups consisting of two or more age levels; the same peer group may remain together for more than one year. Students may work with one teacher, a team of teachers, or interact with several different teachers during the school day.

Multiage classrooms are based on the belief that students benefit from interactions with other students who are at varied stages of development. It is also felt that "mixing" of ages provides greater diversity, and more accurately mirrors life in the family and the community. This approach differs markedly from the traditional notions of sorting and scheduling students by age or ability alone.

Cooperative Learning

There is now substantial evidence that students working together in small cooperative groups can master material presented by the teacher better than can students working on their own (Slavin, 1987). What is cooperative learning? Cooperative learning refers to a set of instructional methods, in which students work in small, mixed-ability learning groups. For example, the groups may have four members—one high achiever, two average achievers, and one low-achiever. The students in each group are responsible not only for learning the material being taught in class, but also for helping their groupmates learn. Often, there may be some sort of group goal.

Like continuous progress approaches, cooperative learning has been found to boost the achievement of average and high achievers as well as low achievers. In addition, cooperative learning has a consistent positive influence on self-esteem and human relations. Four student team learning methods have been extensively developed and researched. Two are general cooperative learning methods adaptable to most subjects and grade levels: Student Teams—Achievement Divisions, or STAD, and Teams-Games-Tournament, or TGT. The remaining two are comprehensive curricula designed for use in particular subjects at particular grade levels: Team Accelerated Instruction (TAI) for mathematics in grades 3-6, and Cooperative Integrated Reading and Composition (CIRC) for reading and writing instruction in grades 3-5. These four methods all incorporate team rewards, individual accountability, and equal opportunities for success, but in different ways (Slavin, 1988).

A substantial body of research has established that two conditions must be fulfilled if cooperative learning is to enhance student achievement substantially. First, students must be working toward a group goal, such as earning certificates or some other recognition. Second, success at achieving this goal must depend on the individual learning of all group members (Slavin, 1983, 1984)

Success for All

Success for All (Slavin, 1988) combines the most effective programs and requires a comprehensive restructuring of the elementary school. In Success for All, the school takes responsibility to insure that no child falls behind in basic skills and that every child will reach the third grade on time with adequate skills. The program integrates several components from the research cited earlier. It uses a structured one-to-one tutoring program for students (especially first graders) who are falling behind in reading; preschool and extended-day kindergarten programs focusing on language skills and self-esteem; a continuous-progress program for grades 1-3 that uses many elements of cooperative learning; and a family support program to encourage parent involvement and home support of the school's goals.

The Accelerated School Model

Generally, low-achieving students are assisted with remedial services, which often pulls them out of regular classrooms. Unfortunately, experience has shown that this strategy will keep these students from becoming academically able because: 1) it institutionalizes them as slow learners, thus reducing expectations for their success; 2) it slows down the pace of instruction so that they get farther and farther behind their peers; 3) it emphasizes the mechanics of basic skills without giving them the substance that will keep them interested and motivated; 4) it provides no way to close the achievement gap between *disadvantaged* and *advantaged* students; and 5) it does not help teachers and parents formulate strategies to improve the learning of their students and children (Levin, 1989).

The Stanford Accelerated Schools Project has designed an accelerated elementary school that will help these children catch up with their nondisadvantaged peers by the end of the sixth grade. The entire school is dedicated to this objective, and this commitment is reflected in the involvement of many participants. Teachers, parents, and students have high expectations, and set deadlines for students to meet particular educational requirements. The educational staff tailors the accelerated school's dynamic, instructional programs for its own needs. And the program uses all available resources in the community—including parents, senior citizens, and social agencies.

The philosophy of the accelerated school is the notion that we can and must treat at-risk students in the same way that we treat "gifted and talented" students. In short, we must accelerate, not remediate.

Teacher Education: Preparation and Programs

Educational journals are filled with articles about teacher education programs; accounts of curricular revisions, surveys of teachers' opinions of their preparation programs, effects of student teaching/or internships, field-based experiences, preparing teacher candidates for a multicultural society, five-year or extended programs, and more recently, reorganization. This body of literature suggests some of what is wrong with and some of what is needed for teacher education programs. However, most of the research uses the individual as the unit of analysis. It therefore becomes difficult to interpret what this research on individuals means for institutions.

The reports seem to have one thing in common;that is, the poor quality of teachers is a contributing factor for the crisis in public education. The National Commission on Excellence (1983), for example, found that the quality of America's teachers had slipped dramatically in recent years. The Commission concluded that not enough of the academically able students were being attracted to teaching; that teacher preparation programs needed substantial improvement; that the professional working life of teachers was on the whole unacceptable; and that a shortage of teachers existed in key fields.

All observers agree that any efforts to reform the schools must pay careful attention to the teaching force. How have teacher education programs responded to these allegations?

Reforms in Teacher Education

Research about Teacher Education, (RATE, 1990) cited the recent activity within teacher education programs across the country. The report indicated (See Figure 10):

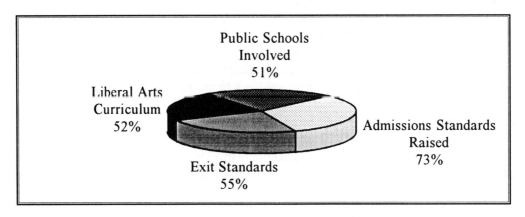

Figure 10. Reforms in teacher education.

73% have raised admission standards for their teacher education programs; 55% have changed exit standards for their teacher education programs; 52% have changed the liberal arts curriculum for preservice teachers; and 51% have begun using public school teachers as teacher educators.

Accreditation Standards for Teacher Education Programs

National accreditation of colleges and university programs for the preparation of all teachers and other professional school personnel at the elementary and secondary levels is the responsibility of the *National Council for the Accreditation of Teacher Education (NCATE)*. The mission of NCATE is two-fold: (1) to require a level of quality in professional education that fosters competent practice of graduates, and (2) to encourage institutions to meet rigorous academic standards of excellence in professional education. NCATE provides a mechanism for voluntary peer regulation of the education unit that is designed to establish and uphold national standards of excellence, to strengthen the quality and integrity of professional educational units, and to ensure that requirements for accreditation are related to best professional practice. NCATE has been authorized by the *Council on Post-Secondary Accreditation (COPA)* to adopt standards and procedures for accreditation and to determine the accreditation status of institutional units for preparing teachers and other professional school personnel. NCATE is also recognized by the U.S. Department of Education as the only authorized accrediting agency in the field of school personnel preparation.

The NCATE Standards

NCATE's standards address five categories: 1) Knowledge Bases for Professional Education, 2) Relationship to the World of Practice, 3) Students, 4) Faculty, and 5) Governance and Resources. The focus of these standards is on the overall quality of the professional education unit, and not on individual programs in the institution. However, the unit's policies, procedures, governance, administration, staffing, and other resources should ensure that programs are accountable.

NCATE Standards and Equity

In the NCATE standards, effective January 1, 1979, the term "multicultural education" appeared and was explicitly addressed in the standards for the first time. In essence, those 1979 standards implied that all teacher education programs needed to meet this new focus by providing provisions for multicultural education which must be evident in undergraduate and graduate programs in order to receive full accreditation. New and revised standards have been implemented in 1987 and most recently in 1990. The equity dimension within the five categories is evident throughout the standards. For example, under Knowledge Bases—*Standard I.E. Content of the Curriculum-Professional Studies* (22) "The unit provides for study and experiences that help education students understand and apply appropriate strategies for individual learning needs, especially for culturally diverse and exceptional populations." Under Relationship to the World of Practice—*Standard II.A.: Clinical and Field Based Experiences* (27) "Education students participate in field-based and/or clinical experiences with culturally diverse and exceptional populations." The NCATE accreditation process can be a vehicle to provide direction for Schools of Education to address the equity perspective within the preparation of future educators and those currently in the field. Eighty percent of all the teacher education programs in the country belong to NCATE.

A Growing Shortage of Ethnic Minority Teachers

The decline in the number of teachers from culturally diverse backgrounds focuses on the numerical disparities between African American, Hispanic, Asian and American Indian teachers and White teachers. (See Figure 11.)

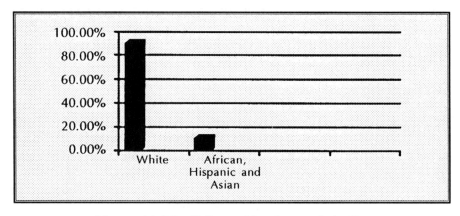

Figure 11. The U.S. teaching force ethnically.

Whites comprise 89.7% of the nation's teaching force and 71.2% of the student population, while African Americans, Hispanics, Asians and American Indians make up only 10.3% of the teaching force and nearly 30% of the student population. (Snyder, 1987; National Education Association, 1987) While the number of students from diverse backgrounds climbs, the number of teachers from culturally diverse backgrounds rapidly declines. (See Figure 12.)

More specifically, African Americans represent 16.2% of the children in public school and only 6.9% of the teaching force. Hispanics make up 9.1% of the children in public school and 1.9% of the teaching force. Asian/Pacific Islanders are 2.5% of the children in public school, but only 0.6% of the teachers.

According to the American Association of Colleges for Teacher Education (AACTE, 1988) while the current supply of teachers now approximates the demand, by 1995 more than one million teaching positions will need to be filled. At that time, the racial and ethnic composition of the teaching force will be diametrically opposed to the racial and ethnic composition of the nation's classrooms.

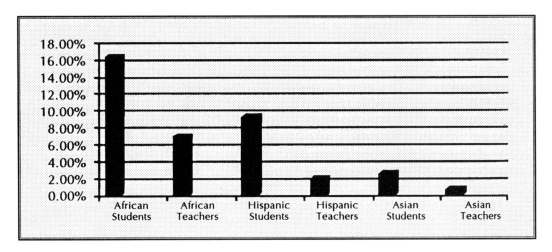

Figure 12. Ethnic breakdown of students and teachers.

The AACTE study reported that 33 states have elementary and secondary minority enrollments of 20 percent or more; however, only six have higher education institutions with schools, colleges, or departments of education with minority enrollments greater than 15 percent. The study stated, the lack of highly qualified minority teachers impedes efforts to change the nature and level of achievement in our schools, both for underserved ethnic minority students and for those students who traditionally meet prevailing school standards. Coordinated action is required to attract a greater number of able ethnic minority teacher candidates, prepare them better in institutions of higher education, and demonstrate effective programs for state policymakers and administrators.

The challenge facing teacher education programs is attracting and retaining the best qualified students available. Equally as important, but a more difficult task, will be the role and responsibility of teacher training programs to recruit and retain ethnic minority students who are interested in the education profession. There is a growing concern being expressed by teacher training programs across the country with the current and projected shortage of ethnic minority teachers. The traditional methods of recruiting students into teacher training programs will not work for the needs of the future. Teacher training programs must first be committed to attracting the non-majority student and then provide enough incentives for those students to make any real difference in the current trends.

Teacher Testing and Certification

State mandates to test teacher competence are becoming increasingly popular. According to the American Association of Colleges for Teacher Education (AACTE) in 1984, thirty

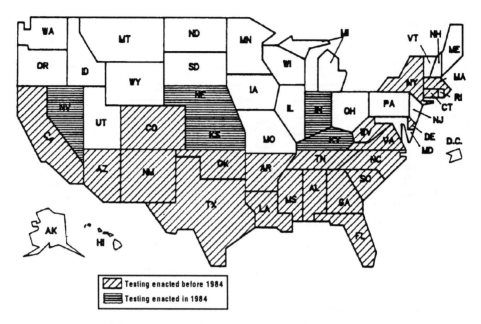

Figure 13. State required testing for initial certification of teachers.

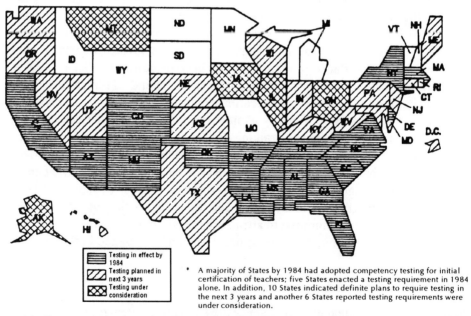

* A majority of States by 1984 had adopted competency testing for initial certification of teachers; five States enacted a testing requirement in 1984 alone. In addition, 10 States indicated definite plans to require testing in the next 3 years and another 6 States reported testing requirements were under consideration.

Figure 14. State-required testing for initial certification of teachers, testing in effect, planned in next 3 years, and under consideration.

states had such mandates, and twelve other states were planning such requirements. See Figure 13—State-Required Testing for Initial Certification of Teachers.

There is a widespread variation in the states' efforts. Tests may address: (1) basic skills such as English, Math, and Science; (2) professional or pedagogical skills; and (3) academic knowledge of a particular subject matter. Testing may occur before admission to the teacher education program or before certification. Some states have developed and use their own tests; others rely on nationally standardized exams. The source of the mandate for teacher testing also varies; in eleven cases it is state law, whereas in twenty-two others it is state education agency regulations (three states have both). See Figure 14—State-Required Testing for Initial Certification of Teachers Testing in Effect. The impact of teacher competency tests has and continues to affect drastically the number of teachers from culturally diverse backgrounds. Expanding rapidly across the country, the competency movement has evolved into an elaborate practice that includes testing for admission, certification, and classroom effectiveness. Among the various tests, the Pre-Professional Skills Test (PPST) and the National Teachers Examination (NTE) are the most common. Documentation that reflects teacher testing activity in 19 states estimates that such examinations have eliminated some 37,717 prospective candidates and teachers. This estimate includes 21,515 African Americans, 10,142 Hispanic; 1,626 Asians; and 716 Native Americans. (Smith, 1987). Regardless of the state and the type of competency tests used, disproportionate numbers of prospective teachers from culturally diverse backgrounds are being screened from the teaching profession.

The debate as to whether or not the examinations are fair or useful tools by which to assess a teacher's ability in the classroom, raises the issue of preparedness. For example, only one-third of African American high school students are enrolled in the college prep track of their high schools.

The Holmes Group

The Holmes Group is a consortium of nearly 100 American research institutions committed to making the programs of teacher preparation more rigorous and connected—to liberal arts education, to research on learning and teaching, and to wise practice in the schools. All these new thrusts have lead to the establishment of Professional Development Schools (PDS).

The Holmes Group defines Professional Development Schools as a regular elementary, middle or high school that works in partnership with a university to develop and demonstrate (1) fine learning programs for diverse students, (2) practical, thought-provoking preparation for novice teachers, (3) new understandings and professional responsibilities for experienced educators, and (4) research projects that add to all educators' knowledge about how to make schools more productive.

A PDS will be a center of responsible innovation where new programs and technologies can be tried out and evaluated. It will be a place where faculty of the school and of the university both experience the collaborative feeling of working at the edge of their knowledge. It will be a place where new teachers, just forming their knowledge and technique, taste the reality of classrooms similar to those where they're likely to get their first jobs, and where they also see the skill, hear the counsel, and feel the support of expert teachers.

University schools of education and public schools all over the country are engaging in long-term partnerships based on the PDS model. One of the encouraging signs with the PDS is the type of partner the university schools of education have engaged with—typically schools with diverse student populations. The efforts of the PDS will be one more avenue in addressing the needs of schools to be truly equitable in the delivery of the educational programs offered at the site. One of the principle doctrines of the PDS is holding ambitious learning goals for everyone's children. Unlike the traditional laboratory school, a Professional Development School will grapple with problems that have been seen as roots of failure—the poverty of students families, the lack of resources in the school, and the disconnection in students minds between school now and their lives in the future.

A PDS will be a regular school where teachers, administrators, and professors collaborate in giving prospective teachers practical experiences of how schools run and how teachers work. These experiences will be integrated with both the professional course of study at the university and the instructional program of the school.

A PDS will not be simply the university's clinic or lab. It will be a center of inquiry with its own agenda, dealing with the school's tough questions.

Summary

Educational doctrines and practices in the United States were developed largely before 1945, following the structure of the society and the characteristics of the clientele of earlier times. When most people were employed as unskilled or semi-skilled laborers, and only 5 percent were in professional or managerial occupations, most persons could survive with little or no formal education and only a few would utilize college education in their work. Under those conditions, a major function of the schools and colleges was to sort children and youth, pushing out those who were judged least promising for further education and encouraging a few to go on. The lock-step process of instruction and the grading system were developed to sort students, rather than to help every child and youth get an education. By moving the whole class at the same rate from topic to topic, pacing the movement in terms of the performance of the average student, those with more difficulty in school learning would be certain to get further and further behind, and many would give up trying. This was reinforced by the grading system, which year by year gave low marks to those having difficulty, thus helping to discourage them from going on. At the same time, the system assigned high marks to those who learned school tasks easily and quickly, thus encouraging them to continue their formal education.

These policies and practices have existed for so long that we rarely know how sharply they differ from those of an institution devoted to effective teaching and learning. An institution concerned primarily with teaching and learning follows procedures based on the available knowledge of how people learn; whereas our schools and colleges, while only partly concerned with helping each student learn, have been preoccupied with grading, classifying and other sorting functions. This was appropriate for society in an earlier era when the positions available for the occupational, social and political elite were few in number. Then the schools and colleges were a major means for rationing educational opportunities to conform to the social structure. It seemed sensible to give everyone a chance to jump the hurdles and to record the results, reporting them in a way that would influence children, youth and their parents to seek further educational opportunities based only on earlier success.

Today we have a different situation. The critical task is no longer sorting students but rather educating a much larger proportion to meet current opportunities. An inappropriate attitude which has widespread acceptance is the practice of assessing the "deficiencies" of students, that is, the aspects in which they deviate from the norms of middle-class students. These deficiencies must be overcome, it is argued, before this student is really ready for learning what the school seeks to teach. The conception overlooks the many positive characteristics of at-risk students and thus furnishes no suggestions about strengths on which their school learning can be built. Success has been slow and will continue to be slow as long as educators have the notion that a student's learning capacity, rather than learning experience, is the main factor in limiting a student's education.

Accepting the idea that many students have limited capacity for learning and that the procedures of teaching and learning which are effective with middle-class students are the appropriate ones for all students leads naturally to the common practice of making small revisions in these practices in efforts to develop programs for educating at-risk students. In contrast to this, the recognition that all students can learn when effective conditions for their learning are provided stimulates an effort to construct new programs based on a systematic consideration of these conditions for effective learning.

The issue of who is educable has become a function of whom society wants to educate, rather than who is most likely to benefit from the opportunity to learn. Education has traditionally provided services to learners and has left the responsibility for learning to the student. If the learner did not learn, we questioned the quality of the learner, not the quality of the education system. If we seek to assess quality of learning we must examine much more carefully the delicate balance of interactions among learning behavior and learning environments, including the quality of teaching and learning task demands.

Teachers have long been seen as the obvious focus for intervention. After all, teachers are ultimately the ones who either teach students or fail to teach them. As Adler states, "There are no unteachable children. There are only schools and teachers and parents who fail to teach them."

When the learning situation does not reflect the background of the student, a gap exists between the contexts of learning and the contexts of performing. This gap exists, as we have seen, most often for those students who are not a part of mainstream America. The evidence gathered throughout the past decade demonstrates that educational failure rests in the institution of schooling, and the promise of equity can only be accomplished through the transformation of schools—a restructuring of policies and practices. This growing gap between expectations and achievement is most serious. It affects the quality of our lives and the lives of all our students—especially those students who are not being well served by our schools.

What must concern us is the *degree* to which many schools fail to come within striking distance of being anywhere near the quality-with-equity goal. The current school reform emphasis on excellence offers an opportunity to focus on those aspects of schooling that limit learning and foreclose opportunity. Inappropriately narrow instructional activities, incomplete and unbalanced curricula and erroneous conceptions of individual differences and abilities must be corrected. For mainstream, middle-class youth, these are issues of excellence replacing mediocrity. For students at risk of school failure, they become matters of survival.

The nation needs to go beyond basic assurances of fair access to schools and school programs and expect more than equal access to mediocrity. Schools, themselves—in their organization, in curriculum and instruction and in the professional preparation and work lives of educators—limit the learning opportunities they profess to provide.

 END NOTES

Adler, Mortimer J. *The Paideia Proposal—An Educational Manifesto*. Macmillian Publishing Co., New York, 1982.

American Association of Colleges for Teacher Education. "Teacher Education Pipeline: Schools, Colleges, and Departments of Education Enrollments by Race and Ethnicity." Washington, D.C. Author. ED 305 346 1988.

Boyer, Ernest. *High School: A Report on Secondary Education in America*. Harper and Row Publishers, New York, 1983.

Conant, James B. *The Comprehensive High School*. McGraw Hill, New York, 1967.

Goodlad, John I. *A Place Called School: Prospects for the Future*. McGraw Hill Book Co. New York, 1984.

Goodlad, John I. *Teachers for Our Nation's Schools.* Jossey-Bass Publishers. San Francisco, 1991.

Levin, Henry. "Accelerating the Education of At-Risk Students." An Invitational Conference sponsored by the Stanford University School of Education with support from the Rockefeller Foundation. Conference Papers, November 17-18, 1988.

National Commission on Excellence in Education. *A Nation at Risk: The Imperative for Educational Reform.* U.S. Government Printing Office, Washington, D.C., 1983.

Oakes, Jeannie. *Keeping Track—How Schools Create Inequality.* Yale University Press, New Haven, CT, 1985.

Oakes, Jeannie. "Tracking in Secondary School—A Contextual Perspective." *Educational Psychologist,* 22(2), 129-154, 1987.

Oakes, Jeannie & Lipton, Martin. *Making the Best of Schools.* Yale University Press, New Haven, CT, 1990.

National Council for Accreditation of Teacher Education. "Standards, Procedures, and Policies for the Accreditation of Professional Education Units." Washington, D.C., 1990.

National Education Association. "Status of the American Public School Teacher, 1985-86." National Education Association Response. Washington, D.C.: Author. ED 284 330 1987.

Nieto, Sonia. *Affirming Diversity—A Sociopolitical Context of Multicultural Education.* Longman, New York, New York, 1992.

Research About Teacher Education. "Schools' of Education: Progress and Change." Washington, D.C., 1990.

Rosenthal, R., & Jacobsen, L. *Pygmalion in the Classroom: Teacher Expectations and Pupils' Intellectual Development.* Holt, Reinhart and Winston, New York, 1968.

Slavin, R.E., "Using Student Team Learning." 3rd Edition. Center for Research on Elementary and Middle Schools, 1986.

Slavin, Robert E. "Ability Grouping and Its Alternatives: Must We Track?" *American Educator,* pg. 85-90, Summer 1987.

Smith, G.P. "The Effects of Competency Tests on the Supply of Minority Teachers." A report prepared for the National Education Association and the Council of Chief State School Officers. Washington, D.C: Council of Chief State School Officers and National Education Association. ED 302 521 1987.

Snyder, T.D. "Digest of Education Statistics." Office of Educational Research and Improvement, U.S. Department of Education. Washington, D.C: U.S. Government Printing Office. ED 282 359 1987.

The Education Commission of the States. "Access to Knowledge: Breaking Down School Barriers to Learning." By Keating, Pamela and Oakes, Jeannie. August, 1988.

 ## SUGGESTIONS FOR FURTHER READING

"Learning Styles: Putting Research and Common Sense into Practice" American Association of School Administrators, 1801 N. Moore Street, Arlington, VA, 1991.

Dunn, Rita. "Rita Dunn Answers Questions on Learning Styles." *Educational Leadership*, October 1990, pp. 15-19.

Name _____ **Date** _____

✔ **DISCUSSION QUESTIONS**

---

1. How do you define effective teaching?

_____

_____

_____

_____

2. What are teacher expectations?

_____

_____

What research evidence is most surprising to you with regard to teacher expectations?

_____

_____

_____

_____

3. What is the most common teaching style? Why is this style so prevalent?

_____

_____

_____

_____

4. Do you believe that it is fair to hold teachers responsible when students fail to learn what they are taught? If this is not fair, who do you think should be responsible? Give reasons to support your answer.

_____

_____

_____

_____

_____

_____

_____

_____

5. Students are the workers of the school and the teachers are the managers. Do you agree or disagree with this concept? Give your reasons for agreeing or disagreeing.

_____

_____

_____

_____

_____

_____

_____

6. What should be the role of teacher training programs with regard to equity?

_____

_____

_____

_____

_____

_____

_____

7. There is a growing shortage of ethnic minority teachers. Given that fact, how would you respond to the statement, "You don't need ethnic minority teachers to teach ethnic minority youth."

_____

_____

_____

_____

_____

_____

_____

8. Do you believe that prospective classroom teachers should have to take a competency test prior to certification? Why or why not?

_____

_____

_____

_____

_____

Do you believe that "certified" classroom teachers should have to take a competency test? Why or why not? If yes, on what should the examination be based?

_____

_____

_____

_____

_____

9. What is a professional development school? How is it different than other schools? Identify specific examples of programs, strategies, policies, etc.with that type of partnership arrangement. Explain.

_____

_____

_____

_____

_____

_____

_____

_____

_____

10. Adler states, "There are no unteachable children. There are only schools and teachers and parents who fail to teach them." Do you agree or disagree with his assessment? Explain your position.

_____

_____

_____

_____

_____

_____

_____

_____

ASSIGNED GROUP WORK

Over the past decade there has been a simultaneous decline in the number of African American, Hispanic, Asian and American Indian teachers and an increase in the number of students among these same groups. This demographic shift has drawn national attention to the teaching profession in general, but more specifically teacher education programs.

Task:

Your group (3-4) will prepare a fifteen minute oral presentation that examines the issues surrounding the absence of teachers from diverse backgrounds and to investigate the implications of this decline from an equity perspective.

Each member of the group should contribute to the research and presentation equally. The following questions are intended to provide you suggested areas within which to frame your presentation.

1. If indeed the survival of this nation depends on the successful education of our growing, diverse population, can this be accomplished without a diverse teaching force?
2. What effect does the lack of teachers of color have on the students of color population?
3. What are the benefits of having teachers of color for the majority students?
4. To what degree have the efforts to recruit teachers of color been successful?
5. Does the decline of teacher education students of color reflect the lack of qualified individuals?
6. How can we counteract students' preferences to enter into professions with greater prestige?
7. How can our colleges and universities better prepare future educators to teach culturally diverse populations? What strategies should be implemented to address this issue? What are the strengths of your institution's teacher education program? The weaknesses?
8. What can be done in your community to reduce the attrition rate of teachers of color?
9. What existing state/local policies or initiatives promote the development of a diverse teaching force? What policies, procedures and programs can be developed to promote balance in the racial/ethnic composition of the teaching force?
10. What role can the business community play in the effort to recruit teachers of color?

INDIVIDUAL OR GROUP WORK

An Experience in Choice, Discrimination, Prejudice and Values

Purpose

▶ To provide students with an experience that will sensitize them to the inter-workings of choice, discrimination, prejudice and values.

▶ To provide students with an experience that will sensitize them to the concept of student learning styles and teaching styles.

▶ To provide students with an experience that will sensitize them to the inter-workings of grouping one tracking of students.

▶ To provide students with an experience that will sensitize them to the inter-workings of a classroom with a diversity of students; with a diversity of needs and problems encountered on a day-to-day basis.

Introduction

You are a member of a team of teachers who must establish a seventh-grade classroom. You are to select only 15 students from the list for the class, from the descriptions of the candidates provided. The school has recently implemented a plan to limit class size to 15. Those students not selected for your classroom will be considered for other classrooms. The only criteria to be used in completing this task are the following:

Individual Work

1. Each teacher is to independently list his/her personal choices of the 15 students to be included (by name). Strong consideration should be given to those with whom you believe you would be most effective;
2. Selections and rejections should be made thoughtfully, with the teacher prepared to provide a rationale for their choices;

Note: To save "in-class time," it is highly recommended that participants do their individual selections before group work.

Group Work

1. When completed, teachers should be randomly divided into groups of 4-5. Each teacher will then share his/her choices and a brief reason for each selection. Also, each teacher will share in the group reasons why students were not selected.
2. The collective task for the team of teachers will be to establish a consensus regarding which of the 15 students will be a part of their class. It is important to reach a consensus because your team will "team teach" this class of students. Be prepared to provide a brief oral presentation for each choice.

Note: Instructors should plan to allow 30-45 minutes for small group work in class.

CONFIDENTIAL

CANDIDATES FOR CLASS ROSTER

7th Grade

Vicki   Vicki is a truly gifted student with an I.Q. of 140. She knows it and flaunts it. She is excellent in all academic subjects and demands a lot of extra preparation time from her teachers. Her work is all above grade level. She does receive two hours of instruction (out of the classroom) a week with the gifted consultant. Prefers to work alone. Scores in the top 10% of the State in competency assessments. Strong parental support from the home. In fact, her parents believe that the school is not meeting her academic needs or challenging her enough. She has only a small circle of friends in school which come from her involvement with the debate team and the drama club.

Sara   Sara is just a good student. She is always polite and mannerly. Her classmates however see her as the "teacher's pet." She is willing to assist her teachers in daily routines. Sara has good grades overall; especially good in language arts. She scores well on State minimum competency (strong in math, reading and writing assessments). Single goal oriented, wants to finish assignments before taking on another. Prefers a relaxed environment. Good parental support. Works well in small group activities and projects. Shows some leadership qualities. A popular student with the teachers and the student body. A very promising writer. Recently selected debate team captain.

Chad   Chad is constantly seeking adult approval. He confides regularly with his male teachers, almost to the point of being a nuisance. He is campus wise to the rumors and gossip that exist—and eagerly shares the information with the adults in the school. His grades are poor. Scores well below average on State minimum competency in math and reading. Has been identified to be "at-risk" of not completing school. His strength is in music. His parents were recently divorced and lives with his mother. Very little support from the home at this time. Chad's older brother, Rick (17 years old) committed suicide last year. Chad works well in small group activities. His friends are from his participation in basketball and track. Has recently formed a local rock band.

Travis   Travis is generally rejected by his peers. He is noticeably financially poorer than his classmates and always appears to be untidy. His grades are about average and he is especially good in art and physical education. He is from a single-parent family, with the father in the home. His three older brothers and sisters have not completed high school. He is very quiet and shy, and presents no behavior problems. Needs a lot of one-to-one instruction. He is struggling with mathematics and history; but recently has become very interested in the computer. Scores below average on State competency assessments (math, comprehension and writing skills). Prefers a structured classroom. He has been participating regularly in an after school tutoring class with volunteer teachers from the local college. Travis is not involved in any extra-curricular activities. His father has attended all teacher conferences that have been scheduled.

John   John is a low-achieving student. He is a hard worker, but needs a lot of one-to-one instruction. He has made significant progress during the past two years. He responds well to small group work. He comes from a family that has moved four times in the past 6 years, thus, attending 4 different schools in 8 years. He has an irregular attendance pattern, and comes to school unprepared. Socially, he is never seen with any of his classmates. Academic profile is not complete to properly identify past efforts or special programs he has been involved with. Has performed poorly on other States' competency assessments. He has recently shown an interest in associating with a newly formed gang in the community. There is no parental support from the home. He has written several thought-provoking pieces of poetry. He has been encouraged to participate in an after school tutoring class with volunteer teachers from the local college, but has not.

Pat   Pat is best described as a free spirit. She does things such as attempting math and reading work simultaneously, and ends up doing neither accurately nor completely. Her grades are generally fair; although she is capable of much better work. She requires constant reminders and always needs the instructions for work at least twice. Pat doesn't perform well on the State competency assessments, but the school believes it is not a matter of ability, but on the structure and her willingness to take them seriously. She is a promising artist. Her mother was recently remarried and her father, remarried two years ago, lives out of the state. Very little parental support provided. Pat is extremely creative; but doesn't like rules or deadlines. She prefers a relaxed classroom atmosphere. Very popular with her classmates. Recently selected to display her artwork at the local art gallery.

Susan   Susan is a very mature youngster who presents no problems to her teacher. She does her work, minds her own business, is socially well-adjusted, and is a favorite with her classmates. She is academically sound in all subjects and has excellent grades. She is often used by her teachers, as a very helpful peer-tutor to her lower-achieving classmates. Susan enjoys reading. She scores well above average on the State competency assessments. Recently recognized in her community for her involvement with the elderly. She seems to be adaptable to various classroom settings. Very strong parental support. Her mother is the building principal's administrative assistant. Extra-curricular activities include volleyball, basketball, track, and serves as class president and student council member.

Mike Mike is a braggart who exaggerates most personal experiences to fantastic proportions. He is always "one up" better than anyone in class or out of class. His story telling is somewhat disruptive to the class and he demands a great deal of attention. He is constantly seeking approval from his classmates. He longs to be accepted by his peers and desperately wants to be liked. He has not recognized his lack of social skills as an inhibiting factor in accomplishing his desire. Has a very small circle of friends. He is from a single-parent family with the mother in the home. He has been identified as B.D. (behavior disorder). He is pulled one-hour a day with the special education consultant. Good parental support. In fact, his mother is a strong advocate for special education inclusion and would rather not see Mike being pulled out of his classes. His grades are average; he is good in history and computer literate. State competency assessments identify poor reading and comprehension skills. Works well in structured situations and seems to be a morning learner. Extra-curricular activities include football.

Laurie Laurie is a very bossy and talkative young person who is constantly ordering her classmates around. Her classmates get very angered by her behavior and as a result, she has very few friends. While generally well-behaved, she often presents classroom management problems engaging in power struggles with teachers. According to school records, she has been abused and neglected by her parents. Records indicate that alcohol is a family problem. Her grades are generally good and she is especially strong in history. State competency assessments identify poor math and writing skills. She was caught with alcohol at a school function last year and was suspended from school for three days. Enjoys evaluating solutions, doesn't like to create them. Little parental support from the home, although her mother is more likely to come to conferences when asked. Prefers to work alone. Laurie is not involved in any extra-curricular activities.

Neil Neil is a smart-aleck, sarcastic youngster. He can be described as a "motor-mouth" who is always quick with "put downs." There is nobody he can't and won't put-down, teachers included. He has a long track record of spending a great deal of time in the principal's office. He is a high-achieving student (I.Q. 127), but isn't motivated most of the time. A classic student who is an under-achiever. Scores well above average on State competency assessments (very high in math, writing, comprehension). Students do not enjoy him in group work, therefore, he prefers to work alone. Two years ago, Neil's older brother was killed in an alcohol-related car accident. Comes from a lower-socioeconomic home, where unemployment has been a problem during the past year. Good parental support. Neil shows signs of leadership, in fact he recently attempted to start an Environmental Concern Group, but it was not successful.

Jacob   Jacob, not "Jake," is upper-middle class, an academically good student, and the class pest. He always finishes his work quickly and accurately. Then he proceeds to pester, tease, and generally annoy his slower-working classmates in a wide variety of imaginative ways. He cannot sit still for any length of time. Seems to enjoy group work. All of his grades are good. State competency assessments are well above average (especially math and science). Because of both his academic quickness and his disruptive behavior, it is a constant strain on his teacher's resources to keep him meaningfully busy. Good parental support. Jacob is highly opinionated, judgmental and especially enjoys oral reports. Works best in structured environments. Jacob always seems to volunteer and is willing to spend time after school on worthwhile projects. Extra-curricular activities include SADD and the quiz bowl team.

Andy   Andy is from a very poor background. His family is large and is widely known in the community as the welfare family. He is considered a compulsive liar and a thief. He has a long record of stealing from the school system and in the community. Andy, along with a buddy, were recently caught with stolen computer equipment. He was placed on probation for three years and ordered to perform fifty hours of community service. He is good in class, with no management problems, but a constant eye is always needed. His friends are all not in school. His grades are generally good, very promising in mathematics. State competency assessments indicate very strong skills in mathematics, but low in comprehension. Works well in small group activities. Likes to read and work on the computer. Very little parental support, however, his oldest sister (26 years old) comes to the parent conferences when scheduled. Mornings are hard for him and he works best in the afternoon. Extra-curricular activities include the technology club.

Jan   Jan is physically more mature than the other young ladies in class. Her clothes are constantly challenging school policy and has had to be sent home several times in the past. She was the first student to have a tattoo and colored spiked hair. She doesn't appear to care what other people think about her or her appearance. She is from a single-parent family (recently divorced during the last school year). Socially, she is never seen with students her own age and is very quiet in class. She has average grades in most subjects, (State competency assessments indicate low performance in comprehension and writing skills). Recently she seems to be losing interest in school. It is difficult to get her involved in class discussions. She prefers to work independently. She has been identified by the school administration as "at-risk," for not completing school. She has refused to visit with her school counselor. She is not involved in any extra-curricular activities.

Tim   Tim comes to school when things are going good for his family—which isn't that often. Tim lives on the "other side of the tracks." Financially, he is very poor and his family is unemployed. He has displayed average academic ability, but his number of absences are more of a problem than his ability. (Scores below State minimum competency in math and writing.) Tim is two years older than his classmates—he didn't start school until he was six and he repeated the fourth grade. He creates no management problem, but is always late with homework and unprepared when he does come to school. Has a good circle of friends in school and is well liked by his classmates. No parental support. Enjoys reading and is more responsive to instruction in the afternoon. The administration fears that Tim will not complete school. Tim is a promising vocalist. Extra-curricular activities include the choir and SADD.

Ann   Ann is the class comedian. While she is a very bright and a capable student, she would rather invest her time and energy to get a laugh and attention from her classmates. While she is very capable in math, science, and social studies, her State assessments indicate only fair scores in these three subjects. She needs, and in fact, demands constant attention, supervision and structure from her teachers. She enjoys group work, and is very popular with her classmates. She has a difficult time completing goals. Because of her popularity, she seems to get away with more than the average student. She has been caught with alcohol on school grounds—in-school suspension (ISS) for four days. Mother recently remarried, and step-father has two children from previous marriage. Good parental support. Her older sister dropped out of school when she turned sixteen. Her best subject is language arts. Extra-curricular activities include cheerleading and debate.

Ed   Ed is of bi-racial parentage and an only child (African American mother, White Father). He tends to be the class bully because of his considerable size advantage over the other students in class. Ed received in-school suspension (ISS) twice for fighting. The school has identified Ed as "learning disabled (LD)," but his parents refuse to acknowledge the classification. Therefore, Ed is not receiving any "special education" assistance. His father recently ran for the School Board, but lost in the primary election. His father believes the school does little to acknowledge the diversity of its students or the community at-large. Overall, Ed's grades are below average with the exception of math. State competency assessments support the skill in mathematics. Good parental support. Works well in small group activities. Classmates are fully aware of his reputation as a fighter and has a relatively small number of friends. Enjoys field experiences and is a morning learner. He is very knowledgeable with computer graphic programs. Extra-curricular activities include the technology club and basketball.

Paula Paula is a student who is nondescript. She is extremely shy and reluctant to socially interact with other students. She never volunteers nor participates in any activities other than the required class work. She is in class every day and assignments are always on time. Her grades are average; she is especially strong in reading and enjoys working on the computer. State competency assessments indicate high skills in comprehension and writing skills. She is easily overlooked by teachers if they didn't make a conscious effort to include her in class discussions and activities. He older brother is an all-state athlete in football and track. Paula has a good circle of friends who are good students. Paula prefers to work independently. Good parental support. Extra-curricular activities include SADD.

Kelly Kelly comes from a long line of prominent and wealthy relatives. Her family is well known in the community and they have one of the finest homes in town. Her father is a School Board member and a prominent lawyer in town. She tends to be verbally and socially abusive and insensitive to some of her classmates. She dresses in the very latest and trendiest fashions. Her older sister and brother are currently attending Ivy League schools. Her grades are generally good; she is especially strong in language arts. State assessments indicate strong skills in comprehension and writing. She has been caught with drugs (marijuana) once in school—with great controversy, she was suspended from school for three days. She is very opinionated and shows little patience. She consciously picks her friends and associates only with the elite circle in the school. Works well in small group activities, but prefers to choose her partners. She is involved in the Spanish Club and volleyball.

Chris   Chris is an athlete. He has been the best at all sports for a number of years. He is athletically ahead of his classmates by at least 2 years. He lives and breathes sports. As a result, he is average in all subjects; he excels in physical education. He does not score well on State competency assessments. Lately, his grades have been slipping—which threatens his eligibility to participate in sports—because of the new school policy. He is an extremely capable young man, but his priorities are not with academics. In fact, academics take a back seat to sports and girls. Chris is somewhat of a day-dreamer in class and has to be "pushed" to get his work completed. He often comes to school without his homework completed. He has been caught twice cheating on assignments and examinations—received in-school suspension (ISS) both times. He has very few friends his own age, in fact his girlfriend is three years older than he is. This is a concern of his parents and they have shown strong support for the school. Works well in small group activities. Enjoys computer work. Extra-curricular activities include football, basketball and baseball. He has been occasionally attending SADD meetings.

Diana   Diana is the third generation of Romeros' in the community. Because of her family's strong Hispanic culture, she is limited-English proficient. She has been assigned to an ESL class (pull-out) that meets twice a week. As a result of her language background, she is academically below grade level. Her State competency assessments are very low; with the administration believing the scores reflect her difficulty with the language. She has difficulty completing assignments and understanding classroom discussions. She requires a lot of one-to-one instruction. She is well liked by her classmates and her very good looks make her a popular student. She is very strong in music (piano). Diana's mother died five years ago and she lives with her father and two brothers. One brother has dropped out of school; while the other is a junior in high school. There is very little parental support. Extra-curricular activities include the Spanish Club and Band.

List Those Students Selected to Your Class

_____

Your Name

List Those Students NOT Selected to Your Class

_____

_____

_____

_____

_____

FOLLOW-UP QUESTIONS

1. What criteria did you base your decisions on? Your group's selections? Do you believe you were consistent?

_____

_____

_____

_____

_____

_____

2. As we have seen, each class has a diversity of students, not only in terms of ethnicity, but of behavior, learning rates, learning styles, social backgrounds, family lifestyles, etc. Based on this activity, how do you feel about tracking or sorting students based on academic performance?

_____

_____

_____

_____

_____

_____

3. Is there a common denominator for those students who were not selected to your class? What is it?

_____

_____

_____

_____

_____

_____

4. Which student is the most "acceptable to you?" To your group? Why?

_____

_____

_____

5. Which student would pose the biggest challenge for you? For your group? Why?

_____

_____

_____

_____

_____

_____

6. What are your thoughts regarding optimal class size?

_____

_____

_____

_____

_____

7. Without necessarily accepting what is written in Chapter Four, what do you think are the needs of teachers? of students? of parents? Are their needs different?

_____

_____

_____

_____

_____

_____

Diversity: An American Trademark  5

Introduction

Understanding diversity in our country could be viewed from two perspectives. First, what is our personal viewpoint with regard to the increasing diversity of the United States? Secondly, from an educational perspective, what should be the role and responsibility of the school in addressing this growing diverse student population? Because of the diverse character of the United States, the educational policies and practices of the past have and continue to be debated today.

The population of the United States is changing gradually, but profoundly. Soon after the turn of the century, one out of every three Americans will be non-White. According to the U.S. Bureau of Census, in 1990, we were a nation of 248.7 million. Different racial and ethnic groups increased at vastly different rates, as can be seen in Figure 15.

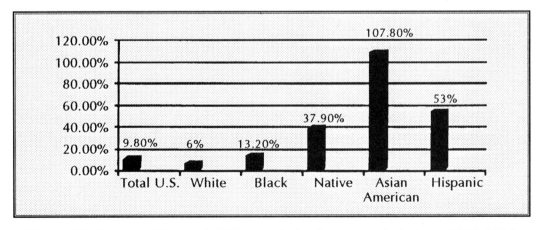

Figure 15. Percent of change in U.S. population by race and ethnicity, 1980–1990.

How the United States total population in 1990 was made up by race and ethnicity can be seen in Figure 16. While about 22% of the total population can be described as ethnic minority, 30% of school-age children are ethnic minority, a number that will reach 36% shortly after the year 2000.

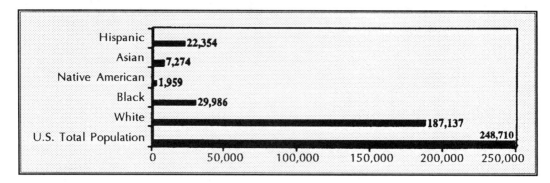

Figure 16. U.S. total population by race and ethnicity—1990 (in millions).

Figure 17 displays the percentage of the total population based on race and ethnicity—1990.

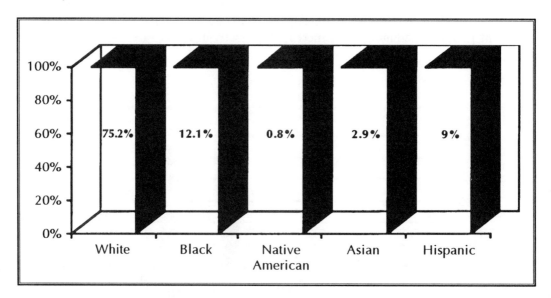

Figure 17. Percent of U.S. population by race and ethnicity—1990 (in millions).

A fundamental question will have to be answered in the very near future: What are the implications for the preparation of new classroom teachers; as well as those professionals currently in the profession?

Chapter 5—**Diversity: An American Trademark** is intended to help focus our direction and planning with regard to one dimension of equity—the ethnic diversity of its students. There are three fundamental questions that this chapter is designed to raise: (1) What should be the role of the school in addressing our ethnic diversity? Should a school highlight the differences or minimize them? (2) How much diversity are we as Americans willing to allow in our society? In our schools? (3) What is the future of diversity in this country? Do we want our rich diversity to remain a part of our American fabric? Or, do we believe that our diversity will contribute to our unraveling? How we address these important questions would seem to guide us on how we will perceive these differences within our society and specifically within our schools and classrooms.

Terminology

The term "minority" gained national acceptance some years ago when it referred almost exclusively to the African American population and a small number of Hispanics, Asians and American Indians. The term connotes inferior or lesser status in relation to the majority. Furthermore, minority is often confused with numerical minority, when in fact a numerical minority may control a numerical majority. Many define minority in terms of a subordinate position, as a group of people who, because of their physical or cultural characteristics, are singled out from others in the society in which they live for differential and unequal treatment and who therefore regard themselves as objects of collective discrimination. These cultural/racial groups made up a relatively small percentage of the United States population and constituted a distinct segment of the population. The term served to denote all people who were non-White.

Today, the term is inappropriate as a designation for African Americans, Hispanics, Asians, and American Indians for three primary reasons. First, its reference to four different cultural groups assumes that the essential characteristics and needs of all the groups are the same and can be addressed as a whole. The issues of Hispanics differ from those of African Americans, Asians and American Indians and as is the case with all cultural/ethnic groups, need to be specifically addressed. Also, it is a term that is never used to describe Polish Americans, Scottish Americans or French Americans. Yet, strictly speaking, these groups being a numerical minority, should also be referred to as such. Second, the term minority is inaccurately used to reference groups of non-Whites who comprise, in many school districts, counties, and states, the numerical majority. Third, minority infers an inferior status. To categorize people as minorities places the relationship to the majority in a subordinate position. Not only have African Americans, Hispanics, Asians and American Indians expanded numerically, but the vague meaning of the term has encouraged its adoption by any segment of the population that is anything other than White, heterosexual and male. Hence, in some circles, minority has come to refer to such populations as the physically disabled, women, senior citizens, gay and lesbian people. The term minority is now being perceived by many to be obsolete and misleading.

Language seems to be constantly changing. In many ways, the language responds to social, economic and political events and is therefore an important yardstick of a society at any given point. Language is important because it describes and defines people of many different groups. A simple word association may be helpful here. For example, what groups come to mind when you hear the following words: lazy, savage, rhythm, stupid, penny pinchers? Taken by themselves, these words are not negative, but they have become code words to categorize an entire group of people. In most cases, negatively. Therefore, in an attempt to be both sensitive and appropriate in the use of language the following terms have been used to describe the following groups: African American, Hispanic, Asian, and American Indian in this text as ethnic minority or people of color. Specifically, each group has its own language preferences based on political or regional affiliation at any given time. Today, the term African American is being more commonly used than Afro-American or Black. The term may be more accurate because it implies a cultural base rather than only color or racial differences. For several years, the term Native American referred to the many indigenous nations that exist in the United States. The term has evolved to Indian or American Indian in recent years. Native American is sometimes being confused because it is often used by others to mean a citizen of the United States whose ancestors came from Europe who are now "native" to this land.

As Nieto suggests, the term "European American" may be a more appropriate term than "White American." (Nieto, 1992). As stated earlier, the traditional "majority" of U.S. society, often may not think of themselves as "ethnic," which has historically been the term reserved for the more easily "identifiable" groups. The term European American more accurately implies a cultural background or heritage. Equally important to understand is the frequently used term "Anglo or Anglo-American" which is an inaccurate term to use when describing all "white" Americans. It is a term that is only appropriate when specifically referring to those with an English heritage.

The decision to be made by educators should be whenever possible, specific distinctions of particular groups should be made because otherwise fundamental differences in ethnicity, national origin, self-identification and length of time in this country are easily overlooked.

A Shift in Our Diversity

A look at immigration rates can provide us with a portrait as to why the shift that is highlighted above is so. Between 1820 and 1945, the nations that sent us the largest numbers of immigrants were (in rank order): Germany, Italy, Ireland, the United Kingdom, the Soviet Union, Canada and Sweden. The nations that send us the most immigrants now and that are projected to do so through the year 2000 are (in rank order): Mexico, The Philippines, Korea, China/Taiwan, India, Cuba, the Dominican Republic, Jamaica, Canada, Vietnam, the United Kingdom and Iran (Hodgkinson, 1992). It is rather evident that from the first wave of immigrants the United States was a nation of Europeans. There was a common European culture that the schools could use in socializing millions of immigrant children. The most recent immigrants pose a brand-new challenge: the population of American schools today truly represents the world. The most diverse segment of our society is our children. While these children bring new energy and talents to our nation, they also represent new challenges for instruction. How accepting will we be of the racial and ethnic diversity coming into the system?

The Children of the 21st Century

The nation's population will continue to grow, reaching 265 million by the year 2020, and much of that growth will be among the ethnic minority groups. Although there is a growing recognition of the importance of such demographic changes, there is also apprehension that this society's major education institutions are not responding quickly or adequately enough in developing policies and practices that will maximize the contributions made by the escalating numbers of ethnic minorities in the population.

These findings portray the dramatic change in the pattern of children entering our schools. Obviously, children come to school today with different diets, different religions, different individual and group loyalties, different music, and different languages. In the fall of 1993, more than 3.6 million children began their formal schooling in the United States. These children are highlighted below:

- ▶ 1 out of 4 were from families who live in poverty
- ▶ 14 percent were children of teenage mothers
- ▶ 16 percent were mentally or physically handicapped
- ▶ 15 percent spoke a language other than English
- ▶ 14 percent were children of unmarried parents
- ▶ 40 percent will live in broken homes before they reach 18 years of age
- ▶ 10 percent had poorly educated, even illiterate parents
- ▶ 25 percent or more do not finish high school

Although the students identified above are not necessarily ethnic minority students, coupled with their diverse backgrounds and these demographic shifts in our student population, the conclusion for American education is inescapable: American public schools are now experiencing larger enrollments of ethnic minority students, will continue to, and an increasing number of these students will be eligible for a post-secondary education.

A potential problem in studying the diversity within the United States is its complexity. This complexity, coupled with the rapid changes of particular groups from generation to generation, makes the task more difficult. In a diverse nation such as the Untied States, the indigenous population, American Indians, make-up less than one percent of the total population. The other 99 percent are recent immigrants or have ancestors who were immigrants. The fact that many people continue to maintain this ethnic identity over generations is the most remarkable quality of the United States. What is this phenomenon ethnicity? Reference to ethnicity can be found in such diverse arenas as political elections, folk festivals, intergroup conflicts, judicial proceedings, hiring policies, federal forms, education, etc.

The Struggle. . .Continues

The call for educational reform is in many respects a declaration from the society the public schools were to serve. It has changed so radically in the last 40 years that the old system and its inequities are no longer socially, morally or intellectually acceptable.

One of the most apparent and significant reasons for change in our society has been the result of the civil rights movement. We uniformly declared as a nation that we will no longer accept the inequities that this society has often placed on people of color, our immigrant populations, and on all our poor. Socially, there are inequities that are visibly overt, while others are increasingly more subtle, yet they exist all across this country. They remain the struggles that will continue through the '90s and into the 21st century.

Ethnicity

What is an ethnic group? Who belongs? Who doesn't belong? An ethnic group is defined as a group of people within a larger society that is socially distinguished or set apart, by others and/or by itself, primarily on the basis of racial and/or cultural characteristics, such as religion, language, and tradition (DeVos, 1975). Ethnicity applies to everyone; people differ in their sense of ethnic identity. Everyone, however, has an ethnic group. Banks (1981) states, "All Americans are members of an ethnic group, since each of us belongs to a group which shares a sense of peoplehood, values, behaviors, patterns, and cultural traits which differ from those of other groups." However, one's attachment and identity with his or her ethnic group varies greatly with the individual, the times of his or her life, and the situations and/or settings in which an individual finds himself or herself. Ethnicity is extremely important for some individuals within our society and is of little or no importance to others.

Ethnicity is an attribute of membership in a group that is set off by its ethnic or racial uniqueness. It is a sense of social belonging and ultimate loyalty to that group. Individuals in the groups share a history, a language (whether or not they can speak the language), the same value system and structure, and the same customs and traditions. To maintain the group identity throughout the generations, the attitudes, values, behaviors, and rituals have been and continue to be practiced in the family, the church, and social clubs.

Many researchers believe that in the United States, boundaries of ethnicity are mainly psychological in nature rather than territorial. A person does not have to live in the same community with other members of the group in order to identify strongly with the group. The boundaries are maintained by ascription from within as well as from external sources that place persons in a specific group because of the way they look, the color of their skin, the location of their home, or their name. Although all members of society can identify with one or more ethnic heritages, not all members choose to emphasize their ethnicity. In fact, some even choose to function as non-ethnics. The degree of identification with the ethnic group varies from person to person. This is certainly the cause of great debate concerning ethnicity in this country. There are individuals who prefer not to identify with any ethnic group, while others do. Why do some individuals maintain their ethnicity and others chose not to identify with their ethnic background?

Ethnic Minority Groups

As discussed earlier, the label "minority" group is confusing as well as inaccurate. Ethnic minority groups are those who because of their physical or cultural characteristics are singled out from others in society. In the U.S., there are four groups who historically represent this description. They are African Americans, Hispanic Americans, Asian Americans and American Indians.

The degree to which an ethnic group (microculture) retains ethnic minority group status depends upon how it is received by and/or receives the host society (macroculture). Does it experience long-term segregation? Is it quickly absorbed into the mainstream? Does it wish to retain its own cultural traditions?

A Nation of Immigrants

America has always been a nation of immigrants. Many citizens believe the resulting ethnic and cultural diversity has given this society a distinctive quality. Others may argue that the sooner one rids himself/herself of these distinct qualities and becomes "American"—the better off they will be—and the better the country will be. These opposing perspectives have strained the social fabric of this country even as it has strengthened it.

The first great period of immigration in this country was between 1910 and 1930, when the number of foreign-born Americans reached a peak of 14.2 million. In 1984, some 544,000 people immigrated legally to the United States—roughly as many as the annual average during the 1920s. Add the estimated 300,000 to 500,000 people who entered the country illegally and 1984 becomes the greatest year for immigration in our history. Immigrants entering the United States each year account for two-thirds of all the immigrants in the world.

As stated earlier in the chapter, during the early part of this century, the majority of immigrants to the United States were of European heritage, and the color of their skin undoubtedly eased their *assimilation* into the predominantly European American mainstream. Today, however, most are Hispanic and Asian. Most parts of the nation feel little impact from this wave of immigrants because the majority of newcomers are choosing to settle in relatively few places. But in those areas, the effects have been astounding.

Ninety percent of the growth in the U.S. happened in the south and west, while only three states received half of the nation's growth: California, Texas and Florida. Never in the 200-year history of census-taking have only three states had half the nation's growth. In 1990, nine states made up half of the U.S. population: California, New York, Texas, Florida, Pennsylvania, Illinois, Ohio, Michigan and New Jersey. The states that are growing most rapidly tend to be states with a high percentage of ethnic minority youth.

The Melting Pot

The concept of the melting pot was proposed by the playwright Israel Zangwill in his 1909 play *The Melting Pot*. In that work, a Russian-Jewish immigrant described the United States in this speech: America is God's crucible, the great Melting Pot, where all races of Europe are melting and reforming! Here you stand, good folk, think I, when I see them at Ellis Island, here you stand in your fifty groups with your fifty hatreds and rivalries, but you won't be long like that, brothers, for these are the fires of God. A fig for your feuds and vendettas! Germans, and Frenchmen, Irishmen and Englishmen, Jews and Russians—into the Crucible with you all! God is making the American. . . the real American has not yet arrived. He is only in the Crucible, I tell you—he will be the fusion of all races, the coming superman. (Zangwill, 1909)

The melting pot was quickly adopted as a promising ideal for fusing persons from various new and old immigrant groups into a new common American society. One of the problems or disadvantages (depending upon your perspective) of the melting pot was that it never proposed to melt all ethnic and cultural groups. Even in Zangwill's speech there is no mention of adding American Indians, African Americans, Hispanics, or Asians to the crucible.

Although the prospect of being a part of the pot that would create the "real American" seemed an attractive idea to many immigrants, other groups, particularly American Indians, fought against becoming the "one model American." To melt into the American society required abandoning customs, dress, and language so that one would think, feel, and act like an American. However, there were many immigrants who strived to rid themselves of their accents and often anglicized their names. Although the unmeltable groups might anglicize their names and show no signs of an accent, they were unable to rid themselves of their skin color or physical characteristics that marked them as different from the idealized model American who was supposed to emerge from the melting pot. Even when these unmeltable groups chose to be the fused American, they were not accepted primarily because they were not "white."

In an important sense, then, the ethnic diversity factor in the United States has been given a particular view by the ideology of the melting pot. By tying ethnic diversity to the melting pot, the basic direction given was that the immigrants were to intermarry on a large scale, denounce their Old World heritage by changing cultural patterns to those of the dominant or majority group, and impart positive meaning to an otherwise chaotic and highly fluid social situation.

Thus, to the immigrant and the established American, the ideology of the melting pot gave support to the belief that the American experience was a new historical epoch for humanity; human history was being given an entirely new direction by the melting pot of America.

First, it was believed that the process called for was totally a biological one, the fusion of races by interbreeding and intermarriage. Second, it was believed that the melting pot meant a process by which persons or groups who were unlike in their social heritage somehow came to share and cherish the same body of tradition, loyalties, and attitudes. The first belief is commonly referred to as amalgamation, the second as assimilation. Some ideologists of the melting pot looked at both of these as called for, and many older Americans as well shared this view. The melting pot was thus an ambiguous ideology for shaping thought and action regarding ethnic diversity, but the ambiguity was no obstacle and allowed for a number of groups to work together to direct social change in a particular way.

The fact remains, however, that the melting pot was a passionate belief by which many people lived and continue to believe in and live by today.

The Role of the School

What role, if any, did the schools play in the ideology of the melting pot? The mixture of the myth and reality in America has produced numerous legends, not the least of which is found in public education. If one were to ask the so-called individual on the street what role, if any, does schooling play in the success of the melting pot, the answer would most likely be that the public school is a prime factor. Indeed, many Americans look on schooling as the chief vehicle for assimilation.

As was so vividly expressed by the educational historian Cubberly (1909): Everywhere these people (immigrants) tend to settle in groups or settlements and to set up their own national manners, customs and observances. Our task is to "break up" their groups and settlements, to assimilate or amalgamate these people as a part of the American race, and to implant in their children, so far as can be done, the Anglo-Saxon conception of righteousness, law, order, and popular government, and to awaken in them reverence for our democratic institutions and for those things which we as people hold to be of abiding worth.

The success or miracle of the melting pot was accomplished with schooling serving as the prime agent in the process. The legend has it that an enlightened body of teachers and administrators led the immigrants in establishing themselves as 100 percent Americans. The school, without hesitation, did its best for the immigrants and the country by making a new American out of the "wretched refuse." For some, the public school legend makes of schooling the primary means of Americanization.

Are You Saying...The United States Is Not a Melting Pot?

While a core of reality lies behind the legend (myths usually have some basic connection with reality), the legend, as it stands, simply is not true. The twin elements of the melting pot magic and public schooling alchemy are largely pseudo-historical, tending to ignore the fact that the school was, after all, only one institution that stood ready to meet the melting pot's demands. Moreover, the schools were not supported on a grand scale, and in large cities where the crush of immigrant children was heaviest, teachers were hard put to teach the basic three Rs, let alone socialize the students in terms of the melting pot ideal. If ethnics were Americanized, the school did so in terms of imposition of White Anglo-Saxon Protestant (WASP) values and standards, not the ideal of the melting pot. The main point is that although most Americans have assumed that schooling was essential to the success of the melting pot, the fact is that immigrants were not educated with the melting-pot ideal at all—they were indoctrinated in the schools with the values of the dominant White Anglo-Saxon Protestant (WASP) culture.

The common view offered with regard to ethnic diversity is that American schooling was a highly effective vehicle in achieving the success of the melting pot. But whether we recognize the fact or not, most immigrants and their children experienced little of the melting pot ideal. The myth continues, but the reality is that schooling promoted an Anglo-conformism that virtually denigrated the ancestral heritage of immigrants. Moreover, some groups were never allowed to melt into the American pot. And it is largely the latter groups who are now determined to be more self-assured, more proud of themselves and better prepared to be more self-determining about their own fate.

The view of schools as the inevitable assimilators of students must be challenged. The boundaries of diversity are being disputed daily. Given the different social and historical context in which we are living, schools need to accommodate diversity in more humane and sensitive ways than they have in the past. Formerly, just one major option existed, and it was quickly, if not always eagerly, seized by most immigrants: quick assimilation in the so-called melting pot. There may be two reasons why assimilation occurred so quickly in the past: one was hope and the other was shame. Hope contributed in a major way in holding out the promise of equality, economic security, and a safe haven from war and devastation. Most important is the fact that the main fuel for the American melting pot was shame. The immigrants were best instructed in how to repulse themselves; millions of people were taught to be ashamed of their faces, their family names, their parents and grandparents, and their class patterns, histories and outlooks.

A Difficult Choice

The students currently enrolled in our schools are some ways more fortunate than previous students. They have more freedom in maintaining their language and culture. Nevertheless, the choice of having no choice is still largely true. On the one hand, if they choose to identify with their culture and background, they may feel alienated from this society; on the other hand, if they identify with U.S. (generally meaning European American) culture, they may feel like traitors to their family and community. The choices are still very difficult ones for many students.

The Anglo-Conformity Theory

As mentioned earlier, many educators believed that schooling promoted more of an Anglo-conformity perspective. For many researchers, primarily Milton Gordon (1954), the Anglo-conformity theory best describes what was actually expected of immigrants and ethnic groups during this period. Distinct ethnic groups were not expected to contribute equally to the making of a new American as idealized in the melting pot theory. Instead they were expected to adopt the WASP culture that historically molded most of the political and social institutions of the country. They were required to attend school to learn the language, values, traits, dress, and customs of the dominant culture. To be accepted as an "American," members of these immigrant groups had to conform to the patterns of thinking, feeling, and behaving of the WASP culture.

The Anglo-conformity theory described what was expected of immigrant and ethnic minority groups, but it did not describe how these particular groups were actually behaving as members within the larger society. Although some members of these groups chose to adopt the WASP culture as their own, many refused to assimilate into the dominant culture and maintained separate ethnic communities and enclaves within the society. They developed within-group institutions, agencies, and power structures for services within their ethnic communities.

This "within-in" group movement may also be referred to as Separatism. Today, in virtually all sizes of cities across this country, communities of ethnic groups still remain vital links to maintaining group cohesion and a sense of kinship. Obviously, the actual amount of isolation within all these separate entities depends upon the amount of language, custom and tradition that are maintained and lived by on a daily basis. My point is that, we still have large numbers of ethnic groups, in many cities and towns across this country, that are living and functioning in a separatist manner for a variety of reasons.

As many suggest in all probability, neither the Anglo-conformity nor the melting pot concept adequately describes the complex process which occurred and is still occurring in the development of American society. Both concepts are in some ways incomplete or misleading because non-Anglo ethnic groups have had (and are still having) a much more cogent impact on American society than is reflected by either theory. WASP culture in the U.S. has been greatly influenced by other ethnic and immigrant cultures. Such ethnic groups as Italian Americans and Polish Americans retain many more ethnic characteristics than are often acknowledged or recognized.

The rather strong ethnic cultures existing within many Hispanic and African American communities are usually more often recognized by scholars and practitioners. As Novak (1973) insightfully pointed out, however, "ethnicity within White ethnic communities is often subconscious and subtle. Ethnic individuals themselves, especially White ethnic group members, are often unaware of the extent to which they are ethnic." Glazer and Moynihan (1975) also recognized the tenacity of ethnicity within modern American society, writing in their classic book, *Beyond the Melting Pot*, "Individuals, in very considerable numbers to be sure, broke out of their mold, but the groups remained. . . . The point about the melting pot is that it did not happen."

Cultural Pluralism

The melting pot concept has been highly criticized and challenged because of its inaccuracy and how it has been misleading. The Anglo-conformity concept suggests that the WASP culture changed very little in America and that other ethnic groups did all the changing. Following World War II, ethnic minority groups became increasingly powerful, both politically and socially, and refused to tolerate discrimination by the dominant cultural group and its political and social institutions. In the 1960s, the concept of cultural pluralism became popular in education circles. However, this idea of cultural pluralism was born near the turn of the century when great numbers of European immigrants were entering the United States at the same time that Nativism, designed to stop the massive flow of immigrants, was becoming pernicious and widespread. Philosophers and writers, such as Kallen, Bourne, and Drachsler, strongly defended the rights of the immigrants, arguing that they had a right to maintain their ethnic cultures and institutions in the United States, and used the concepts of cultural pluralism and cultural democracy to describe their philosophical positions.

Ravitch (1985) stated "the principle of cultural pluralism is as thoroughly American as the melting pot idea. What pluralism means in practice is that diverse groups have the right to be left alone, so long as their members fulfill the basic obligations of citizenship."

Like the concepts of the melting pot and Anglo-conformity, however, cultural pluralism may not adequately describe the complex nature of ethnic relations and cultural development in the United States. When Americans urge one concept or the other on the public schools, they usually have in mind a certain kind of society that the schools are supposed to produce. Since American society is made up of hundreds, perhaps thousands, of different cultures and subcultures, the schools are incessantly torn between pressures to enforce unity and pressures to reinforce diversity.

Some members of cultural groups strongly support the development of identity and commitment with their cultural group almost to the exclusion of influence from the dominant culture. Under such a pluralist ideology, the rights of the group membership are more important than the rights of the individual. These particular groups assume that an ethnic group can attain inclusion and full participation within a society only when it can bargain from a powerful position and when it has little or no influence from competing groups. In its strongest form, the cultural pluralist idea suggests that ethnic groups live within tight ethnic boundaries and communities and rarely, if ever, participate within the universal American culture and society. To this extent, cultural pluralism denies the reality of a universal American culture and national identity which every American, regardless of ethnicity and ethnic group membership, shares to a large extent.

Many believe that most Americans highly value their national identity and significant ethnic behaviors and characteristics. This common national culture and identity should be accepted, respected, appreciated and promoted by the schools in any reform effort related to ethnicity.

While some members of cultural groups strongly support a pluralist ideology, there is little overall support for a cultural entity separate from the dominant culture of the United States. If we were to develop a continuum that defined assimilation theories, we could place the melting pot at one end of the continuum, and separatism at the other end, with cultural pluralism between, as shown below:

Melting Pot	**Cultural Pluralism**	**Separatism**

If a representative sample of the U.S. population were asked to indicate whether citizens should be expected to conform to cultural patterns, values, and traits of the dominant culture or be allowed to maintain a separate cultural identity, they would probably indicate that neither end of the continuum is desirable. Somewhere between the two ends of the continuum is desirable, although responses would be likely to favor the Melting Pot. If we were to study the cultural patterns of individuals in the United States, we would again find individuals scattered across the continuum. Such findings would support the idea that ethnic attachments exist simultaneously with shared cultural traits. How culturally diverse we are does not seem to matter as long as we agree on certain basic values, one of which is respect for one another's cultural differences. As Gollnick and Chinn stated, "We need to learn to live together, not how to become alike."

Learning Styles

The instructional techniques currently in use in many classroom across the country were developed when "one best system" was considered both desirable and attainable. The school's role, according to popular belief, was to teach the basics and instill good working habits adaptable to the industrial age. The idea that innovation, problem-solving, cooperative work, or analytical skills were the educational right of all students was unthinkable. That these skills could be achieved by recognizing and fostering individual potential hardly was considered.

As a result in many school systems today, the traditional curriculum follows the traditional course and is still linear and limited. It does not allow much room for differences in how students learn. And too often its structure and organization blames students when they fail to respond to the one best system.

All children must learn, and they must achieve at a level and with the lifelong adaptability formerly reserved for only the few at the top. And every child has different strengths and talents which must be nurtured in order to produce the high standard of performance needed. As Resnick (1987) pointed out:

> "Although it is not new to include thinking, problem solving, and reasoning in *someone's* school curriculum, it is new to include it in *everyone's* curriculum. It is new to take seriously the aspiration of making thinking and problem solving a regular part of a school program for all of the population, even minorities, even non-English speakers, even the poor. It is a new challenge to develop educational programs that assume all individuals, not just an elite, can become competent thinkers."

Using what we know about learning styles is one way of ensuring that the curriculum, including high content and high expectations, engages all students.

We've always known it—people learn differently. Students differ in the way they approach learning. All students learn in different ways. Some are better listeners. Some work well in groups; others prefer to work alone. Some are more visual. Some students grasp oral instruction quickly; others need to see the directions in writing. Some learn best in a formal environment, while others prefer a more relaxed atmosphere. Lately, we've learned that some are more "right brained" and some are more "left brained," and we may have "multiple intelligence's" (Gardner and Hatch, 1988; Glasser, 1990).

Learning styles may be defined as those characteristics of a learner that tend to reflect how the learner perceives, interacts with and responds to the learning situation (Fisher, 1988). There are all kinds of learning styles, however, the most practical and meaningful to the teaching process are the five most commonly identified learning styles. (1) *Social*—which relates to how the student prefers to learn in relationship to others in the class. If the student has an *independent* learning style this student enjoys working on their own. Once the student understands the assignment, he or she is willing to work on his or her own. If the student is a *dependent* learner, he or she enjoys working on a one-to-one basis usually with the teacher or perhaps with another student. These students respond well to tutors and need consistent support. These students tend to enjoy being with people. *Interdependent* style students prefer to work and learn in situations where there is ample discussion and interchange between classmates. The student prefers to learn through the sharing of ideas. This student tends to be more outgoing than the other two styles of learning. (2) *Cognitive* refers to the student's preferred sensory mode (visual—student prefers to learn through seeing; auditory—student prefers to learn through listening). (3) *Structure* refers to the student's need for direction, for organization of material, and for the outlining of responsibility. It is the students need for structure. There are two primary categories that students fall into: (a) *Field Dependent*—this student needs a high degree of structure or organization in relation to the information being learned. The student requires specific directions, sequential tasks, frequent feedback, and continual support. (b) *Field Independent*—this student requires very little structure in relation to the information being learned. The student tends to be self-directed and responsive to making choices. They tend to be able to apply structure to the learning task. It is important to note that there are students who have no preference for either and in fact, can learn in both styles. (4) *Experiential* refers to whether or not the student prefers to learn through concrete experiences (pictorial material, charts, graphs, maps, and hands-on) as compared to abstract material which may include symbols (words, numbers) and semantic material. (5) *Participation* refers to whether or not the student prefers to learn by observation, or whether they tend to learn by doing. Those who tend to learn by observation are more passive and tend to take their time before acting. They look at all sides of an issue and are very aware of what's going on around them. Those who prefer doing tend to enjoy trying things out, participating, or experimenting.

The Issues of Culture and Ethnicity

The effect of culture and ethnicity upon learning is only beginning to provide useful signals to the classroom teacher. The key questions researchers are addressing are these: what are the individual learning styles preferred by a student's African American, American Indian or Hispanic cultural heritage and how should educators use them to enhance student learning? We can only hope that the field of learning styles among specific cultures will hold promise of moving toward a more accommodating, responsible and energetic vision of learning as a truly equitable opportunity. As with any research agenda, a word of caution is in order. As Hilliard (1988) has studied variations of learning styles among cultural groups, he identified three problem areas: (1) errors in estimating a student's intellectual potential, leading to misplacement and mistreatment; (2) errors in estimating a student's learned achievement in subjects such as reading; and (3) errors in estimating a student's language ability.

There has been a body of research with children from various cultural backgrounds and the implications they have for learning styles. Ramirez and Castaneda's research discovered that European American students tend to be the most field independent learners. Hispanic, American Indian and African American students, in contrast, tend to be closer to field dependent. Exactly how culture influences learning is not clear. Many believe that the values, attitudes, and behaviors taught at home are the basis for how children learn to learn. However, what remains a puzzle is that it is not as simple as the statement implies. For example, there are great differences in Hispanic learners. To be sure, there are many Hispanic students who may indeed be field dependent learners, but many will also be field independent learners. It is becoming clear that while child-rearing practices may contribute to a student's preferred learning style, it is by no means a sufficient criteria.

A student's social class background, many believe, may be as equally or more important than ethnicity in influencing learning style. Social class refers to membership within a particular social grouping, based on both economic variables and values (Nieto, 1992). Thus, the working class may differ from the middle class not only in economic resources but also in particular values and practices. The logic, many believe, is that social class is a more important influence on learning style than is ethnicity—that the intellectual environment of children in the home may be due more to economic than cultural factors. However, Banks (1988) found in general that ethnicity seemed to have had a greater influence on cognitive style than did social class. He also found that ethnic differences persist in spite of upward mobility. This line of research points out the apparently strong and continuing link between culture and learning.

There are important implications for teaching and learning in this research area. Some researchers suggest that all students should be exposed to and become adept at both styles of learning (field independent/dependent), with the acknowledgment that students probably still will maintain their preferred style.

The continued discussions about learning styles of students in many ways runs the risk of oversimplification. Although it is helpful in identifying learning differences among students that may be related to ethnicity and culture, it will inevitably come down to how teacher's approach and use of the information. The teacher's role and responsibility is to analyze the student's learning style by using: 1) an inventory (i.e. Dunn, Dunn and Price), 2) observing, and 3) visiting with the student or parent(s). Once the learning style is determined then the teacher can relate instruction to that particular style, or can provide supplemental instruction to meet the learning style. Of course, the teacher may also choose to simply be flexible in terms of instruction and utilize several methods which appeal to a broad number of learning styles.

Because The National Task Force on Learning Style and Brain Behavior recently offered only a *tentative* definition of learning style this should be enough to alert educators to the fact that learning style research is still evolving. Despite decades of research, there are more questions than answers about learning styles. On the other hand, to simply ignore the current knowledge base and impact that learning styles may play in our classrooms is also foolhardy. We must be careful not to view learning styles research as the panacea that will eliminate failure in the schools. To address only teaching and learning styles in isolation is to ignore other conditions of the school that contribute to inequities.

Addressing Diversity: A Five-Level Approach

McCune and Wilbur (1988) identified five levels of integration efforts which have emerged as viable means to reduce the existing disparity in opportunity. The following is a description of their five levels of equity.*

> **Level I: Physical Desegreation**
>
> **Level II: Equal Access**
>
> **Level III: Equal Treatment**
>
> **Level IV: Equal Outcomes**
>
> **Level V: Quality Outcomes**

Each differs in terms of effect, but each has been a necessary outgrowth of specific concerns over time. Heretofore integration efforts have focused on improvement primarily

* Wilbur, Gretchen, **Equity: Have We Arrived?** Reprinted with permission of the author.

within the existing structures of the school system. The first three levels of responses have been: physical desegregation, equal access and equal treatment. The remaining two, equal outcomes and quality outcomes, require the actual restructuring of the educational process itself. The latter are the levels which can fundamentally achieve the goals of equity by enabling the relevant preparation of all students for the information society.

Level I: Physical Desegregation

Physical desegregation was deemed necessary as a result of the 1954 Supreme Court decision of *Brown v. Topeka* which determined that separate schooling was not equal. The operating belief was that by dismantling the dual system of schooling, inequalities would be eliminated and students would be given equal opportunity regardless of race. However, it has been found through experience that even though students are placed in the same classroom, inequalities continue to remain. This is because inequities continue to exist in the expectations people hold and, thus, in their subtle treatment of students. Although desegregation is a vital step, further efforts are needed to eliminate these mental barriers.

Level II: Equal Access

When race discrimination began to be more substantively addressed as a result of the 1964 Civil Rights Act, and when sex discrimination became a legal matter through Title IX of the 1972 Educational Amendments, the question of equal access to opportunity became an issue. Disparate patterns in placement, enrollment and achievement highlighted the systematic conditions which abridged equal access. Pursuing alternative methods for providing access have been significant and deal with the more subtle characteristics of bias and stereotyping behavior. Although once access to classrooms and programs was granted, the problems of student treatment remained.

Level III: Equal Treatment

Equal treatment issues were dealt with by attempting to treat all students alike. This contradicted the initial intent of the treatment question as it denied the different needs of each student. For example, if all students were treated alike and some did not speak English, then access to equal opportunity would still be denied to the non-English speaking students. It was during this stage that a clarification of terminology emerged. Addressing the problems of discrimination, bias, and stereotyping (more than the concept of sameness) was needed. Doing the same for everyone ignored individual differences and past histories, and in fact, perpetuated the inequalities. So the issue became more clearly defined as equity, that is striving for equal outcomes.

Level IV: Equal Outcomes

Equitable practices are concerned not with treating everyone alike but with treating people in accordance with their specific needs, thus giving them perhaps different opportunities so they can have equal chances for pursuing their unique potential. This approach is guided by the goal of equitable participation in society for all people. In all areas of an equitable society—government, workforce, and education—participation would reflect the composition of the population in terms of sex, ethnicity, disability and religion. The achievement of proportional representation would signal achievement of equity.

Level V: Quality Outcomes

Educators are now asking another question—whether the schools we have had in the past will meet the needs of the future. And if they do not, then equal outcomes mean less if we are not providing a relevant education. Pursuing the fifth level, quality outcomes, becomes critical in achieving the full intent of educational equity. To achieve quality outcomes means that we must rethink the priorities of education and restructure the educational culture so that the achievement of all students reflects the skills required by the information society. An equitable educational system does not only consider equal outcomes but analyzes the worth of those outcomes in terms of ensuring a meaningful and productive life for individuals and society.

Have we achieved the mission or the concept of an equitable educational system? Have we provided opportunities for all students to pursue their interests without holding stereotypic expectations of their abilities and potential? Are we satisfied merely by providing students with an equal chance?

In the '90s, we are still facing desegregation/integration issues. Schools have not successfully desegregated their faculty or student populations to accurately reflect the local population composition. In 1990, more than 40 years after the *Brown* decision, a majority of America's school children still attended predominantly segregated schools. Equal access is not yet accomplished as course enrollment and achievement figures continually show the discrepancies between male-female (gender), majority-minority (ethnicity) and socioeconomic (status) representation. This inadequacy is sometimes rationalized by claiming that the choice is there but schools should not promote non-traditional enrollments. However, schools do have a responsibility to break down past barriers, whether internal or external, and be proactive in identifying the benefits of each option. Although we are not striving for the same treatment for all students, we continue to find that treatment is stereotypic and that lower expectations are held for students who are poor, African American, Hispanic, or female. The treatment should differ, but it should be motivated by the same goal for all students in the pursuit of their obvious and hidden potential. Equal outcomes have not yet been attained. This is clearly evident in achievement scores, in the workforce, in educational administration, and in political positions. As for quality outcomes, as mentioned in previous chapters, the curricula driving many educational programs continue to reflect the needs of an industrial society. In analyzing the populations of unemployed and under-employed, we may also find that there are overwhelming proportions of African Americans, Hispanics and women represented. This seems to be a clear statement of the inadequacies in our present system for achieving equitable opportunities for all people.

The Role of Equity in Our Schools

The first step to understanding equity is to acknowledge that successful school reform efforts are contingent upon the attainment of an equitable educational system. Unless we take these issues seriously and institute proactive efforts to respond to the changing needs of students and society, we will continue to perpetuate the inadequacies. Quality cannot be realized without equity.

Quality-with-equity is a reform movement that is attempting to change the schools and other educational institutions so that students from all backgrounds will have an equal opportunity to learn. This reform movement will require changes in the total school or educational environment; it is not limited to curricular changes.

Second, the driving mission of the school must be articulated and must reflect equity goals. Consensus of the concept is necessary for commitment and authentic action by all those who are a part of the school.

Quality-with-equity is also a process whose goals will never be fully realized. Equity, like liberty, justice, and democracy are ideals toward which human beings work but never fully attain. Because the goals of equity can never be fully attained, schools must have the vision of working continually to increase the prospects of a quality-with-equity education for all students.

Third, day-to-day behaviors, policies and practices should be analyzed as to their consistency with the intent of the mission. This also means that colleagues hold one another accountable to the mission. The new culture committed to equity must also be supportive of individual differences and encourage the behaviors which enable the meaningful growth of all persons.

To achieve social equality is a continual process, and it requires a commitment in belief and in action to the goals of equity. Attainment is dependent upon responsiveness to on-going change and respect for diversity. To proclaim and believe that we have attained equality is only to obscure the reality and deny human rights for all people.

Summary

The demographic data and the theories offered in this chapter indicate that America's population is becoming more diverse, not more homogeneous. There seems to be an increasing resistance to the old, majority American philosophy of assimilation reflected in the melting pot ideology.

In addition to a more diverse population, the nation will have larger numbers of ethnic minorities in proportion to the majority population. In many larger cities, ethnic minority groups already are in the majority, and the trend will continue.

The ethnic minority population grows younger and increases at a faster rate, while the majority population ages and slows down in growth. In education, the wave of declining enrollments now rolling through the system will reverse itself, but a very different education environment will emerge regionally, ethnically, culturally, and economically.

Demographic forecasts can permit policymakers to peer into the future to discern the kinds of problems and opportunities that await. The challenge to the schools is less clear. What policies, what approaches, will ensure an excellent educational system for the generation now growing up and for the future generations? Clearly, an approach that seeks to treat all alike will end up continuing to benefit some more than others and to leave still others with no benefits at all. An educational policy that focuses on the needs laid out by the demographics will have to be more targeted and tailored than has been the case up to now. Based on the demographic data and the changing nature of the economy, it seems clear that much greater attention will have to be paid to the needs of an ever-growing diverse population. The demographic future is rather predictable: Much less predictable is the nation's capacity (the schools in particular), or willingness, to initiate changes in policy, practices and resource allocation patterns to cope with that future.

Schools will have to answer some important questions. First, what is or will be the policy addressing the diversity within our society in general? Second, what is or will be the policy and practices of their school in addressing diversity of individual students or groups?

Today's education must include the development of skills and concepts students can use to form their own cultural perspective to allow them to function actively and effectively in our ever-changing society. Raw knowledge of ethnic or cultural differences will not be enough. Tomorrow's adults will need constructive attitudes toward the differences which exist between people and cultures. They will require a set of values which will allow them to deal effectively with change in our diverse society. As the self-interests of one group interacts with the self-interests of persons from other segments of our society, there will be a search for common ground so the interest of both parties will be protected.

Tomorrow's citizens will find differences between themselves and other people, and they will have to look for strength in those differences. They will have greater opportunities to interact with people whose values do not match their own; and as a result, they will need attitudes that will help them build strong working relationships. They will need an appreciation of the interdependency of the people in our diverse society which goes beyond knowledge of contributions, holidays, and cultural characteristics. Students must now begin to learn to respond positively and easily to change because change is the only thing we can promise them in the future. In short, leaders of business, industry, government, science and education will be most effective in the future if they who can cope with change, deal with a society as a system, and appreciate and accept human diversity.

END NOTES

Banks, James A. *Multiethnic Education: Theory and Practice.* Allyn and Bacon, Inc., Boston: MA, 1981.

Banks, James A. *Teaching Strategies for Ethnic Studies.* 2nd Edition, Allyn and Bacon, Boston, MA, 1979.

Banks, James A. "Ethnicity, Class, Cognitive and Motivational Styles: Research and Teaching Implications," *Journal of Negro Education,* 57, 4 (1988), 452-466.

Bennett Christine I. *Comprehensive Multicultural Education—Theory and Practice.* Allyn and Bacon, Boston, MA, 1986.

Brown v. Board of Education, 347 U.S. 483 (1954).

Chinn, Philip A. & Gollnick, Donna M. *Multicultural Education in a Pluralistic Society.* The C. V. Mosby Company, St. Louis, MO, 1983.

Cubberly, Ellwood P. *Changing Conceptions of Education.* Houghton Mifflin, Boston, MA, 1909. p. 16.

Dunn, Rita, Dunn, Kenneth, and Price, Gary. *Learning Style Inventory.* Price Systems, Inc. Box 1818, Lawrence, KS 66044, 1991.

Fisher, Richard I. *Learning Difficulties: Strategies for Helping Students.* Kendall/Hunt Publishing Co., Dubuque, Iowa, 1987.

Gardner, Howard and Hatch, Thomas. "Multiple Intelligences Go to School." *Educational Researcher,* November, 1988, pp. 4-9.

Glasser, William. *The Quality School.* Harper & Row, Publishers, New York: New York, 1990

Glazer, Nathan & Moynihan, Daniel P. (Eds.) *Ethnicity: Theory and Experience.* Harvard University Press, Cambridge, MA, 1975.

Hilliard, Asa, "Behavioral Style, Culture, and Teaching and Learning," paper presented to the New York State Board of Regents, March, 1988.

Hodgkinson, Harold L. "A Demographic Look at Tomorrow." Institute for Educational Leadership, Inc., Center for Demographic Policy, Washington, D.C., 1992.

McCune, Shirley & Wilbur, Gretchen. "Equity: Have We Arrived?" McRel Center, Kansas City, KS, 1988.

Nieto, Sonia. *Affirming Diversity.* Longman, New York, NY, 1992.

Novak, Michael. *The Rise of the Unmeltable Ethnics.* MacMillian Publishing Co., Inc., New York, NY, 1973.

Oakes, Jeannie. *Keeping Track—How Schools Create Inequality.* Yale University Press, New Haven, CT, 1985.

Ramirez, Manuel and Castaneda, Alfred. *Cultural Democracy, Bicognitive Development and Education.* Academic Press, New York, NY, 1974.

Ravitch, Diane. *The Schools We Deserve.* Basic Books, Inc., New York, NY, 1985.
    U.S. Bureau of Census Washington, D.C., 1990.

Resnick, Lauren. *Educating and Learning to Think.* National Academy Press, Washington, D.C., 1987.

Zangwill, Israel. *The Melting Pot.* MacMillian Publishing Co, New York, NY, 1909.

SUGGESTIONS FOR FURTHER READING

Kozol, Jonathan. *Savage Inequalities—Children in America's Schools.* Crown Publishers Inc., New York, NY, 1991.

Nieto, Sonia. *Affirming Diversity.* Longman Publishing Co., New York, NY, 1992.

Odell, Sandra J. & O'Hair, Mary J. *Diversity and Teaching—Teacher Education Yearbook I.* Harcourt Brace and Javonovich College Publishers, Ft. Worth, TX, 1993.

Name _____ **Date** _____

☑ **DISCUSSION QUESTIONS**

1. What are the demographic projections for the near future—in terms of children entering our schools?

_____

_____

_____

_____

   What are the implications for educators?

_____

_____

_____

_____

2. Three different models for addressing our diversity are:
   a. *Melting Pot*—all newcomers "melt" to form a new American.
   b. *Anglo-Conformity*—all newcomers need to conform to the dominant European American, middle-class, English-speaking model.
   c. *Cultural Pluralism*—all newcomers maintain their languages and cultures while combining with others to form a whole, which is a uniquely U.S. society.

Choose one of the above and argue that it represents the dominant ideology in U.S. society. Provide examples.

_____

_____

_____

_____

_____

_____

_____

_____

Which model is most apparent and successful?

_____

_____

_____

_____

_____

_____

What are the advantages and disadvantages of each model?

_____

_____

_____

_____

_____

_____

3. Define an "American."

_____

_____

_____

_____

_____

_____

4. Why do some ethnic groups isolate themselves from the mainstream of American society? Explain.

_____

_____

_____

_____

_____

5. Do schools have a role to play in "assimilating" students in society? Why or why not? If so, how do they do it?

_____

_____

_____

_____

_____

_____

_____

Why should schools teach more about various cultures?

_____

_____

_____

_____

_____

6. In what ways can a school promote cultural pluralism? Provide examples.

_____

_____

_____

_____

_____

_____

_____

_____

7. Explore ways in which teachers can become "multicultural" people. Propose specific examples in their attitudes, beliefs and behaviors.

_____

_____

_____

_____

_____

8. In pursuing a "multicultural curriculum," one of the first challenges that teachers and curriculum developers must confront is choosing which groups to teach about, which groups should the curriculum feature, and why?

_____

_____

_____

_____

_____

9. What do we know about culture, ethnicity and social class regarding learning styles? What implications does this information have with Question #3?

_____

_____

_____

_____

_____

_____

_____

10. Identify your learning style based on the five presented in the chapter. Cite an example with each category.

_____

_____

_____

_____

_____

_____

_____

SMALL GROUP WORK

In groups of 4 or 5.

Task:

On a large sheet of paper, list the 15 largest ethnic groups in the U.S. (Number 1 should be the largest ethnic group in number). Once your group has identified and listed the fifteen groups in order—to the right of each group identify either a fact, myth or stereotype of the group. Identify a recorder and a reporter.

Once each group has reported, each group will pick a number from a "hat" with the designated ethnic groups numbered. Each group will prepare a 15-minute report about the group they have selected. The report should have educational implications for teachers.

INDIVIDUAL OR GROUP WORK

Different Viewpoints on America's Ethnic Composition

Directions:

Each of the following items presents a particular view of the nature of American society with regard to its ethnic composition. Some clearly illustrate a belief in the melting pot while others represent a separatist point of view, and still others may represent a middle ground between these two extremes, cultural pluralism. Under each item place an X on the continuum to indicate the perception of America's ethnic character as the individual makes the statement.

1. "My parents decided never to teach us Spanish. They hoped that by not doing so, we would gain a generation in the process of becoming full Americans."

Melting Pot   Cultural Pluralism   Separatism

2. "Outwardly I lived the life of the white man, yet all the while I kept in direct contact with tribal life. While I had learned all that I could of the white man's culture, I never forgot that of my people. I kept the language, tribal manners and usages, sang the songs and danced the dances."

Melting Pot   Cultural Pluralism   Separatism

3. "That's right! I was ashamed of my name. Not only that, I was ashamed of being a Jew. There you have it! Exit Abraham Isaac Arshawsky... enter Art Shaw! You see, of course, how simple this little transformation was."

Melting Pot   Cultural Pluralism   Separatism

4. "I am not referred to as our seventh-grade math teacher, but as our minority math teacher."

Melting Pot   Cultural Pluralism   Separatism

5. "It makes no difference to me whether my students are Black, Hispanic or Asian. They are students and I treat them all the same, I don't see any differences."

Melting Pot   Cultural Pluralism   Separatism

6. "There are many regions of the United States where the third generation of Americans do not speak English."

Melting Pot   Cultural Pluralism   Separatism

7. "Why all the attention to the "minorities?" "Why not include and emphasize Irish Americans, German Americans and Swedish Americans?"

Melting Pot   Cultural Pluralism   Separatism

8. "Americans who do not speak English should learn it or go back to where they came from!"

Melting Pot   Cultural Pluralism   Separatism

9. "The Amish want to keep to themselves—a separate people. They are tied together by their religion and its values, by kinship (most are related), and by customs that make them appear different from everyone else."

| Melting Pot | Cultural Pluralism | Separatism |

10. "What the United States needs at this time, more than at any other time in our history, is an official language—English."

| Melting Pot | Cultural Pluralism | Separatism |

11. "More and more, I think in family terms, less ambitiously, on a less than national scale. The difference in being Slovak, Catholic, and lower-middle class, seem to be more important to me."

| Melting Pot | Cultural Pluralism | Separatism |

12. "I am not a 'minority,' I am a Japanese American."

| Melting Pot | Cultural Pluralism | Separatism |

13. "We demand that Spanish be the first language of the school and that the textbooks be rewritten to emphasize the heritage and the contributions of Hispanics in the United States."

| Melting Pot | Cultural Pluralism | Separatism |

14. "Black people just don't want to help themselves. They just keep together in their groups and they will never learn what it takes to make it in this country."

Melting Pot   Cultural Pluralism   Separatism

15. "Bilingual education is detrimental to the progress a student can make in school and in society. Teach them English as quickly as possible because that is what they will need to learn in order to succeed in American society."

Melting Pot   Cultural Pluralism   Separatism

16. "I don't consider myself 'ethnic,' I am an American. The only traditions we maintain in my family are the major holidays, birthdays, family reunions and the importance of our religion."

Melting Pot   Cultural Pluralism   Separatism

17. "My grandparents came to America not knowing a word of English, with no formal education and made a pretty good life for themselves. I don't understand why the new immigrants are not able to adapt and become Americans like my grandparents did."

Melting Pot   Cultural Pluralism   Separatism

18. "There is nothing wrong with an all Black school—as long as the programs meet state requirements for graduation and accreditation standards. As a matter of fact, they will probably get along better with their own kind."

Melting Pot   Cultural Pluralism   Separatism

A Generation in Jeopardy

6

> *If an unfriendly foreign power had attempted to impose on America the mediocre education performance that exists today, we might as well have viewed it as an act of war.*

> —*A Nation at Risk*, April 1983

Introduction

The above quote—and the landmark report it introduced—may well have pushed a nation down the long road to education reform. It has been eleven years since the *"Nation at Risk"* report. Where are we now? Are we still a nation at risk? Are we winning the war against mediocrity? The education of "at-risk" students has continued to be one of the major challenges of our time. These students are heavily concentrated among ethnic minority groups, immigrants, single-parent families, and the poor. At-risk students begin school without many of the standard skills upon which the school curriculum is based. As they move through school, they drop farther and farther behind the academic mainstream; by sixth grade they are about two years behind grade level in achievement; by 12th grade, they're four years behind, and half don't graduate from high school. In 1988, Levin predicted that about one-third of all students in the public schools would be at-risk, and many agree he was correct in his prediction. Unfortunately, the proportion of at-risk students is still rising rapidly.

Concurrently, there was a growing recognition that the movement toward school reform had sparked concern that the routes to achieving quality in our schools may bypass those students for whom traditional methods of education have often failed. There are risks for these students and their families in society at large and the risks to their educational attainment and entry into productive lives of employment are increasing.

Chapter 6, **A Generation in Jeopardy** is based on the following:

▶ That the series of national educational reforms is not likely to be successful in addressing the problems of the at-risk students because the reforms do not address the pertinent issues.

▶ That there are effective ways of providing appropriate educational services that must be implemented so that the rapidly increasing population of at-risk youth does not automatically grow up as a rising population of at-risk adults.

▶ That the benefits of such policies far exceed the costs.

▶ That failure to address the problems of at-risk youth will have serious consequences for the nation as a whole.

Growth of the At-Risk Population

The at-risk student population is growing at a far more rapid rate than that of the rest of the population. Although not all ethnic minorities are at risk, and many at-risk students are not members of an ethnic minority group, the ethnic minority population can be used as a proxy for assessing the size of the at-risk group in the public schools. From 1970-80, U.S. public school enrollments from pre-primary level to twelfth grade declined from about 46 million to 41 million students (National Center for Educational Statistics, 1986). At the same time, ethnic minority enrollments rose from about 9.5 million to about 11 million, or from about 21 percent to 27 percent of the total student population. As mentioned in the previous chapter, ethnic minority enrollments have been increasing at a more rapid pace than the general population because of a considerably higher birth rate and immigration—both legal and illegal—that is unprecedented in recent decades. Both factors create rapid growth, particularly among school-age populations, since immigrant families tend to be young and to have children.

State figures vary widely. California is at one extreme where ethnic minority student enrollment rose from about 27 percent of the total in 1970 to about 43 percent in 1980; as expected, ethnic minorities became the dominant component of California's student body in 1990. While growth has not been as rapid in Texas, the proportion of ethnic minority students was about 46 percent in 1980, rising from about 37 percent in 1970. During the same period, the ethnic minority student population rose in Connecticut from 12 to 17 percent; in Florida from 28 to 32 percent; in Massachusetts from 6 to 11 percent; in New York from 25 to 32 percent; in Oregon from 5 to 9 percent and in South Carolina from 41 to 44 percent. As for the major cities, by the year 2000, fifty-three major cities will have "majority" ethnic minority enrollments.

An additional reason for the growth of at-risk groups in the schools is the increase among all racial groups in the number of children in poverty families. Under family structure and poverty, the proportion of children in poverty stayed about 16 percent between 1969 and 1979, but it rose precipitously to 22 percent from 1979 to 1983 (Korentz & Ventresca, 1984). This represented an increase of about 3.7 million in only four years to a total of almost 14 million children. Some 45 percent of African American school-age children and some 36 percent of Hispanic school- age children live in poverty. Although some increase was associated with a rising incidence of single-parent, female-headed households, most was due to a higher poverty rate created by a changing economy in the late '80s and early '90s.

The evidence suggests that the proportion of at-risk students in American education is high and is increasing rapidly. While there is no precise method of estimating the total number of at-risk youth in the U.S., an estimate must include students in poverty and those whose chances of educational success are handicapped by virtue of language and cultural difference. If we assume that about three-quarters of all the ethnic minority students meet the economic and/or cultural-linguistic criteria, that accounts for almost 8 million at-risk students. Nearly ten years ago, about 40 percent of ethnic minority students met the poverty criteria alone (Levin, 1985). If we augment that total by the estimated 14 percent of non-ethnic minority students who live in poverty, another 4 million students are included for a total of 12 million at-risk students out of 40 million. This suggests that at-risk students accounted for about 30 percent of elementary and secondary students, and the proportion has continued to increase. For the purposes of comparison, it should be noted that in 1982, the U.S. Department of Education estimated that 42 percent of all students between the ages of 5 and 14 had limited proficiency in English. This estimate was based on the performance of a large national sample of students who were tested on their English proficiency. Even this total does not include the high number of at-risk dropouts who have left school but are less than 18 years old. Further, the evidence suggests that the degree of educationally disadvantaged youth is probably rising as the at-risk population is augmented by poor immigrants.

Both of these factors suggest that the challenge to American education posed by at-risk students will rise precipitously at a time when even the present needs of at-risk students have not been addressed satisfactorily. Accordingly, it is important to consider the consequences of ignoring these trends.

When the at-risk population represents a relatively small percentage of school enrollments, the failure of the schools to educate this group is tragic for its members and contrary to the principles of a democratic society. But its immediate effects were mainly confined to the at-risk population itself. For this reason, the issues could be ignored by the more advantaged majority without immediate consequences. As the at-risk groups have increased in school populations—and ultimately the overall population—the problem is no longer confined to that group. The potential consequences of inaction accrue to the larger society as well. The consequences include: (1) reduced economic competitiveness of the nation as well as states and industries that are most heavily impacted by these populations, (2) higher costs of public services associated with the impoverished and crime, (3) massive disruption in higher education, and (4) ultimately, the emergence of a dual society with a large and poorly educated underclass.

At-Risk Students

It is generally acknowledged that a growing proportion of young people are at risk of not making a successful transition to productive lives. There are a number of categories of risk that can be found in national, state and local reports on the topic. For our purposes, at-risk students will be defined as "those students who are likely to fail in some important way in school." For example, if a school believes that it is important for students to attend school daily, perform well on assessments, and make progress academically etc., when a student is not meeting those expectations and is developing a predictable pattern, that particular student is at-risk of not being successful in school.

The U.S. schools' track record in meeting the needs of special groups of students is not good, in fact, our schools are least successful with this population. U.S. schools, generally, are most successful in assisting youth from families in which: the parents have graduated from high school and have successfully completed some college coursework; the income level covers basic needs and allows some discretion in expenditure; the housing provides adequate shelter and individual privacy for reflection or study; and the language spoken in the home is a standard version of English. All of these factors contribute to the educational process by supporting the skills, values and languages that schools emphasize and by providing the additional resources in the home that reinforce schooling practices. In addition, it is important for children to be surrounded by persons who have succeeded both educationally and economically, so that the connection between education and future economic success is made. When students lack these advantages, conventional schooling tends to be much less successful in meeting their needs (Levin, 1988).

While a number of the following categories represent social phenomenon that educators cannot address alone, it seems valuable to identify the universal conditions of youth that create the most serious at-risk circumstances.

School Drop-outs

In a 1986 report to members of Congress, the United States Government Accounting Office (GAO) indicated that in October, 1985, there were approximately 4.3 million drop-outs (ages 16-24) and of those, about 3.5 million were White, about 700,000 were African American, and about 100,000 were from other ethnic groups. Fourteen percent of youth (ages 18-19) were drop-outs—16 percent of young men and 12 percent of young women. Drop-out rates of Hispanics, African American and other non-White groups as well as Whites from low-socioeconomic groups are considerably higher than the average for other groups. Drop-out rates for African Americans and for students in large cities with high concentrations of ethnic minorities are reported to exceed 50 percent (Kolstad & Owings, 1986). About 14 percent of sophomores in 1980 had dropped out of secondary school by the spring of their senior year in 1982. But the rates for African Americans and Hispanics were fully 50 percent higher than that of White, non-Hispanic students. Even these data understate the true disparity, since they do not account for dropouts prior to the spring of the sophomore year. Data suggests that about 40 percent of Hispanic drop-outs leave before the tenth grade (Lyke, 1986)

It's difficult to compare student drop-out rates accurately because of variations in the methods of reporting student attrition. In some school districts, the "drop-out" count may include students who have graduated early, had long hospitalizations, or died. But graduation rates can serve as a proxy for dropout rates. The statistics from the U.S. Department of Education are calculated by dividing the number of public high school graduates by the public school ninth grade enrollment four years earlier. They've been corrected for one variable, interstate population migration. (See Figure 18 — High School Graduation Rates—Percentage.)

Minnesota	89.3%	Missouri	76.2	New Mexico	71.0
Nebraska	86.3	Wyoming	76.0	**U.S. AVERAGE**	**70.9**
North Dakota	86.3	Idaho	75.8	Tennessee	70.5
Iowa	86.0	Colorado	75.4	North Carolina	69.3
South Dakota	85.5	Arkansas	75.2	Rhode Island	68.7
Wisconsin	84.5	New Hampshire	75.2	Kentucky	68.4
Vermont	83.1	Washington	75.1	Nevada	66.5
Montana	82.1	Alaska	74.7	Arizona	64.6
Kansas	81.7	Virginia	74.7	Texas	64.6
Ohio	80.0	Illinois	74.5	South Carolina	64.5
Connecticut	79.1	Massachusetts	74.3	California	63.2
Utah	78.7	Oregon	73.9	Georgia	63.1
Maryland	77.8	Hawaii	73.2	Mississippi	62.4
New Jersey	77.7	Oklahoma	73.1	Florida	62.2
Maine	77.2	West Virginia	73.1	New York	62.2
Pennsylvania	77.2	Michigan	72.2	Alabama	62.1
Indiana	77.0	Delaware	71.1	Louisiana	56.7

Figure 18. High school graduation rates (adjusted for migrant and unclassified students).

Young Offenders

According the *United States Crime Statistics Report* (1985), fifty percent of all arrests for serious crimes are of young people under 21 years of age. The homicide rate for non-White teens increased 16 percent and for Whites 23 percent from 1950-1978. The early '90s have witnessed a sharp increase in the number of young people carrying handguns—and the increase in violent crimes with this young group. In fact, in 1993, the average age of handgun violence was 16 years of age. Serious and repeat teenage criminals are placed in a variety of detention facilities, many offering limited help for continuing their education or for re-entering society. Family members and teachers are frequently victims of teenage crime. Incarcerated youth, when released from penal facilities, have increasing difficulties with school and employment and are at risk of continuing lives of crime or of being economically dependent during most of their lives.

Teen-Age Parents

According to a special report prepared by the Select Committee on Children, Youth and Families and the United States House of Representatives (1986), the number of births to teens under 20 was just under one-half million (499,038). This number accounts for almost 14 percent of all births in the country. Most teenage pregnancies are unintended and it is anticipated that at least one-third of teen mothers will experience a subsequent pregnancy while still in their teens. Most teen births are to women 15 to 19 years of age. Between 1960 and 1973 the number of births to girls under 15 rose from 7,500 to 13,000. Forty-nine percent of the births to the 15-17 year-old group were to unmarried teens.

The Problem Highlighted

▶ Every minute in America, two teens become pregnant.
▶ Every day in America, 40 teenage girls give birth to their third child.
▶ Only half of all teens who become parents before age 18 graduate from high school.
▶ Three out of four single mothers under 25 years of age live below the poverty line.
▶ Teen motherhood repeats itself: 82 percent of teen mothers under the age of 16 are daughters of teen mothers.
▶ A teen mother earns half the lifetime earnings of a women who waits to have children until age 20.
▶ Over $16 billion in government funds were spent in 1986 caring for teen mothers and their babies.
▶ The 385,000 first-babies born to teens in 1985 will receive more than $5 billion in welfare benefits over the next 20 years.
▶ The cost of caring for each low-birthweight baby born to teens runs from $10,000 to $15,000.

Nearly every state reported a serious teenage pregnancy and parenthood problem and 26 states acknowledged that existing prevention and assistance services are inadequate to address the needs.

As these children of teen parents are entering public schools, generally speaking, it can be anticipated that their educational disadvantages may be severe. Parents of these children are typically the at-risk youth from the previous generation who many times are under-educated, frequently did not have positive experiences in school, and many are not in a position to provide early learning experiences for their children in preschool years.

Drug and Alcohol Abusers

The National Center for Health Statistics reports that arrests of teens for drug abuse increased 600 percent between 1960-1980. Arrests for drunkenness among high school seniors rose 300 percent during the same period. Even without statistical evidence, the perspective that drug and alcohol abuse among youth represents a national crisis is currently shared by national, state and local leaders throughout the nation. The incidence of drug and alcohol use among school-age students is found in all geographic sections: urban, suburban and rural schools. Alcohol remains the choice of most school-age youth; and is clearly the drug that is abused the most.

Youth Unemployment

Educationally at-risk students tend to become at-risk adults. As adults, they have less economic opportunity, with lower personal incomes and less rewarding jobs. Society bears the related costs of their reduced productivity. Undereducation may also lead to other social burdens, among them lower levels of adult literacy, more welfare dependency, added health care costs, and more crime. According to Catterall and Robles (1988) the following statistics illuminate these statements:

▶ Only 25 percent of young adults (aged 21-25) who have not finished high school score well enough on a national test to indicate that they can follow directions from one place to another using a map.

▶ Just over 20 percent in the same population show skills that would enable them to balance a checkbook.

▶ The male high school dropout will earn $260,000 less over his lifetime than a graduate; a female dropout sacrifices about $200,000.

▶ The drop-outs from a single graduating class in a large urban district were estimated to lose $200 billion in earning over a lifetime; this would cost society more than $60 billion in lost tax revenues.

▶ Work interruptions due to loss of job are almost twice as likely for high school drop-outs than for graduates, and four times more likely for drop-outs than for college graduates. Such work interruptions are almost 50 percent more likely for Hispanics than for Whites, and almost 100 percent more likely for Blacks than for Whites.

► For young adults, each added year of secondary schooling reduces the probability of public welfare dependency by 35 percent.

► Entrance rates into the food stamp program are more than three times higher for those with only some high school than for those who simply graduate. Attaining some college beyond high school cuts the average entrance rate by more than half. Entrance rates for non-Whites are 3.5 times those for Whites.

Labor market opportunities are poor for high school drop-outs. Low educational attainment also contributes to the failure of youth to compete in the job market. The population survey data for 1985 shows that 1 in 4 drop-outs age 16-24 were unemployed, compared to 1 in 10 high school graduates who were not enrolled in school. In addition, large proportions of drop-outs do not even seek work. It is estimated that approximately 3 million 14 to 16-year-olds are looking for work and another 400,000 have stopped looking. The employment prospective for Black dropouts is more bleak than for Whites. In 1972, the unemployment rate for Black teenagers was 35 percent. It rose to 43 percent in 1986 (Catterall, 1986). However, it should be recognized that the disparity in labor force participation and unemployment between all Black and White youth (drop-outs and graduates) is greater now than in the past.

One can speculate that the effect of low educational attainment among those who do complete high school has significant economic and psychological effects also. These young adults are in the pool of the millions of other functionally illiterate adults. In the fall of 1993, a U.S. Department of Education study released the latest figures on illiteracy. The percentage of illiteracy continues to increase at unacceptable levels. Forty-seven percent of adults were identified as illiterate.

Ethnicity

To a remarkable degree, Americans seem to believe that the ethnicity problem has been solved, that our laws and institutions have been transformed enough so that any remaining ethnic minority achievement differentials can only be attributed to motivational shortcomings or differences in ability. Indeed, some of the long-term trends are encouraging. Black college graduates now attain jobs and incomes comparable to those of White graduates. While only 1.3 percent of Africans had completed college in 1940, by 1982, 12.4 percent had done so. At the same time, it is too easy to become complacent about these short-lived successes. In the early '90s a disproportionate number of ethnic minority students are enrolled in higher education in less prestigious junior and community colleges, and there is evidence that the rates of continuation from high school to college among ethnic minorities is actually declining. African American family income has not increased at all relative to White family income, and trends in residential and school segregation have shown, at best, inconsistent progress.

If ethnic minority access to and participation in higher education is in fact declining, this is a serious and troubling trend. It is not, however, necessarily the most important source of economic differences. Wilson and Aulletta, in their separate studies, indicate growing economic divergence within the African population, with enormous economic disparities persisting between relatively unskilled and poorly educated White and African workers. Bills (1986) interpretation, which seems well supported by the evidence, is that the "race" problem is increasingly a class problem, in that an exceptionally high proportion of African Americans are relegated to low-status jobs. He maintains that while affirmative action programs have had beneficial effects on the careers of African professionals, they have done little to enhance the prospects of the working poor or the underclass.

Past Responses to At-Risk Students

Cuban and Tyack (1988) offer a capsule examination of how schools and teachers described at-risk students, how historically educators have perpetuated misconceptions and implemented flawed solutions that hurt these students rather than helped them.* Cuban and Tyack state that for almost two centuries, explanations for "low achievement" have blamed individuals, families, teachers, educational institutions, or the inequalities embedded in the political economy. Each explanation proposed a solution in keeping with the perceived cause. Over time, the blame shifted somewhat, but earlier explanations persisted alongside the new:

▶ **Low achievers are responsible for their own performance.** This response, which had deep roots in American ways of thinking, has been the dominant way to frame the problem. In the nineteenth century, notions of "intelligence" and cultural differences were rudimentary, so educators typically explained poor academic performance in terms of flawed character: the student was lazy or immoral. In the twentieth century, when "science" informs educational decision-making, psychological interpretations prevail: low I.Q. and inadequate motivation cause academic failure. The solution has often been to educate children by separating them into categories that presumably matched their genetic make-up that is, remedial education.

▶ **Families from different cultural backgrounds fail to prepare and support their children's progress in the elementary and secondary grades.** Moral complaints against the nineteenth-century low-achiever sometimes spilled over onto their families: parents were intemperate, undisciplined, unfamiliar with American standards of behavior. With the rise of social science in the twentieth century, finger-pointing became less

---

* Larry Cuban and David Tyack, professors in the School of Education at Stanford University. This summary is excerpted from their paper, "Historical Background of the Educationally At-Risk." Reprinted with permission of the authors.

moralistic. But still, parents figured largely in theories that stressed the poverty, or the supposed cultural deficits, in the families of "unteachable" children.

▶ **The school system cannot accommodate the range of intellectual abilities and the different destinies of its heterogeneous student body.** Many reformers argued that academic failure stemmed from the rigidity of the standardized curriculum and the inflexible practices of promotion and grading. They did not frontally attack the graded school, for it had served the majority of students well. Rather, they argued that a single, lock-step academic course of studies produced failures because not all students were capable of studying the same subjects at the same rate.

▶ **Schools produce the unequal social relationships of a capitalist political economy.** In this view, schools are structured to produce winners and losers. Because public education reflects in its organization and processes the unequal social relationships of production, certain children will rise to the top and others fall to the bottom because schools are dynamic instruments of the larger political economy. Although educators may be unaware of the systemic character of such class, racial, and gender discrimination, and despite resistance of students and teachers to domination, the overall results are predictable: some pupils are destined to fail because of the imperatives of the economy.

▶ **Children often fail academically because the school's culture differs so greatly from cultural backgrounds of their communities.** In this view, the schools, not the children, should adapt to social diversity. The teachers often unconsciously served as agents of a pervasive cultural system that was geared to standardizing their pupils. Classrooms became cultural battlegrounds, in which teachers communicated lower expectations and failed to connect with their culturally diverse students. Thus, they unwittingly created student failure. (Cuban and Tyack, 1988)

Cuban and Tyack (1988) suggest that each of these diagnoses led to a different conclusion. Blaming the individual student or the family provided an alibi, not a solution. Blaming the rigidity of traditional education exposed institutional faults, but it led to policies that too often sequestered the "abnormal child" in an inferior and segregated corner of the system. Analyzing how the school reflected the inequalities of the larger political economy illuminated the difficulty of correcting social injustices in education and through education, but it offered no practical remedies; it made the school an ally of social injustice, not a cure for it. Spotlighting the gaps between the school's culture and the cultural backgrounds of students provided a useful corrective to the earlier ethnocentric explanations that blamed students and parents—but failed to question the basic structure and processes of schooling. Moreover, because it focused on the unconscious cultural biases of teachers, it ran the danger of personalizing the answer: more sensitive instructors were obviously needed — but where were they to come from? Adding "Black" history to the curriculum or bilingual strategies to the instruction would defuse conflict, but such attempts to make schools "multicultural" merely added to a familiar pattern of instruction; they did not change the institution.

Almost all these diagnoses and the solutions they generated failed to alter the structure of the school. All of the labeling and its specialized programs have become part of the problem; they often reflect and reinforce stereotypes about the genetic or cultural inferiority of certain groups.

Indicators for At-Risk Students

School Attendance

Poor attendance often begins at the earliest stages of schooling. Given the evidence of the relationship of learning time to school performance, number of days of absence from school becomes a significant predictor of low performance. When the pattern of absence is established in the primary grades, it is almost certain that it will worsen as students reach pre-adolescence. Student attendance is undoubtedly the earliest and most visible indicator of potential problems in school. Schools should maintain accurate records with regard to daily attendance rates (DAR), but more importantly, records of specific students and their patterns of attendance. Nationally, 10% of our students are not in school daily.

Academic Performance

School performance is another early indicator of educational risk. When students in third and fourth grades are already two years behind their age counterparts, catching-up becomes a difficult, if not insurmountable, obstacle. There are real differences in academic achievement that are rooted, to a great extent, in the factors discussed in the previous chapters. The cumulative effects of achievement are well documented in a number of sources. A reasonable appraisal of the magnitude and nature of achievement differences is essential for understanding and improving the educational consequences of being at-risk. While a number of successful interventions have been identified and are being tried, it seems obvious that efforts to improve instruction and learning for large numbers of students have failed to affect outcomes of significance. Poor academic performance remains the primary reason students leave school.

Involvement in School Activities

Studies (Pollas & Verdugo, 1986) have examined the participation of school drop-outs in school activities when they were attending. School drop-outs participate in very few of the academic and social activities or recreational-related activities. The practice of isolation from the enrichment activities of schools is another indicator for educators to examine, especially as students make the transition from elementary to secondary school levels. One indicator cited by Pollas was students' participation in antisocial activities outside of school. Gang membership, numbers of hours spent on the streets, use of drugs and alcohol are likely to lead to poor school performance, early school leaving and delinquency. There is strong evidence that suggests that students who are not involved in school activities are disproportionately represented in dropout statistics.

Student Behavior

Antisocial behavior in school is often accompanied by other indicators of educational risk. The manner in which schools address disruptive students can often increase the likelihood that students will increase truancy, vandalism and other unacceptable behaviors. The degree to which these patterns can be altered in the early years of schooling, the more likely students will develop healthier attitudes in later school years. The involvement of families and other community agencies is often a necessity to address the problems of disruptive students. There is also a growing body of literature that indicates the relationship of student behavior to the classroom and school climate and to the implementation of rules regarding student behavior. Many schools are integrating health-related agencies, social workers, and mental health experts to work with students and teachers.

Attitudes Toward School

Closely aligned to student behavior are the attitudes toward school and toward the adults in the school. Negative attitudes that are demonstrated in the early years of school are often indicators of later school problems. As mentioned in earlier chapters, there are numerous survey instruments to gather information about student's perception and attitudes about school—taken seriously by the school, they can provide the administration and staff some very valuable information.

Need for Employment

Some of the indicators cited above may be directly related to the presence of economic difficulties in families. High school students may actually be encouraged to seek employment in order to supplement family income. The awareness of the need for employment by teens may require school schedule changes, the provision of assistance and increased school-work programs. There have been numerous studies with regard to the amount of work and the detrimental effect it may have on students' academic performance in school. Generally speaking, the research suggests that if high school students work more than 20 hours a week, their grades have a greater chance of being negatively effected—by as much as one grade level or more.

Nature of Family Support

Many schools have expressed the difficulty of securing the adequate assistance from families with the student experiencing problems. This is an area where premature judgments can be made. However, it is important to have supplemental services to investigate the extent of family problems that are affecting school attendance, performance, and attitudes. Such knowledge indicates the need to increase the student's support within the school. Not always true, but for a number of these parent(s), schooling was not a positive influence upon them either. In many ways, they represented the first generation in jeopardy; while the schools are currently witnessing their offspring—the second generation in jeopardy.

Involvement with the Justice System

A number of teen crimes are committed by students who are still in school. It is likely that students who are frequently involved in crimes and are on probation to juvenile courts are at risk of failing to stay in school or are doing poorly in school.

It seems clear that the first six of these eight indicators of educational risk are much closer to the business of schools than the last three. They are also the indicators that are most alterable by schools.

Current Responses to At-Risk Students

The call for reform in education, spurred by the *A Nation at Risk* report, was not a response to the plight of the at-risk student. Rather it was premised on the concern that, in the absence of major changes in American education, the U.S. economy might lose in the competitive race for international markets in our age of high technology.

As discussed in earlier chapters, several recommendations seek specific changes that would strengthen curriculum and standards; for example, implementing minimum competency standards for graduation, raising graduation requirements, and teacher testing and certification, are just some of the reforms recommended. For a number of reasons, these requirements are only marginally relevant to at-risk students. Some educators believe that some of the recommendations may actually be harmful, since they create additional barriers to high school completion without providing the resources and assistance necessary for the at-risk student to meet the new requirements.

The states have responded to the reform agenda by legislating some of the recommendations, modifying standards in past legislative mandates and programs, directing attention at the state and local levels by establishing commissions, task forces etc., to address the needs and strategies for at-risk students in their immediate area or region. Even where reform has been converted into legislation, some critics have found that it often takes a rigid, mechanical approach that is unlikely to have the desired results or that provides only a large number of questionable responses, rather than a comprehensive solution to the issues.

Compensatory Education

The impact of poor school performance has far reaching implications for students, and even when poor academic performance is a single factor affecting youth, it represents a very high risk factor. The fact is that poor academic performance is typically accompanied by other risk factors. Poor grades are the most frequently reported reason for dropping out of school. Borus and Carpenter conducted a study of the correlation of dropping out of school and found that among the most important concerns was being two or more years behind grade level (Borus & Carpenter, 1984). While poor school performance is at the center of concern regarding school drop-outs, it is a serious high-risk factor for students who are currently in schools and for those who complete school with a history of low achievement. McDill (1986) and his colleagues, in an examination of the effects of higher academic standards on potential drop-outs, reported that the consistent failure and frustration of low-academic achievement inevitably leads to increases in absenteeism, truancy and school-related behavior problems.

It has been well documented that the low achieving phenomenon often starts in the earliest grades of schooling and increases in severity as students proceed through elementary and middle schools. It was this premise that led to the development of compensatory education programs for "disadvantaged" children in the middle 1960s. The original intent of the Elementary and Secondary Education Act (ESEA) was to promote educational equity for poor and disadvantaged children. This act set a precedent for federal aid to education and was considered an effective way to break the cycle of poverty. Since 1965, $38 billion in federal funds has been spent on Chapter 1 programs (the largest federally funded program in education). Since the passage of the original Elementary and Secondary Education Act in 1965, school districts have wrestled with the problems of educating low-achieving, disadvantaged students. In addition to the difficulties of designing and implementing programs that overcome achievement deficits, schools have been constrained by regulations — to supplement, not supplant, regular programs, to serve only eligible students, to use standardized tests to determine eligibility, and to focus on reading and arithmetic.

A considerable amount of literature exists regarding the evaluation of Chapter I programs. Typically, they have focused on only a portion of the students at risk, and the resources that they have provided have been far short of what is required to make any substantial difference. The evidence suggests that such policies have affected small reductions in the test score gap between White and non-White students over time (Guttmacher, 1981, Catterall, 1986, and Humphrey, 1986). Even so, the educational performance of at-risk students lags considerably behind that of their more advantaged counterparts, and they are more likely to drop-out before completing high school.

However, in the more recent Chapter 1 reauthorization, school districts now have the opportunity to use complete flexibility: Chapter 1 professionals can work in regular classrooms; eliminate pull-out programs; become team-teaching situations; parent-liaison staff can work with parents of special-education students; and all faculty members can participate in Chapter 1 inservice or planning activities. This shift in emphasis means that rather than depending on specialists, teachers will have the opportunity to work collaboratively in addressing the educational problems of low-achieving students. Authority to conduct this school-wide approach is granted directly by the state educational agency upon approval of the plan. There are several schools across the country in the early '90s that are engaged in school-wide reform efforts using the Chapter I resources. These schools are referred to as being a school-wide Chapter I school. In exchange for flexibility, this process will require school-specific accountability and extensive parental involvement. These new approaches and regulations will challenge teachers and parents in schools across the country to provide more effective schooling for the educationally disadvantaged.

Setting State Competency Standards for Receiving a Diploma

On the surface, this may be viewed as a very attractive reform, assuring that all holders of a diploma will have certain proficiencies. But if at-risk students enter secondary schools functioning two or three years below grade level, it is likely that few of them will suddenly catch up to meet competency standards for graduation. More likely, even if they try very hard, they will not meet the stringent standards and will not receive a diploma for their efforts. The additional standards may simply discourage them from trying to remain in school. (See Figure 19—States Using Minimum-Competency Testing).

There are two ways to solve this dilemma. If competencies are set at a very low level for graduation, such as at eighth-grade achievement, they will be relatively easy to satisfy, even for most of the at-risk students who do not drop-out. In the past, most states have chosen low competency standards. An alternative is to choose higher standards and provide educational resources and programs for at-risk students so that they can meet the higher standards. Many of the new standards are likely to be higher than previous ones, and therefore will require remediation for the at-risk student. But without resources and a mandated commitment, this is unlikely to happen.

In the absence of comprehensive compensatory programs, the attempt to raise standards to meet educational and job-related requirements will increase pressure on the at-risk student to drop-out, even for those students who could have met the standards with

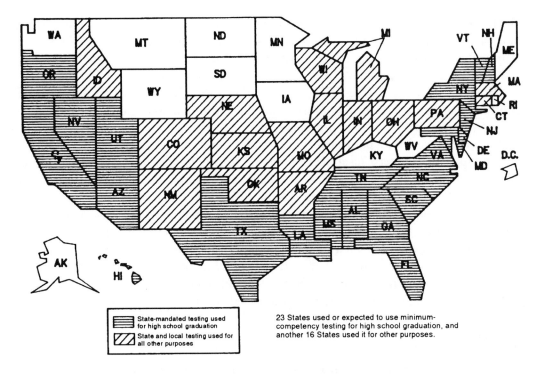

Figure 19. States using minimum-competency testing.

appropriate educational assistance. And failure to meet standards and obtain a competency-based diploma may increase employer rejection of such students, even when they are able to perform the job.

Without a major commitment to the educational problems of the at-risk student in the earliest grades, raising competency standards will discourage them from completing school. This is even true when standards are used for determining promotion in earlier grades. Without major funding and programs to alleviate early deficiencies, many educators believe too many of the at-risk students will be required to repeat grades, at great cost to the schools. Clearly, it would seem to be more effective to put those resources into remediation of achievement deficiencies at each grade level than use grade repetition as a device to meet standards.

Increases in Course Requirements for Graduation

When at-risk students who enter ninth grade are performing at a sixth-grade level, additional course requirements in mathematics, English and science are not likely to be effective in raising performance levels for them. The additional requirements will mean that benefiting from high school level instruction will be made even more difficult. Students who are far behind need to be brought up to those norms before they can benefit from existing high school requirements, to say nothing of additional requirements.

As discussed earlier, the practice and organizational structure of tracking and sorting students in our schools will have to be addressed. As we have seen, the many issues involved with meeting the needs of at-risk students and other related issues, are centered around the issues of tracking itself.

Increasing the Length of the School Day or School Year

General evidence that more instructional time will improve learning outcomes is weak at best. There is virtually no evidence that the present school day or school year is the limiting factor affecting the learning of all students, or the at-risk student in particular (Pollas & Verdugo, 1986). For many of these students, the fact that they are doing poorly and see no hope of catching up reinforces the feeling of school as a oppressive environment. To require them to spend more time in such a situation *without altering educational strategies* to make their learning experience more successful is likely to produce greater dissatisfaction. It is imperative that the learning situation become more vital and exciting, and that the student have some sense of progress rather than feelings of failure and futility. Without these changes, forcing the student to spend more time in school is unlikely to reap much success.

As mentioned previously, most educational reforms currently sponsored by states do not address specific issues affecting at-risk students. Reforms that create more time in school or higher standards—without noticeable changes in the schooling process that will increase learning for the at-risk student—will likely increase drop-out rates among those students who can scarcely hope to meet present standards. It is clear that whatever merits the present reforms have, they are incomplete and foreshadow both a present and future tragedy unless the needs of at-risk students are addressed.

The Care Team Approach

The Care Team approach works with students who have problems that interfere with learning. Typically, the Care Team identifies those students in their building who are considered at-risk of academic failure. The Team attempts to negate any obstacles to learning by providing access to resources available within the school and community at large. Where resources are lacking, the Team identifies deficiencies and makes appropriate recommendations for acquisition and development to the designated representative (i.e., principal). The goal of the Team is to maximize student learning and to help ensure a successful education for the identified students.

The Care Team can be composed of building administrators, classroom teachers, as well as personnel from the counseling staff, school psychologist, social worker and other support staff members. The Team should meet weekly at a designated time and place. Records of the Team meetings should be maintained by the coordinator of the Care Team.

The Team reviews each "active" case at each team meeting until the case is placed on the "inactive" status. This procedure ensures consistent follow-up for each student identified in the program. It is the responsibility of the team to review and assess referrals, to make recommendations and to ensure student access to appropriate educational resources and interventions.

Since the focus of the school is student learning, it is important for the Care Team to keep its activities consistent with that focus. When students have problems which prevent them from learning, it is the responsibility of the Care Team to provide strategies for the assistance needed to maximize student learning. It should not be the responsibility of the Care Team to provide personally all interventions, but is the charge of the Team to identify those strategies which are available and to lead the school in the development of those programs which could help actualize student learning.

Assessing the Needs of At-Risk Students

The unique needs of the at-risk student cannot be effectively addressed by reforms of a general nature such as increasing course requirements or increasing the amount of instructional time or establishing Care Teams. While these reforms may be desirable on their own merits, they should not be viewed as substitutes for direct and comprehensive strategies to solve the problems of the at-risk student. In the absence of specific academic programs, general reforms may overwhelm the abilities of an ever-growing number of at-risk students to meet the requirements for high school completion.

Approaches to change must be viewed in the context of an overall strategy for placing the challenge of the at-risk student on the national, state and local policy agenda and addressing the challenges effectively. Such an agenda should include establishing (1) guidelines for prevention strategies, (2) guidelines for identification strategies and (3) school-wide goals.

Guidelines for Prevention Strategies

Successful prevention strategies can take many forms and involve very different school practices. Some of the more successful strategies, for example, provide special learning experiences for preschoolers; some focus their efforts almost entirely on school improvement plans, while still others deliver services to troubled students. Although successful strategies are often quite different, they tend to share certain characteristics.

▶ Successful strategies will support students during times of personal crises, be unbiased about the cause(s) of student failure, consider the continuity of development, encourage individual competency and self-reliance, be empathetic towards students, address specific developmental needs and maintain a healthy sense of skepticism regarding any programs that are described as the answer to the problems that at-risk students experience.

▶ Prevention programs need to consider how to support students when internal or external demands become personal crises. Programs that provide resources for students at these times, augmenting their own problem-solving skills, prevent temporary failures from overwhelming students and disrupting their development. Prevention programs, therefore, should identify ways in which school personnel can help students during critical times in their development.

▶ Successful preventions are unbiased about the causes of student failure. They neither "blame the victim" nor "blame the system" for the problems that at-risk students often experience. Successful prevention strategies consider the role of students and the school when designing and implementing policies and strategies. They encourage the development of individual students and the improvement of school practices and procedures which affect learning and growth.

▶ There is no special period, no single critical stage in development that determines all or most of whom a child will or can become. Cognitive and emotional development is best described as continuous and divided into many "critical" stages. Prevention strategies, therefore, must be appropriately spread across the developmental continuum. Prevention will be most successful if it aids students at numerous "critical points" in their development.

▶ The most successful prevention programs tend to be those that make students more competent in a regular school setting. Many school failures are defenses against the daily frustrations and degradation that at-risk student experience at school. School-based preventions tend to fail if they do not realistically improve a student's chances of succeeding in school and life and usually that means teaching students to function better socially and cognitively.

▶ Committed, empathetic adults, who understand the nature of child development and have high expectations for themselves and students, are important characteristics of successful prevention strategies. Prevention requires a particular type of understanding and sensitivity toward at-risk students, and those run by empathetic adults tend to be most successful.

▶ Prevention programs with specific goals are more likely to succeed than those with vague objectives. Good intentions, enjoyable experiences and a reprieve from everyday stresses are often not enough to bring about personal change. School failures are always a response to specific internal and external stresses, and preventions that identify those stresses and take actions to make them manageable are more successful than others.

▶ The potential benefits and dangers of early identification and prevention are far too real to proceed haphazardly. Students can be harmed, and money can be wasted on ill-conceived programs and strategies. A healthy sense of skepticism, therefore, is always warranted, especially when strategies are described as the answer to the problems that at-risk students experience. Prevention efforts will be most successful if they are carefully developed, piloted, implemented and evaluated.

Guidelines for Identification Strategies

The following strategies can be used as a guideline for developing your own identification strategies. Additionally, the following are precautionary measures for identifying individual students as at-risk.

▶ Individuals should never be identified as at risk without careful consideration of potential benefits and harm to them. The greater the possibility of harming students, either through negative labeling or denial of educational opportunities, the greater the need for protecting student rights.

▶ Whenever possible, identification should be based on behaviors that students can control. Identification should always afford students the possibility of changing their "at-risk status," by improving their grades, attendance or classroom behavior, for example. Factors should clearly reinforce desirable behavior when educational opportunities are affected.

▶ Factors that are a matter of cultural values or beliefs, such as dress or religious preference, should never be used to identify students at risk. These factors are not appropriate criteria on which to base decisions about educational resources and opportunities.

Identification strategies can be evaluated in different ways, depending on the criteria used to assess them. It may be useful to evaluate strategies according to their fairness, opportunities, completeness, usability and specificity. Every strategy should be evaluated in terms of how well it focuses on at-risk students.

Actual strategies, however, are always a compromise between desired attributes, for many of these criteria are inversely related to each other. Attempts to be fair may, in some instances, make a strategy more time-consuming and less usable; attempts to be complete, that is, to identify *all* students who will eventually fail in some way may result in less specificity, the ability to identify *only* those who do fail.

These criteria can be used as guidelines for developing your own identification strategies. Ask yourself, "How well will our (my) strategies focus attention on at-risk students?"

Fairness

Identification strategies should fairly identify students as at risk, especially when there is the possibility that identification could be harmful or used to deny opportunities. Strategies should be evaluated to determine if they protect students and recognize their rights. The fairness of an identification strategy should be routinely considered.

Opportunities

Identification strategies should provide timely information about students who are at risk. Strategies should be evaluated to determine how promptly they identify at-risk students, giving the student and personnel ample opportunity to prevent school-related difficulties from occurring or getting worse. The opportunities that an identification strategy creates for prevention should be carefully considered.

Completeness

Identification strategies should attempt to identify *all* students who are at risk of failing in some important way. Strategies should be evaluated to determine how completely they identify students who eventually fail, given the actual occurrences of certain school-related difficulties, such as dropping out of school, substance abuse and expulsion. School personnel should consider who, if anyone, a strategy fails to identify and what the implications for that failure might be.

Usability

Identification strategies should be easy to implement and use. Strategies should be evaluated to determine whether or not they are practical, considering the time, coordination and expertise they require of school personnel. Strategies which use straightforward and easily understood techniques for identifying students are always preferable to those which require extensive data collection, record keeping, calculations and education to understand.

Specificity

Identification strategies should attempt to identify *only* those students who will actually fail in some way, limiting, to the extent possible, the number of students who are identified as needing special services. Ideally, that number would always be equal to the number that actually fail if school personnel do not intervene in some way. Strategies should be evaluated to determine how specifically they identify at-risk students. School personnel should consider who, if anyone, a strategy misidentifies and what the implications for that misidentification might be.

▶ Whenever possible, identification should be based on easily observed and interpreted behaviors, so as to assure uniformity and neutrality in how students are identified. Identification should not be based on subjective factors, unless special provisions are made for a thorough consideration of all interpretations.

▶ Factors that are used to identify individuals should be casually related to the outcomes being prevented. Intuitive and statistical proofs of the relationship between at-risk factors and outcomes should be thoroughly considered before using them to identify individuals.

▶ Specific individuals should not be identified as at risk if other less isolating strategies can be used effectively to deliver services to students. The need for individual identification should be carefully considered, as well as the possibility of alternative selection techniques, such as volunteering or monitoring group performance.

▶ Individuals should never be identified as at risk of a specific outcome unless there is a reasonable chance of preventing its occurrence. School personnel should always be prepared to assist individual students who are identified as at risk of failure. Goals for alleviating the educational disadvantages that face all students in our school—especially at-risk students—must be concrete. Just as higher standards are set for the schools, so should specific goals be set for bringing at-risk students up to the required norms. This should be done at the initial stages of schooling so that by the time students enter secondary school, they are able to benefit from regular instruction.

The establishment of prevention strategies and identification strategies serves two purposes. First, it is a policy statement that signals priority. Second, goals are a means for assessing progress. Therefore, specific achievement goals for at-risk students should be set at both state and local levels in the form of measurable standards of achievement.

Summary

Our nation is at risk of starting the 21st Century with one of four students failing to complete the essentials of learning. There was a time in this nation when school failure and little education did not foreclose a person's options for a self-sufficient and fulfilling life nor impede the nation's capacity in trade, defense, environmental condition, or quality of life. That time is gone. Technological advances, demographic changes, international competition, and intense pressures of providing a better life for greater numbers of people on a seemingly shrinking planet today require a citizenry educated at least through high school graduation. This is imperative for our nation.

We are not meeting that imperative. One of four youth does not graduate. The greatest proportions of those who are at risk of not graduating are poor, ethnic minority, and those of limited English proficiency. We must serve them by taking several actions now. The high school class of 2000 entered kindergarten in 1987—one quarter of them living in poverty. Our society must commit more resources for quality and equity. We must strengthen the practice of teaching. We must provide assistance and incentives for schools to change their programs to succeed with at-risk children.

Programs abound in schools to address these students. Dropout prevention programs, sex education programs, delinquency prevention programs, vocational training programs, alternative school programs, counseling programs—each pick out a piece of the at-risk student problem. Several research centers and projects work to address these immediate problems, but they also see clearly that a common thread winds its way through each—poor academic performance in school, usually from the early years onward. Given this common thread, a scenario emerges. If schools could improve the academic performance of at-risk students beginning in the early years, this improvement would have multiple positive effects on student drop-out, delinquency, pregnancy, substance abuse and other behaviors. Thus early improvement of poor academic performance could greatly alleviate multiple aspects of the overall problem.

How can we bring about a state of affairs in which schools are choosing from among proven programs, implementing those programs effectively, and producing measurable benefits for their at-risk students? First, each region, state and local educational agency should establish a valid list of effective programs for at-risk students. Secondly, they should provide the necessary resources to help schools adopt effective practices. For one example, they should establish state or regional centers, staffed by personnel trained in the various effective models and in the dissemination and implementation of successful practice. Third, they should fund research and development of new effective models. Several groups of researchers and developers should be funded to follow a rational sequence of development, pilot-testing, small-scale evaluation, and large-scale evaluation by outside independent evaluators. And Fourth, they should establish independent evaluation centers. These centers would oversee and assist in independent evaluations of programs conducted by state and local evaluation agencies and conduct evaluations of their own. These evaluations would be essential to insure the credibility of program effects.

END NOTES

Bills, David. "Students Who Are Educationally at Risk." In North Central Regional Educational Laboratory, Unpublished Report, University of Iowa, Iowa City, IA, 1986, p. 6.

Borus, Michael E. & Carpenter, Susan A. "Youth and the Labor Market: Analyses of the National Longitudinal Survey." In Michael E. Borus (Ed.), *Choices in Education*, Chapter 4. The W. E. Upjohn Institute for Employment Research, 1984.

Catterall, James & Robles, Eugene. "The educationally at-risk: what the numbers mean." Conference Papers, November, 1988. Stanford University.

Catterall, James S. "On the Social Costs of Dropping Out of School." University of California, Unpublished Report, 1986.

Cross, Patricia. "The Rising Tide of School Reform Reports." *Phi Delta Kappan,* Vol. 66, No. 3, November, 1984.

Cuban, Larry & Tyack, David. "Dunces, Shirkers, and Forgotten children: historical descriptions and cures for low achievers." Conference Papers, November, 1988. Stanford University.

Cuban, Larry. "School Reform by Remote Control: SB 813 in California." *Phi Delta Kappan*, Vol. 66, No. 3, November, 1984.

Doss, Harriet Willis. "Students At Risk: A Review of Conditions, Circumstances, Indicators and Educational Implications." North Central Regional Educational Laboratory Elmhurst, Illinois, October, 1986. Unpublished Report. (Reprinted with permission).

Douglas County Task Force on Teen Pregnancy. "Teen Sexuality, Pregnancy and Parenting: How Can We Respond?" Conference Presentation, May 8, 1987, Lawrence, KS.

Glazer, Nathan. "The Problem with Competence." *American Journal of Education*, Vol. 92, No. 3, 1984.

Guttmacher, Alan. *Teenage Pregnancy: The Problem that Hasn't Gone Away.* The Alan Guttmacher Institute, Washington, D.C., 1981.

H. Hubert Humphrey. Institute of Public Affairs. "Criminal and Juvenile Delinquency." Minneapolis, MN, 1986.

Kolstad, Andrew J. & Owings, Jeffery A. *High School Dropouts Who Change Their Minds About School.* U.S. Department of Education, Center for Statistics, Washington, D.C., April, 1986.

Korentz, Daniel & Ventresca, Marc. *Poverty Among Children.* Congressional Budget Office, Washington, D.C., 1984.

Levin, Henry M. "Accelerating the Education of At-Risk Students." Conference Papers, November, 1988. Stanford University.

Levin, Henry M. "The Educational Disadvantaged: A National Crisis." The State Youth Initiatives Project, Working Paper No. 6, 1985, p. 9.

Lyke, Bob. *High School Dropouts.* Library of Congress, Congressional Research Service, Issue Brief IB 86003. Updated April 4, 1986.

McDill, Edward L.; Natriello, Gary; & Pollas, Aaron M. "A Population at Risk: Potential Consequences of Tougher School Standards for Student Dropouts." *American Education Journal,* Vol. 94, No. 2, February, 1986.

McPartland, James M. & McDill, Edward C. *Violence in Schools: Perspectives, Programs and Positions.* D.C. Heath, Lexington, MA, 1977.

National Center for Education Statistics. *The Condition of Education.* U.S. Department of Education, Washington, D.C., 1984.

National Center for Health Statistics. *Deaths from 72 Selected Causes by 5-Year Age Groups, Race and Sex.* Vital Statistics of the United States, Vol. II, Washington, D.C., 1986.

National Commission on Excellence in Education. *A Nation At Risk: The Imperative for Educational Reform.* U.S. Government Printing Office, Washington, D.C., 1983.

Pollas, Aaron M. & Verdugo, Richard R. *Measuring the High School Dropout Problem.* U.S. Department of Education, Center for Education Statistics, Washington, D.C., 1986.

Slavin, Robert E. "Making Chapter 1 Make a Difference." *Phi Delta Kappan,* October, 1987, pp. 110-119.

Toch, Thomas. "The Dark Side of the Excellence Movement." *Phi Delta Kappan* Vol. 66, No. 3, November, 1984.

 ## SUGGESTIONS FOR FURTHER READING

Frymier Jack. "Growing Up is Risky Business, and Schools Are Not to Blame."Final Report, Volume I, *Phi Delta Kappa,* Study of Students at Risk, Bloomington, Indiana 1992.

Frymier Jack. "Assessing and Predicting Risk Among Students in School." Final Report, Volume II, *Phi Delta Kappa,* Study of Students at Risk, Bloomington, Indiana, 1992.

Hodgkinson, Harold. *A Demographic Look at Tomorrow,* Institute for Educational Leadership, Inc., Center for Demographic Policy. Washington, DC 1993.

Strother, Deborah Burnett "Learning to Fail: Case Studies of Students at Risk" *Phi Delta Kappa,* Bloomington, Indiana, 1991.

Name _____ **Date** _____

| ✔ | **DISCUSSION QUESTIONS** |

---

1. Who, *in your opinion*, are the students "at risk" in our schools today? Explain.

   _____

   _____

   _____

   _____

   _____

2. "The U.S. schools track record in meeting the needs of special groups of students is not good." Our schools are generally most successful in assisting youth from what family characteristics?

   _____

   _____

   _____

   _____

   _____

In your opinion, why have the families you described above been the most successful in our schools?

_____

_____

_____

_____

In your opinion, for those "other" families that you didn't identify, why have they not been as successful in our schools?

_____

_____

_____

_____

3. What are some precautionary measures for identifying individual students as at-risk?

_____

_____

_____

_____

_____

_____

4. What are some common characteristics for successful at-risk policies and strategies?

_____

_____

_____

_____

_____

_____

5. There was a time in this nation when a high school education wasn't essential. However, today, and in the future, this won't be acceptable. Explain this evolution.

_____

_____

_____

_____

_____

_____

_____

INDIVIDUAL AND GROUP WORK

Research suggests that various factors contribute to the extent to which a student may be at risk. Some factors are more subject than others to influence by the school. Furthermore, some factors may place a student more at risk than others. On the following page are ten factors that research suggests cause a student to be at risk.

In the space immediately beside each factor place a number which reflects the rank ordering of items in terms of *your* estimate of the extent to which that factor contributes to a student being at risk. Item number "1" would be the item which you think would be most likely to cause a student to be at risk; item number "10" would be that item which you think would be least likely to cause a student to be at risk. These rankings should be done independently.

The second blank will be your group's rank ordering. You will compare your independent ranking with other members in your group. Your group's task will be to come to a consensus as to a group ranking of the ten items listed.

Worksheet #1

	Your Rank	Group's Rank
Father did not graduate from high school.	————	————
Student's sense of self-esteem is negative.	————	————
Parents were divorced last school year.	————	————
Mother is the only parent living in the home.	————	————
Student was retained in grade (held back).	————	————
Student attempted suicide during last year.	————	————
English is not the language used most in home.	————	————
Student's brother or sister died last year.	————	————
Parent(s) drink(s) excessively.	————	————
Student below 20th %ile on achievement test.	————	————

Worksheet #2

Reviewing the same factors listed on the previous worksheet, indicate the extent to which the members of your group agree that the school does have information about each factor and whether the school *should* have information about each factor. Write "yes" if there is general agreement that the school does have the information; write "no" if there is agreement that the school does not have the information. Use the same terms in the column labeled "school should."

	School Does	School Should
Father did not graduate from high school.	_____	_____
Student's sense of self-esteem is negative.	_____	_____
Parents were divorced last school year.	_____	_____
Mother is the only parent living in the home.	_____	_____
Student was retained in grade (held back).	_____	_____
Student attempted suicide during last year.	_____	_____
English is not the language used most in home.	_____	_____
Student's brother or sister died last year.	_____	_____
Parent(s) drink(s) excessively.	_____	_____
Student was below 20th %ile on achievement test.	_____	_____

Worksheet #3

Listed below are several factors that research suggests relate to being at risk. For purposes of discussion, presume that one child might have several of these problems at the same time. Such a youngster would be seriously at risk.

Can you and your group identify three factors that, if they existed in combination in the life of any student, would be an absolute indication that the student was terribly at risk? Which three factors would you identify? Your group identify?

Your Three Factors: 1._____   2._____   3._____

Your Group's Three Factors: 1._____   2._____   3._____

A. Was expelled from school last year.
B. Was absent more than 20 days last school year.
C. Parents were divorced or separated last year.
D. Has been retained in grade (i.e., "held back").
E. Attempted suicide during the last school year.
F. Has been sexually or physically abused.
G. Average grades were below "C" last school year.
H. Student's sense of self-esteem is negative.
 I. Uses drugs or engages in substance abuse.
 J. Scored below 20th percentile on achievement test.
K. Is a member of a gang.
 L. Was arrested for illegal activity.
M. Was involved in a pregnancy during the last school year.
N. Parent(s) drink(s) excessively.
O. Failed two courses during the last school year.
P. Parents have negative attitudes toward education.
Q. Is recent immigrant.

Worksheet #4

Listed below are several generalizations from research studies. Each generalization reflects the consensus of most researchers. Read each point, discuss the generalizations in your group, then solve the problem at the end.

1. Students who are retained in grade are more likely to drop out of school and more likely to get in trouble with the law than students who are not retained.
2. Students who are retained do not learn more (they learn less) and they do not develop more positive self-concepts (they develop more negative self-concepts) *unless* there is something different about the next year's experience.
3. Most children who are retained in grade *repeat* the same experience (i.e., there is no special effort to provide new experiences for the student).
4. Many teachers (48% to 65%) say that retaining students in grade is sound educational practice.
5. It costs, on the average, about $4,500 to have a child repeat a year in grade.
6. Approximately 1,600,000 students are retained in grade each year in the United States.

PROBLEM: Using the concept of "Cost/Benefit Analysis," try to determine costs and benefits—to the individual and to society—of retaining students in grade. That is, what are the costs to the individual student? What are the costs to society? What are the benefits to the individual? What are the benefits to society?

_____

_____

_____

_____

_____

_____

_____

_____

Worksheets #1–#4 were adapted from a workshop presentation presented by Phi Delta Kappa, 1989.

A Host of Languages: Policies and Issues  7

Introduction

Language variation in the United States has evolved out of a long history of cultural diversity. If equity in education is to succeed either in cultivating understanding and respect for social and cultural diversity, or in providing a truly effective learning experience for all students—especially for students from diverse sociocultural backgrounds—it must be concerned with the diversity in language form and use.

Before Europeans began to colonize this country, native people spoke hundreds of different languages. Colonists brought with them Spanish, French, English, Dutch, and German, as well as slaves who spoke a number of distinct West African languages. In the nineteenth and twentieth centuries, massive immigration has continued to replenish our linguistic resources with a host of tongues from virtually every other nation in the world. Some of these languages have disappeared with hardly a trace, but a surprising number have either continued to be spoken in the United States or have left their mark on American English (Conklin & Lourie, 1983).

As we know, Americans are a diverse group of people, speaking many languages and many varieties of English. But for the most part, we have conducted our public life as if we were all monolingual English speakers. Only in the last two decades have we begun—often reluctantly—to respect linguistic diversity and ethnic minority rights enough to validate nonstandard dialects, offer bilingual education, or make public information available in non-English languages. Since the late 1970s, our non-English speaking population has increased because of legal immigrants, a large number of illegal immigrants, and refugees from Indochina, the former Soviet Union, and Latin America. Consequently, the question of how to treat and address our non-English speakers is more pressing now than it has been at any time since World War I. In 1993, approximately 16% percent of our students beginning school spoke a language other than English.

In the next decade, the United States will confront a complex set of issues that will focus on languages other than English and their speakers. We will have to decide: (1) whether to keep admitting more non-English speakers into the United States, (2) how to plan for the education of those who are already in our schools, (3) which approach best meets the needs of limited-English-proficient students (bilingual education or English as a second language), and (4) whether we wish to encourage or discourage the continued use of languages other than English.

Chapter 7—**A Host of Languages: Policies and Issues,** is intended to provide a variety of viewpoints on the special educational needs of linguistically different students and the most popular methods used in addressing those needs. In order to better understand how we have arrived at such a dilemma in this country, it will be necessary to provide a brief historical and judicial overview. We must be sensitive and understanding to the special needs these particular students bring to our schools. Given the demographics presented earlier in this book, those numbers will more than likely increase. What should concern us is that a significant number of students in our schools have not been recognized, identified or are not being provided for.

The issue of linguistically different students in our schools, the current drive to get English recognized as our nation's "official" language and the heated debate about which program best serves our youth have become national headlines. As educators, we need to have an understanding of the policies, practices and issues facing the schools.

Historical Overview

In assessing the needs of limited English proficient students today, it may be helpful to understand the evolutionary pattern of language treatment that has occurred in the United States. (See Figure 20—Evolutionary Pattern of Language Treatment in the U.S.)

▶ **Permissive Laws**   During the first period, 1780s to 1920s, there was no explicit designation of English as the official language and there was a great tolerance for the use of other languages in the schools. Bilingual education had been part of the immigrant experience in America since the Colonial period, when native-language schooling was the rule rather than the exception. By the late 17th century, at least 18 different tongues were spoken by European ethnic groups, and many more were spoken by Indian tribes. While English was most prevalent, German, Dutch, French, Swedish, and Polish were also common (Castellanos, 1983). New arrivals fought vigorously to preserve their native customs, and language loyalties were strong. Indeed, the Pilgrims had left Holland in part because they feared their children were losing English. Where immigrant groups settled in enclaves, they naturally taught their children in their own languages, despite some attempts to impose English instruction. With mounting pressures for political unity, English became more common at ethnic schools—sometimes as a class and sometimes as a medium of instruction. Still, no uniform language policy prevailed during the 19th century. Bilingual approaches were accepted in areas where ethnic groups had influence and rejected where anti-immigrant sentiment was strong. By the mid-1800s, public and

```
┌─────────────────────────────────────────────────┐
│                                                 │
│       1780s to 1923—Permissive Laws             │
│                                                 │
│    1920s to 1965—English Only Policies          │
│                                                 │
│              1965 to Present                    │
│                                                 │
│      a) Bilingual Education                      │
│                                                 │
│      b) English as a Second Language            │
│                                                 │
│      c) No Identification Process/Program        │
│                                                 │
└─────────────────────────────────────────────────┘
```

Figure 20. Evolutionary pattern of language treatment in the U.S.

parochial German-English schools were operating in such cities as Baltimore, Cincinnati, Cleveland, Indianapolis, Milwaukee, and St. Louis. Wherever immigrant groups possessed sufficient political power—whether it was Italian, Polish, Czech, French, Dutch, or German—foreign languages were introduced into elementary and secondary schools, either as subjects or as languages of instruction. A resurgence of nativism in the late 19th century, a backlash against the foreign-born, led by such organizations as the Know-Nothing Party marked the beginning of a decline for bilingual education. St. Louis canceled its German-English program in 1888 after redistricting watered-down German voting strength. Louisville, KY, and St. Paul, MN, soon followed suit, allowing German to be taught only as a foreign language in the upper grades (Crawford, 1987).

In 1916, the U.S. Commissioner of Education compromised and allowed Spanish instruction in grades 1–4, Spanish and English in grade 5, and only English thereafter—a policy that lasted until 1948. With the approach of World War I, anti-German feeling spelled trouble not only for German-language instruction, but for all bilingual-education programs.

► **English-Only Policies** During the second period, 1920s to 1965, specifically in response to massive immigration and a growing hatred of the "foreigner," fourteen states had passed laws requiring English as the medium of instruction. By 1923, (*Meyers v. Nebraska*) the number of states requiring English had soared to thirty-five (Anderson & Boyer, 1970). In its 1923 ruling, the Supreme Court struck down a Nebraska law prohibiting foreign-language teaching before the 9th grade. "The protection of the Constitution extends to all those who speak other languages as well as to those born with English on the tongue," the Court said.

"Perhaps it would be highly advantageous if all had a ready understanding of our ordinary speech, but this cannot be coerced by methods which conflict with the Constitution—a desirable end cannot be prompted by prohibited means" (1923).

Still, the trend had been established: bilingual approaches were virtually eradicated throughout the nation by what has been described as "the anti-hyphenation, anti-foreign language, anti-immigration movement." According to Castellanos (1983), roughly during the same period, the study of foreign languages, including Latin, declined dramatically, from 83 percent of high school students in 1910 to 22 percent in 1948. "This linguistic equivalent of 'book burning' worked admirably well in forcing assimilation," Gonzales (1975) writes, ". . . it worked best with the Northern European immigrants," who had a "cultural affinity" with American values and shared a Caucasian racial history. For other language minorities, English-only schooling brought difficulties. While their cultures were suppressed, discrimination barred these groups from full acceptance into society.

▶ **Present Practice**   As a result of several pieces of legislation, the third period (1965 to the present) brought alternatives and different approaches to the language diversity in our schools. Presently, languages other than English are once again recognized in the schools and by the courts.

Most Americans take it for granted that English is the official language of the United States and even imagine that every American speaks it fluently. According to the 1990 Census, however, 14 percent of Americans come from non-English speaking homes, while in 1993, the percentage of children starting school—with a language other than English— was estimated at 16 percent.

Non-English speakers live in all fifty states of our union. (See Figure 21—Number of Persons with Non-English Mother Tongues by State.)

The figure displays their relative population densities. In two states—over 25 percent of the population is non-English speaking—Hawaii with its large proportion of Asian Americans and New Mexico with its many Spanish speakers and American Indians. In California, Arizona, Texas, Louisiana, New Jersey, Connecticut, Rhode Island, Massachusetts, New York, and North Dakota, between 16 and 25 percent of the population claims a non-English speaking background. In twenty-three states, the non-English language minority comprises 10 percent or more of the total population. Clearly, non-English languages can be heard today in every region of the country.

The Role of the Federal Government

Historically, the federal government had played a limited role in financing public instruction. By the middle of the 1960s however, the pattern was to change drastically. This shift was clearly demonstrated with the introduction and passage of the Elementary and Secondary Education Act of 1965 (commonly referred to as Chapter 1). As mentioned

States with 1,000,000+	States with 500,000–999,000	States with 100,000–499,000	States with 50,000–99,000	States with 25,000–49,000
California	Connecticut	Colorado	Arkansas	Alabama
Florida	Illinois	Delaware	Mississippi	Alaska
Illinois	Louisiana	Georgia	South Carolina	Idaho
New York	Massachusetts	Hawaii	Tennessee	Kentucky
Pennsylvania	Michigan	Indiana	Vermont	Montana
Texas	New Mexico	Iowa	West Virginia	Nevada
	Ohio	Kansas	Wyoming	North Carolina
		Maine		North Dakota
		Maryland		South Carolina
		Minnesota		South Dakota
		Missouri		Utah
		Nebraska		West Virginia
		New Hampshire		
		Oklahoma		
		Oregon		
		Virginia		
		Washington		
		Wisconsin		

Figure 21. Number of persons with non-English mother tongues by state.

in the previous chapter this new program was intended to provide financial assistance for schools in meeting the particular needs of impoverished and "educationally disadvantaged" school-age children. The Elementary and Secondary Education Act supported reform, in that it provided recognition for the need of other types of educational and instructional approaches regarding the educational needs of students of limited-English-speaking abilities or students from low-income family backgrounds. Proper implementation of federally sponsored educational programs was aided and regulated by the federal guidelines of the Civil Rights Act of 1964. Section 601 of the Act states:

"No person in the United States shall, on the grounds of race, color, or national origin be excluded from participation in, be denied the benefits of, or be subjected to discrimination under any program or activity receiving federal financial assistance."

The political pressure of the 1960s further recognized the special needs of the many limited-English-speaking students in American public schools. These efforts culminated in 1967 with the introduction of the first bilingual education bill ever to be considered by Congress. Final passage of the bilingual bill was to create Title VII of the Elementary and Secondary Education Act of 1965, better known as the Bilingual Education Act of 1968.

Section 702 of the Bilingual Education Act asserted:

▶ that there are large numbers of children of limited-English-speaking ability;
▶ that many such children have a cultural heritage which differs from that of English-speaking persons;
▶ that the use of a child's language and cultural heritage is the primary means by which a child learns; and
▶ that, therefore, large numbers of children of limited-English-speaking ability have educational needs which can be met by the use of bilingual education methods and techniques;
▶ that in addition, all children benefit through the fullest utilization of multiple language and cultural resources.

Furthermore, Congress thereby declares it to be the policy of the United States:

▶ to encourage the establishment and operation of educational programs using bilingual educational methods and techniques and;
▶ to provide financial assistance to local educational agencies in order to enable such agencies to carry out such programs in elementary (including preschool), and secondary schools which are designed to meet the educational needs of such children (The *Bilingual Education Act*, 1968).

In 1978 the *Bilingual Education Act* was further amended and this became P.L. 95-561. Through these amendments the definition of the target population changed from Limited-English-Speaking Ability (LESA) to Limited-English Proficient (LEP). This expanded the population of eligible participants. Limited English proficiency was defined to include children with limited-English reading, writing, speaking, and understanding. The 1978 statute formally included the American Indian and Alaskan Native language groups. The new law also instructed grant recipients to use native-language instruction to the extent necessary for children to become competent in English. In order to promote a multicultural environment and to protect LEP students from segregation, the law set up a 60:40 ratio requirement. This meant the monolingual English speaker could participate in the program but only up to a maximum of 40 percent of the total number of students.

The uses of the native language and culture in bilingual education were maintained in the legislation, but as Leibowitz pointed out, they were subordinated to a stronger English language emphasis. Title VII came under increasing fire after the Lau regulations were withdrawn in 1982. Soon after taking office, Former President Reagan declared that it was absolutely wrong and against American concepts to have a bilingual education program that is now openly, admittedly dedicated to preserving native language and never getting adequate in English. In 1981, a Department of Education review of bilingual education research concluded that the case for the effectiveness of transitional bilingual education is so weak that districts should be encouraged to experiment with alternative methods. Under a compromise, 4 percent of Title VII funds were authorized for special alternative instructional programs—those using no native language. For example, if total appropriations exceeded $140 million, half of the excess would go to the alternative programs, up to 10 percent of total grant awards. The Reagan administration cut Title VII funding from a high of $171.7 million in 1980 to $133.3 million in fiscal 1986 and grants for English-only programs remain capped at 4 percent. In the Fall of 1985, then Secretary of Education, William Bennett, had called for a more flexible, national bilingual education policy. The consensus at that time seemed to indicate that the native language component in a bilingual program was being slowly phased out and a stronger move toward English as a Second Language (ESL) was being encouraged by the Department of Education. For example, the Commissioner suggested that bilingual education had failed. Federal policy, he said, had lost sight of the goal of learning English as the key to equal educational opportunity. Instead, native-language instruction had become an emblem of cultural pride. With this assault, he initiated a three-part plan. First, the Department of Education issued new regulations for bilingual education grants, which gave preference to programs that moved children as quickly as possible from native-language instruction to mainstream classes. Second, it informed the 498 districts that had adopted bilingual education as part of Lau plans that they were free to renegotiate the agreements with the Office of Civil Rights. Finally, the Administration, citing the inconclusiveness of research, proposed legislation to remove all restrictions on Title VII funding for English-only approaches (Crawford, 1987).

The Bilingual Education Act of 1968 has had and appears to be continuing to undergo a number of significant changes over the past 25 years. The changes have gradually expanded the population of eligible students, but as noted, the most recent changes have put more emphasis on the acquisition of English language proficiency through English-only approaches.

Bilingual Education

Few programs are as poorly understood as bilingual education. So stubborn is the resistance to this concept that it has now permeated the press and other popular media to a degree that baffles many observers.

Certainly, the reasons for this lack of understanding and support for programs of bilingual education have been debated and have been centers of controversy for years. However, given the current demographic projections and the numbers of limited-English-proficient students currently in our schools—the issue becomes more critical, and perhaps more controversial. Some are deeply rooted in history and tradition, and in habits of thought that are difficult for society to break. Other reasons can be traced directly to the lingering effects of racism, discrimination and ethnocentrism.

Bilingual education is generally defined as an educational program that involves the use of two languages as a means of instruction. This definition is broad enough to include the many program variations that are classified as bilingual education. For example, a student who speaks a language other than English, say Spanish, may receive instruction in content areas in Spanish while at the same time learning English as a second language. The culture associated with the primary language of instruction is generally part of the curriculum, as is that of the second language. This approach is sometimes called bilingual/bicultural education and is based on the premise that the language and culture students bring to school are assets that must be used in their education.

The primary goal of bilingual education is to get a limited-English-proficient student to speak English. The basic definition of bilingual education, generally agreed upon by scholars and laypersons is the use of two languages as a medium of instruction. In other words, there is an agreement regarding what the process of bilingual education is, but confusion arises when the philosophy and goals of bilingual education are discussed.

There are numerous interpretations of bilingual education in the schools, ranging from English as a Second Language (ESL) to developmental bilingual education. Some of these will be briefly described.

The goals of bilingual education can be organized into four categories: cognitive development, affective development, linguistic growth and culture. The consensus of experts in the field of bilingual education agree that the primary goals of bilingual education are the areas of cognitive and affective development rather than in the linguistic and cultural realms. In other words, it is not to teach English or a second language per se but to teach children concepts, knowledge, and skills through the language they know best and to reinforce this information through the second language.

When educators, legislators, or parents lose sight of cognitive and affective development as the primary goals of bilingual education, then confusion, controversy and disagreement are likely to be the outcome. What occurs most often is that the linguistic and cultural goals are taken out of context and made the primary purpose of the program. As Baca and Cervantes (1984) have stated,

> "Legislators might say: The main purpose of this program is to teach them English as soon as possible and get them into the mainstream of education. On the other hand, parents might say: The main purpose of this program should be to maintain their native language

and culture while they learn English. The issue of transition versus maintenance is certainly an important one, but it should not become the central issue when discussing the primary goals of the program."

Transitional Bilingual Approach

The most common model of bilingual education in the United States is the transitional bilingual education approch. Over 90% of all bilingual programs are transitional in design. In this approach, students receive their content area of instruction in their native language while learning English as a second language. As soon as they are thought to be ready to benefit from the monolingual English-language curriculum, they are "exited" out of the program. A transitional model is one that utilizes the native language and culture of the student only to the extent that it is necessary for the student to acquire English and thus function in the regular school curriculum. The rationale behind this model is that native-language services should serve only as a transition to English. The primary objective of a transitional program is to teach students English as quickly as possible so that they can continue their education in a monolingual English classrom. The transitional approach does not teach the student to read or write in their native language.

Maintenance Bilingual Approach

A bilingual program with linguistic and cultural maintenance as a goal also promotes English acquisition. In addition, it endorses the idea that there is value to linguistic and cultural diversity. Therefore linguistic and cultural maintenance encourages students to become literate in their native language and to develop bilingual skills throughout their schooling even into their adult lives. The maintenance approach is a more comprehensive and long-term model. The objective is for the student to become fluent in both languages by using them both for instruction. Students may, in theory, remain in a maintenance bilingual program throughout their education. The longer they remain in the program, the more functionally bilingual they become and, therefore, the more balanced is the curriculum to which they are exposed. That is, they can potentially receive equal amounts of instruction in English and in their native language. In recent years, the term developmental bilingual education has been substituted for the term maintenance.

All state and federal legislation supports the transitional approach to bilingual education. These laws, however, do not prohibit local districts from going beyond the law into a maintenance program using local resources. Although legislation favors the transitional approach, local school districts are free to implement a maintenance approach if they so desire.

Two-Way Bilingual Approach

This is a program model for integrating students whose native language is English with those for whom English is a second language. The purpose of this approach is to develop bilingualism in both. Therefore, all students learn content in their native language while they learn the other language as a second language. For example, let's look at a Spanish-English bilingual program. English-speaking students would learn Spanish as a second language, and those who speak Spanish as their native language would learn English (ESL). They would each learn content in their stronger language, but they would be integrated for some academic work. The more fluent students become in their second language, the more time they are integrated for instruction. This approach also lends itself quite well to cooperative learning and peer tutoring since all the students have important skills to share with one another.

Immersion Bilingual Approach

This is an approach that is quite different to learning a second language. In these programs, students are generally immersed in their second language for a year or two before their native language is introduced as a medium of instruction. By their fifth or sixth year of schooling, they may be receiving equal amounts of instruction in their two languages, or they may continue to receive the majority in their second language. Immersion has been found to be quite effective with middle-class students whose language is the dominant language of the society. For example, in Canada, English-speaking students have been quite successful learning in French (Cummins, 1978). Unfortunately, the success of this kind of program has been used by opponents of bilingual education as a basis for suggesting submersion bilingual education for linguistic minority students in the United States. It has been suggested that linguistic minority students be placed in a totally English-language environment in order for them to learn English as quickly as possible and thus benefit from their schooling.

Assessing the School's Perspective

No bilingual program should be designed without a comprehensive needs assessment of the students who will be involved in the program. This needs assessment should focus on first and second language proficiency, on academic needs, and on affective needs. This information should be provided for both the linguistically different as well as the non-linguistically different students who wish to participate in the program. Once the school knows the needs of its students, it can then begin to review and select an appropriate dual-language instruction schedule model. The program design is selected when compatibility exists between the needs of the students, the linguistic ability of the staff, and the philosophy of the school. For example, there is evidence that teachers interact more negatively with students who do not speak English than those who do (U.S. General Accounting Office, 1987). If this is the case, the language dominance of students is not really the issue; rather, the way in which teachers and schools view their language may be even more crucial to student achievement.

Shifting the focus from teacher behavior to program design, Troike (1986) has found the following seven elements to be important for effective bilingual instruction.

▶ Emphasis must be given to the development of native language skills, including reading, and the overall amount of English used should not exceed 50 percent.
▶ Teachers must be trained and be able to teach fluently in the language of the students.
▶ The program should extend over at least five grades, and preferably more.
▶ The program must be integrated into the basic structure of the school administration and curriculum, and a supportive environment must exist.
▶ There should be support from the community and parents.
▶ High standards for student achievement should be set and every effort made to maintain them.

Successful bilingual education approaches also have common beliefs and characteristics that are platforms of their programs.

▶ Language development in the home language as well as in English has positive effects on academic achievement.
▶ Language proficiency includes proficiency in academic tasks as well as in basic conversation.
▶ An LEP student should be able to perform a certain type of academic task in his or her home language before being expected to perform the task in English.
▶ Acquisition of English language skills must be provided in contexts in which the student understands.
▶ The social status implicitly delegated to students and their languages affects student performance.

Unresolved Issues in Bilingual Education

Although bilingual education represents an important advance over monolingual education, there are a number of problems with proposing it as the only alternative. One is that it is often perceived as a panacea for all the educational problems of language minority students. Yet even with a bilingual education, many students are likely to face educational failure, which is true in other programs in general as well. No approach or program can cure all the problems, educational and otherwise, facing our young people if is does not also address the fundamental issues of discrimination and stratification in schools and society. Only a comprehensively conceptualized approach can hope to achieve success for most students. Simply substituting one language for another, or books in Spanish, will not guarantee success for language minority students. Expecting too much of even good programs is counterproductive because in the absence of quick results, the students are again blamed for their failure.

One of the implications for teachers to consider is how modifications can be made in their instruction and curriculum to help students achieve. Effective pedagogy (as discussed in an earlier chapter) is not simply teaching subject areas; in this case teaching in another language, but rather finding ways to use the language, culture, and experiences of students in their education.

Bilingual programs are in constant limbo because of several factors. Too many rely on outside funding sources on a year-to-year basis. Couple this concern with the dilemma of implementing what was stated in the funded proposal to the reality in the school and community. Many proposals are quickly written without a solid foundation of educational research and programatic design. Once funded, schools often scramble to either start or continue their programs from a weak foundation. The number of students of limited-English proficiency may vary from year-to-year. Equally troubling for some schools is that they have numerous language groups in their student population. Several schools, because of the concerns listed above, may be perceived as being unstable, and may be granted low priority in the school. Often in these schools, bilingual approaches are never institutionalized. There continues to be a shortage of bilingual certified teachers. There are many bilingual citizens in the United States, however there are, relatively speaking, very few certified bilingual teachers. The teacher training programs at the university level; often experience the same "unstable" environment that local schools do. In spite of the short duration of funding, and immediate expectations for success, much of the research has documented that students generally need a minimum of five to seven years to develop the level of English proficiency needed to succeed academically in school (Cummins, 1989). This research evidence is in direct contrast to the reality of program implementation in many bilingual schools across the country. Generally speaking, bilingual education is widely misunderstood and is more of a political issue than an academic concern. Bilingual education has a problematic feature that concerns its need to separate students. Bilingual education has been characterized by some as tracking because students are separated from their peers for instruction. Although the reasons for this separation are legitimate and based on sound research and pedagogy, tracking as a practice runs counter to the equity concept. These issues need to be sorted out carefully. Although this particular dilemma seems particularly disturbing from an equity perspective, there are ways in which the needs of limited-English-proficient and mainstream students can be served at the same time. Within every bilingual approach, there are opportunities for integrating students for nonacademic work. Students in the bilingual program can take nonacademic classes with their English speaking peers. In addition, the greatest impact will be realized when bilingual programs are truly integrated into the school rather than separated in a wing of the building, so that teachers from both bilingual and non-bilingual classrooms are encouraged to collaborate on various projects.

English as a Second Language

One approach to remedying the school problems of linguistically different students has been instruction in English as a Second Language (ESL). English as a Second Language is a component of virtually all bilingual education programs in the United States. And because of a shortage of bilingual teachers, for many limited-English-proficient students it is the only special assistance available. Especially in school districts where many language groups are represented, students may receive ESL instruction only through pull-out classes a few times each week. Critics contend that the student plays catch-up all the time, trying to learn both a new language and new subject material.

With ESL, as with bilingual instruction, methods vary tremendously. The most common approaches remain Grammar-Based, such as the Audio-Lingual Method, which emphasizes memorization of vocabulary and drills in the structure of the week. The Grammar-Translation Approach, an older, less-used method, concentrates on learning a language by perfecting reading and writing skills, with less attention to listening and speaking.

While Grammar-Based ESL has produced students who can formulate grammatically perfect sentences—given enough time—it has often failed to make them proficient communicators, according to many researchers. And the tedious content of instruction, for students and teachers alike, appears to impede learning (Baca & Cervantes, 1984).

Increasingly, Communication-Based ESL is superseding the old methods. The new approaches are grounded in the theory that language proficiency is acquired through exposure to comprehensible messages, rather than learned consciously through the study of syntax and vocabulary. Representatives of such innovative methods, The Natural Approach and Total Physical Response, stress simplified speech and visual or physical cues to help students comprehend second-language input. Also, they aim to create low-anxiety environments that lower the affective fiber that prevents comprehensible input from getting through. For example, teachers focus on meaningful and interesting communication, resist the impulse to correct students' errors overtly, and avoid pressuring students to "produce speech" in the second language before they are ready (Carlos & Collier, 1985).

The ESL model for educating students with limited English proficiency is an attractive remedy for several reasons. It is less expensive than a full bilingual program and requires fewer specially trained teachers. It can accommodate students from a large number of language backgrounds in a single class. It allows minority language students substantial opportunity to improve their English skills by interacting with native-English-speaking teachers and peers in regular classes. And in many cases, ESL is the best and only viable alternative available for many school districts.

The major criticism of ESL is that it ignores the student's language and culture. Also, the ESL model usually fails to teach minority language students enough English to keep up in other classes—unless they are also getting ample practice in using English at home and in the community. In addition, the pull-out method segregates children with limited English in a way that invites their English-speaking classmates to stigmatize them, particularly if the non-English speakers are also economically and socially disadvantaged (Garcia, 1982). There is also mounting evidence that students who feel alienated from school are highly prone to academic failure.

Legal Implications

The force which may have brought about the greatest recognition for bilingual education, and to which such national entities as the National Education Association (NEA) and the Civil Rights Commission contributed, were the education lawsuits. These lawsuits challenged the disproportionate placement of Hispanics and other linguistically and culturally different students in special education programs.

In considering the developmental history of bilingual education, it is vitally important for all educators, at all levels, to be aware of the significant lawsuits that have taken place and that have set school policy in many instances. These lawsuits were the first legal challenges to early testing, standardized testing, the selection process, and the caliber of instruction in special education classes. In essence, they found that standardized tests were used to measure the capacity to know and speak English, rather than to measure a student's general achievement.

The first of these special education lawsuits—*Arreola v. Board of Education*—was in Santa Ana, California and was argued in the state court. Although this particular case did not have the significant impact that followed, the Santa Ana case broke new legal ground. It focused blame where, up to this point it had not been placed; it brought about significant state legislation and subsequent state education policies; and it generated important awareness of this type of educational neglect and damage to school children. Most significantly, the Santa Ana case helped to pave the way for *Diana v. State Board of Education*.

Unlike the Santa Ana case, *Diana v. State Board of Education* was argued in Federal court. The judgment of the court was that Hispanic and Chinese speaking students already in special education classes must be retested in their primary language and must be re-evaluated only as to their achievement on nonverbal tests or sections of tests. Although this case was concerned with special education classes, it became clear that it was the teachers, counselors, and administrators who were referring linguistically and culturally different students to such classes because, to quote one Administrator at the trial, "we just do not know what to do with them." The basis for most of the judgments which placed these students in special education classes was their inability to speak or to function well in English, which had nothing to do with their mental or psychological capacities. It was evident that in too many instances, the language and culture of the schools could not or would not adapt to the language and culture of a significant community of students.

The special education lawsuits made their own impact on educational reform. Specifically, they contributed to an acceptance of the notion that there was a serious problem, that it started very early in the student's life, that it had to do mainly with the student's language and culture, and that what the schools were doing was not working. If anything, what the schools were doing was educationally and psychologically damaging the student, and a new educational strategy had to be developed. In addition to the special education cases, a number of other education lawsuits have contributed significantly to the rise in bilingual education and English as a Second Language (ESL) programs throughout the country.

Lau v. Nichols

Following the desegregation of the San Francisco school system in 1971, there were 2,856 students of Chinese ancestry in the school system who did not speak English. Of these, about 1,000 received supplemental courses in the English language. The remaining 1,800 did not receive supplemental or bilingual instruction.

The class action suit was brought by 13 non-English speaking Chinese American students who alleged that they were being denied an education because they could not comprehend the language in which they were being taught. They argued that the failure either to teach them bilingually or teach them English should be prohibited on the grounds that (1) failure to do so was a violation of equal protection under the Fourteenth Amendment, and (2) it was a violation of the Civil Rights Act of 1964.

The facts clearly supported the claims that the non-English speaking Chinese were not benefiting from their educational experience. Indeed, the school district noted the frustration and poor performance created by the students' inability to understand the regular work. Predictions were made that substantial numbers would drop out and become another unemployable in the ghetto. The district argued, however, that discrimination was not being practiced because the students were being taught in the same facilities, by the same teachers, and at the same time as everyone else.

The district court and the circuit court of appeals both ruled in favor of the school district. The arguments in support of this ruling focused primarily on the fact that the alleged violation was not based on prior segregation. The court suggested then, that the students' failure was of their own making, not state-related, and thus of little consequence when school resources were limited. The court further observed:

> "Every student brings to the starting line of his educational career different advantages and disadvantages, caused in part by social, economic and cultural background, created and continued completely apart from any contribution by the school system. That some of these may be impediments which can be overcome does not amount to a "denial" by the school district of educational opportunities. . . should the district fail to give them special attention. . . ."

On appeal to the Supreme Court, (*Lau v. Nichols*), the lower court's decision was reversed. The High Court's opinion supported the arguments presented at trial by the Chinese-speaking students:

> "Basic English skills are at the very core of what these public schools teach. Imposition of a requirement that before a child can participate effectively in the educational program he must already have acquired these basic skills is to make a mockery of public education. We know that those who do not understand English are certain to find their classroom experience wholly incomprehensible and in no way meaningful."
>
> "Under these state-imposed standards, there is no equality of treatment merely by providing students with the same facilities, textbooks, teachers, and curriculum; for students who do not understand English are effectively foreclosed from any meaningful education." (*Lau v. Nichols*, 1971)

While the court laid to rest the argument that equal access to facilities provides equal treatment and equal educational opportunity, it did not base its decision on the constitutional requirement; rather, support was found in the Civil Rights Act of 1964. The act forbids discrimination on the grounds of race, color, or national origin by any agency receiving federal financial assistance. Because the support for the ruling came from the Civil Rights Act, there is still not a constitutional right to a bilingual education or even an education from which one can benefit. Thus, a district that does not receive federal funds would not be compelled to offer non-English-speaking students bilingual education. The constitutional issue has been raised elsewhere, however, with some support.

State Involvement

In compliance with federal legislation and regulations, many state governments have adopted measures to fund and otherwise encourage bilingual education. By 1990, twelve states had stipulated conditions under which bilingual education was mandatory: Alaska, California, Connecticut, Illinois, Indiana, Iowa, Massachusetts, Michigan, New Jersey, Texas, Washington, and Wisconsin. Eleven other states had laws permitting bilingual education, and twenty-six had no provisions regarding language of instruction. Only one state, West Virginia, still required instruction to be exclusively in English.

The English-Only Movement

English-only or English-plus, that's the question currently being debated in several states and considered by some members of Congress. In the fall of 1986, Californians voted by a 3-to-1 margin to declare English the state's official language. In the Fall of 1988, Arizona, Colorado and Florida also declared English as the official language of their states. Since then, Arizona has repealed the legislation.

In a national context, the measure's approval has been a boon to the English-only movement, the best organized opposition that bilingual education has yet faced. In 1987, 31 states had considered official language laws. There are now 17 states that have English as their official language.

Legally, these statutes and constitutional amendments may have no direct effect on bilingual programs. But voter enthusiasm for such measures—as well as the letter writing campaigns that the issue has generated—usually featuring attacks on native language instruction—has not gone unnoticed by politicians.

The drive to get English recognized as our nation's "official" language began in 1981, when S. I. Hayakawa, then U.S. Senator from California, introduced a congressional proposal for an English language amendment to the U.S. Constitution. The amendment has been reintroduced as a joint resolution in each succeeding Congress but has never received action. The group's premise is that bilingualism poses a growing threat to English as the unifying force in American society. The group warns that the nation is being divided along language lines, as ethnic minorities, particularly Hispanics, insist on retaining their native languages and cultures instead of joining the English-speaking mainstream (Crawford, 1987).

While the current publicity about California had implied that the U.S. English movement was a national ground-swell, the movement had been successful in only three other states. The following states have enacted state legislation recently: Arizona (1988), Colorado (1988), Florida (1988), Arkansas (1987), California (1986), Georgia (1986), Indiana and Tennessee (1984). The current U.S. English movement had nothing to do with the nation's four other English-only state laws: Virginia (1981); and Illinois, Kentucky and Nebraska have been on the books for over 60 years.

Fishman (1987) questions the sudden concern for the "functional protection of English." "How," he asks, "is English endangered in a country where it is spoken by 97 percent of the population; where linguistic minorities overwhelmingly lose their mother tongues by the second or, at most, the third generation and where no ethnic political parties or separatist movement exists?" Fishman maintains that U.S. English and like-minded groups have a 'hidden agenda' of equating cultural differences with disloyalty, of seeking scapegoats for social ills that have little to do with language, such as terrorism abroad and economic dislocations at home. The English-only movement, he argues, is a displacement of middle-class fears and anxieties from difficult, perhaps even intractable, real problems in American society, to mythical, simplistic, and stereotypic problems.

English-Plus

To counter the growing influence of the English-only movement, in the late 1980s, the League of United Latin American Citizens and the Miami-based Spanish American League Against Discrimination launched a campaign known as English-Plus. There is no question that English is the nation's common language, says Soto, president of Spanish American League Against Discrimination, and the groups favor every effort to help limited-English-proficient children become proficient in it. But English is not enough, we don't want a monolingual society. This country was founded on a diversity of language and culture and we want to preserve that diversity. The English-plus campaign has concentrated on urging states and municipalities to declare themselves officially multilingual and multicultural. Such measures have passed in Atlanta, Tucson, and Oscelola County, Florida, and are pending in Arizona and New York State (Crawford, 1987).

Summary

The surprising multiplicity of U.S. languages has direct ramifications for public policy. As the institution that most embodies and perpetuates our language attitudes and policies, public education requires particular attention. What happens in this nation's classrooms will largely determine whether we continue efforts to homogenize the American language or view this linguistic diversity as a valuable and enriching asset.

Throughout its first century, the United States was an openly multilingual nation. There were treaties, public notices, and education in a variety of indigenous and immigrant languages. Subsequently, in the latter half of the nineteenth and first half of the twentieth centuries, the rights of non-English speakers were eroded by anti-foreigner and racist sentiment and action. In recent years, however, the Supreme Court, and federal court rulings and legislation have reinstated many minority language rights. In the 1990s, we are witnessing large-scale legal and illegal immigration from Mexico, resettlement of Southeast Asian refugees, and an influx of refugees from various Caribbean and Central American countries. What will be the reaction from the federal government? The public schools? The '90s have also produced a new surge of English-Only policy in many states and discussions of a national language are beginning to become more frequent.

As we witnessed, the recent developments surrounding the government-sponsored ESL and bilingual education programs—both approaches still suffer from uncertainty about their effectiveness and widespread confusion remains about their differing aims and implications. Clearly, however, they represent the largest legal, moral, and financial commitment this country has ever made to minority languages and their speakers.

Language variation in the United States has evolved out of a long history of cultural diversity. Chapter 7 was intended to provide a variety of viewpoints on the special educational needs of linguistically different students and the proposed methods of addressing those needs. In order to understand the current debate on which approach should be endorsed, it was necessary to provide a brief historical and judicial review. Politically, the issue of limited-English-proficient students has recently taken on a new opponent—the English-only policies—from national and state levels. As we have learned, each of the two approaches—bilingual education and ESL—may be the best solution, given the particular variables within a community and school system.

Misunderstandings about the nature of language evolution and negative attitudes toward linguistic diversity make rational debate of such matters extremely difficult. As long as attitudes of any individual or group are the sole basis for policymaking, it will remain impossible to discover the most effective means of meeting the needs of limited-English-proficient students.

 END NOTES

Arreola v. Board of Education, Santa Ana Unified School District, 150577, California.

Baca, Leonard M. & Cervantes, Hermes T. *The Bilingual Special Education Interface*. Times Mirror/Mosby Publishing Co, St. Louis, MO, 1984., p. 64.

Bilingual Education Act, P. L. 90-247, 81 Stat. 783 816 January, 1968.

Carlos J. & Collier, Virginia P. *Bilingual and ESL Classrooms: Teaching in Multicultural Contexts*. McGraw Hill, New York, NY, 1985.

Castellanos, Diego. *The Best of Two Worlds: Bilingual- Bicultural in the U.S. New Jersey State Department of Education*, Trenton, NJ, 1983.

Conklin, Nancy Faires & Lourie, Margaret A. *A Host of Tongues—Language Communities in the United States*. Free Press, New York, NY, 1983.

Crawford, James. "Bilingual Education: Language, Learning and Politics." *Education Week*, Washington, D.C., April 1, 1987.

Cummins, Jim. "The Role of Primary Language Development in Promoting Education Success for Language Minority Students," in Office of Bilingual Bicultural Education, *Schooling and Language Minority Students: A Theoretical Framework*. Sacramento: Evaluation, Dissemination, and Assessment Center, California State University, 1981.

Cummins, Jim. "Linguistic Interdependence and the Educational Development of Bilingual Children," *Review of Educational Research*, 49 Spring, 1978.

Cummins, Nancy L. "Language and Affect: Bilingual Students at Home and at School," *Language Arts*, 66,1 January 1989.

Diana v. State Board of Education, Soledad, C70-37-RFP, California.

Garcia, Ricardo L. *Teaching in a Pluralistic Society: Concepts, Models, and Strategies*. Harper and Row, New York, NY, 1982. p. 142.

Gonzales, J. "Coming of Age in Bilingual/Bicultural Education: A Historical Perspective." *Inequality of Education*, February, 1975.

Gonzales, Josue M. Coming of Age in Bilingual/Bicultural Education: A Historical Perspective. Inequality in Education, February, 1975, pp. 5-17.

Lau v. Nichols, 94 S. Ct. 786 (1974).

Leibowitz, A. H. *The Bilingual Education Act: A Legislative Analysis*. National Clearinghouse for Bilingual Education, Rosslyn, VA, 1980.

Meyer v. Nebraska, 43 S. Ct. 625 (1923).

Troike, Rudolph C. "Improving Conditions for Success in Bilingual Education Programs," in *A Report of the Compendium*, 2. 1986.

U.S. General Accounting Office, *Bilingual Education: A New Look at the Research Evidence*, Washington, D.C: U.S. Government Printing Office, March 1987.

 SUGGESTIONS FOR FURTHER READING

Association for Supervision and Curriculum Development. *Building an Indivisible Nation: Bilingual Education in Context*. A.S.C.D., Alexandria, VA, April, 1987.

Fuentes, Carlos. *"Myself with Others: Selected Essays"* Farrar, Straus & Giroux, New York, NY 1988.

Hakuta, Kenji. Mirror of Language: The Debate on Bilingualism. Basic Books, New York, NY, 1986.

Krashen, Stephen D. Inquiries and Insights: Second Language Learning, Immersion & Bilingual Education, Literacy Alemany Press, Hayward, CA, 1985.

Ovando, Carlos J. & Collier, Virginia P. McGraw-Hill, New York, NY, 1985.

Ramirez, David. "Study Finds Native Language Instruction Is a Plus" *NABE News* 14, No.5, March 15, 1991.

Stein, Coleman B. Jr. *Sink or Swim: The Politics of Bilingual Education*. Praeger, New York; NY, 1986.

Zamora, Gloria R. "Understanding Bilingual Education." National Coalition of Advocates for Students, Backgrounder Series. Boston, MA, 1987.

Name _____ Date _____

DISCUSSION QUESTIONS

1. What are the three evolutionary periods of language treatment that the United States has experienced?

_____

_____

_____

_____

_____

What are the differences between the first and third periods? Explain.

_____

_____

_____

_____

_____

2. Why were the special education cases so important? Explain.

_____

_____

_____

_____

_____

_____

3. What is the significance of the *Lau v. Nichols* case?

_____

_____

_____

_____

_____

What were the arguments presented by the San Francisco school district?

_____

_____

_____

_____

What was the Supreme Court's interpretation of equal treatment ?

_____

_____

_____

_____

_____

4. English-Only or English-Plus—define each and then explain your preference.
English-Only:

_____

_____

_____

_____

_____

English-Plus:

_____

_____

_____

_____

_____

What is your preference?

_____

_____

_____

_____

_____

5. **What is bilingual education?**

_____

_____

_____

_____

_____

What are the goals of bilingual education?

_____

_____

_____

_____

_____

What are the advantages of bilingual education?

_____

_____

_____

_____

_____

What are the disadvantages of bilingual education?

_____

_____

_____

_____

_____

6. What is English as a Second Language (ESL)?

_____

_____

_____

_____

_____

What are the goals of ESL?

_____

_____

_____

_____

_____

What are the advantages of ESL?

_____

_____

_____

_____

_____

What are the disadvantages of ESL?

_____

_____

_____

_____

_____

7. How should programs for limited-English-proficient students be defined—according to local schools, state departments of education or the federal government? Explain your position.

_____

_____

_____

_____

_____

Who will monitor or evaluate your position stated above? Explain.

_____

_____

_____

_____

_____

8. Where should the funding for limited-English-proficient students come from? Explain your response.

_____

_____

_____

_____

_____

9. In what type of school system would bilingual education be more effective and beneficial for all students involved? Explain.

_____

_____

_____

_____

_____

In what type of school system would ESL be more effective and beneficial for all students involved? Explain.

_____

_____

_____

_____

_____

10. What staff development or teacher training should be provided for school staffs working with limited-English-proficient students?

_____

_____

_____

_____

INDIVIDUAL OR GROUP WORK

Individually read the following case study of Fox Hollow. Then in small groups discuss the case study with your group members. You should address each of the questions at the end of the case study.

A Host of Languages

A Case Study of Fox Hollow High School

Fox Hollow is one of five high schools in a community of 235,000. There are 1,285 students attending Fox Hollow, 81 full-time instructional staff and 14 support service personnel (i.e., special education, psychologist, counselors). Of the student body attending Fox Hollow, there are 18% ethnic minority students (predominately African American, Hispanic, and Vietnamese). Twenty-six percent of the students are on free or reduced lunch, although school personnel believe that figure should be higher, but students do not want to be singled out as "low-income." During the last school year, school records indicate that 11% of the students dropped out of school. Although 34% of the students attended a post-secondary education after graduation, the 11% figure is a concern, because three years ago the figure was 6%. Another figure that concerns the staff at Fox Hollow is the increasing number of students whose language is not English. Although there are programs at the elementary schools and the two junior high schools that feed into Fox Hollow, the number of students not proficient in English is increasing annually. Three years ago Fox Hollow had only 27 students whose first language was not English, the following year there were 68 students; and the following year 94 students. This year the number is 127 students. A breakdown of the 127 students is as follows: Spanish Speaking: 67; Vietnames, 31; Chinese, 4; Arabic, 8; Russian, 13; and Hmong, 4.

Last year, Suzanna, a four-year veteran greeted her ninth graders each morning in the three languages she knows best: English, Spanish and a personal greeting of acknowledgement. Of the twenty-six students in her first hour class, 8 are from 6 different countries. If she called roll, it would sound like this: Aziz, Joyce, Fong, Jasmine, Matias, Raven, Felipe, Jeremiah, Azeneth, Jan'tel, Diane, Nakisha, Renata. . . . Suzanna has seen over the past four years the number of students for whom English is not the language spoken at home, and knows the variety of languages spoken is increasing nationwide and in her community of Fox Hollow. Fellow educators are struggling to keep up with the increasing numbers, planning for the future, and trying to predict from where the next wave of immigrants will come. However, it should be noted that not all of these students are "recent immigrants;" in fact, many of the Hispanic students are second and third generation American citizens. Some of the surrounding school districts also are grappling with the increased enrollment of Limited English Proficient (LEP) students, although not at such dramatic increases.

The staff of Fox Hollow is divided as to the best approach to meet the needs of LEP students. Quietly, there are a number of staff members who would rather see these students return to their country of origin, but keep their viewpoints only among a small circle of their colleagues. Another group of faculty members, whom Suzanna represents, are asking the question: "What is the best approach that we can take here at Fox Hollow? How do we plan? How do we get the resources needed?" Still, there are a number of faculty members who remain untouched by the recent increase in LEP students, as they are primarily teaching the advanced placement courses—typically not represented by LEP students at Fox Hollow.

Those staff members who are asking the questions remain concerned, because the number of LEP students who eventually graduate from Fox Hollow is very low—in fact of last year's graduating class, only 8 LEP students graduated. It appears that many students who attend Fox Hollow become literate in neither language.

Currently, Fox Hollow has one English as a Second Language certified classroom teacher. His responsibility is to work with the classroom teachers on assignments and secure resources that teachers need. Students who are limited-English proficient are identified by the school and offered, on a voluntary basis, ESL instruction after school daily. The ESL instructor is currently planning to offer ESL classes for community members two nights a week beginning with the next school year. Many staff members believe that more needs to be done for these students. The administration is asking the staff to develop a plan for Fox Hollow. The Principal has assigned a committee to develop a plan that would best meet the needs of Fox Hollow's limited-English-proficient students. What would you recommend to the committee?

1. What "other" information (data, numbers, personnel, community, etc.) would you need to better understand Fox Hollow? Explain your reason for needing the information.

_____

_____

_____

_____

_____

2. What approach do you think Fox Hollow should take in meeting the needs of it's limited-English-proficient students? What is the rationale for the approach you have selected?

_____

_____

_____

_____

_____

3. What should the role of the building principal be in this school?

_____

_____

_____

_____

The ESL certified instructor?

_____

_____

_____

_____

_____

4. What would you recommend to those staff members who are "quietly" against the increasing numbers of LEP students?

_____

_____

_____

_____

_____

5. Who should be on the committee? Why?

_____

_____

_____

_____

_____

6. Identify the recommendations that you would forward to this committee.

_____

_____

_____

_____

_____

_____

_____

_____

What is the basis for your recommendations?

_____

_____

_____

_____

_____

_____

Instructional Materials: A Matter of Use

 **8**

Introduction

Throughout the past two decades, there has been an increased research effort and acknowledgment of the role textbooks and instructional materials play in education. The conclusion of these efforts is that textbooks and instructional materials do play an important part in education—transmitting not only facts and figures, but ideas and cultural values. The words and pictures students see in school influence the development of the attitude they carry into adult life—these words and pictures not only express ideas, but are part of the educational experience which shapes ideas.

Today many educators continue to discuss the need for improving the quality of instructional materials by including diverse perspectives and by excluding bias content. Bias and stereotyping in the content of textbooks and other instructional materials continue to stand in the way of educational equity at the national, state, and local levels. Many believe "state textbook adoption" policies can best achieve this goal, others point to the negative effects of state textbook adoption policies. What criteria are used to evaluate texts from an equity perspective? Who are the individuals or groups responsible for the text selection? Are state textbook adoption policies and equity education compatible? More importantly, do classroom teachers rely to heavily on the textbook?

Chapter 8—**Instructional Materials: A Matter of Use**, is intended to: (1) address the importance of instructional materials in education, (2) identify who selects textbooks and instructional materials, (3) examine state-adoption policies, (4) identify criteria for the selection of materials, (5) briefly examine the role technology is playing within the instructional resource arena, and (6) provide you the opportunity to evaluate textbooks and instructional materials. In addition, suggestions are provided for individual classroom teachers and school district personnel in addressing the issue of equity in textbooks and instructional materials.

Because bias and stereotyping are frequently an unconscious practice, teachers-to-be, teachers, administrators and other school personnel limit a student's opportunities without intending to do so. They simply continue biased practices because "that is the way it has always been done." However, in order to make any significant changes in the school environment and build the school's capacity to provide instruction not limited by bias or stereotyping, educators need to make a conscious effort to learn new skills in identifying and compensating for bias.

Impact of Textbooks and Instructional Materials

American schools have been described as textbook dominated. Indeed, researchers have found that textbooks are primary determinants of what is taught in the U.S. classroom. One can easily become overwhelmed by the total number of instructional materials available for use in the classroom. How important are textbooks and instructional materials in the classroom? Researchers suggest that textbooks are the focus of more than 75 percent of a pupil's classroom time. Other studies have shown that as much as 95 percent of all "teaching time" is spent on the use of some type of textbook or instructional material (EPII, 1984).

If this is an accurate portrait of life in U.S. schools, it follows that textbooks and instructional materials must be significant factors in determining the quality of U.S. education.

Who Selects the Textbooks and Instructional Materials?

Review committees are created in a variety of ways. In most adoption states, the state board of education appoints committee members at the state level. In several states, the state board appoints a special textbook committee or commission which in turn appoints the actual reviewers. In local districts, reviewers may be appointed by the superintendent or board or may represent constituent groups. Members of committees are usually appointed on the basis of their roles (teacher, supervisor, principal, parent) or on the basis of location—regions in the state, areas in a school district, etc. According to Cody (1986), educators, especially teachers, make up most of the committee members at both the local and state levels.

Such variance demonstrates the lack of overall consistency with regard to textbook selection. Although local districts are, in general, responsible for identifying and rectifying weaknesses in instructional materials, a growing number of individuals believe states still need to take a more active role in providing bias-free textbooks in the classroom.

State-Textbook-Adoption Policies

What are state-textbook-adoption policies? How do they work? Observers often comment that state-adoption procedures distort the market and allow pressure groups in adoption states to dominate. Although that may be true and in some cases may have a negative effect on the selection of books, centralized book selection also can permit states to have positive influences on the market. In any case, few states indicate that they are interested in changing the way in which books are selected.

In 27 states, local school districts make textbook decisions independently of any state control. These are referred to as open states. In 23 states, mostly in the south and west, districts select textbooks from a preliminary list created and approved at the state level. These are referred to as adoption states.

As of 1988, there were 23 states that had adopted the policy of "state-approved" textbooks. They were: Oregon, California, Nevada, Idaho, Utah, Arizona, New Mexico, Texas, Oklahoma, Arkansas, Louisiana, Mississippi, Alabama, Georgia, Florida, Tennessee, North Carolina, South Carolina, Kentucky, West Virginia, Virginia, Indiana, and most recently Hawaii. (See Figure 22—State Textbook Adoption Policies.) Most state-

Figure 22. State-textbook-adoption policies.
23 states take active role in approving texts.

textbook-adoption policies are a result of legislation passed prior to the 1950s. Several states first enacted such policies just after the turn of the century (e.g., Utah, 1909), and of these, the majority seem to have revised their laws in the decade of the '80s.

The original purpose of such policies on the part of the states was: (1) to ensure that every student had a book, (2) to screen out "inferior" texts and uphold high standards, and (3) to make efficient use of tax dollars via centralized purchasing arrangements. More recently, due to an increased awareness of diversity in the country, state curriculum committees also have served to evaluate potential materials in light of cultural diversity.

Disadvantages of State-Adoption Policies

Tulley and Farr (1985) argue that the actual statutes mandating state-textbook-adoption policies show little evidence of pedagogic intent. Instead, say the researchers, "the data contained in these statutes suggest that the intent of state level textbook adoption may be to control the marketing practices of the publishing industry." Categorizing the content of 23 different states' statutes reveals that out of 20 categories, nine deal with controlling costs and contractual obligations between publisher and state. Out of these nine categories dealing with the publishing industry, one category shows interest in pedagogic quality— to provide evidence of learner verification. But only two of the 23 states, California and Florida, have such a statute. On the other hand, 17 out of the 23 states have a statute requiring publishers to maintain the lowest price.

Adoption Policies and Equity

Bowler (1978) cited that the state-textbook-adoption system tailored their textbooks to suit the needs of the majority of their market, mainly Texas and California, thus slighting the needs of the other parts of the country. Bowler explains why the economic self-interest of publishers in cornering the largest markets leads to limited choice for the rest of the nation's schools. He shares the story of a Maryland educator who wondered why a poem about Harriet Tubman had been dropped from a major textbook and replaced by a poem about White Texas cowboys. This editorial decision, of course, was made in an effort to woo the heart of Texas. Unfortunately, what Texas wants out of textbooks, Bowler says, are topics dealing with family, conflict, sex, love, hate, and violence—in short, much of the reality of children's lives.

In addition to the unreality and lack of diverse perspectives caused by publishers' pandering to big markets such as Texas, researchers cite three other arguments against state textbook adoption policies: 1) State-level adoption implies that district educators, who know the needs of their students, cannot make intelligent textbook decisions; 2) The idea of a uniform curriculum, which was a useful idea for states in the 1800s, is not appropriate in today's society where a diversity of material is what most educators call for; and 3) Contrary to popular belief, a huge amount of money is wasted maintaining the state bureaucracy machine which chooses and buys textbooks and instructional materials. Bowler reported that ten years ago, the California Textbook Commission's operating costs alone exceeded $800,000.

Bernstein (1985) writes, "publishers have tried to accommodate the lists of required topics from several major adoption states in order to have as large a market as possible. The result is a magazine-style book—filled with tidbits but lacking context, adequate explanations, or clarifying examples." Thus, although put-downs based on gender and ethnic slurs virtually have been banished by state-mandated content guidelines, textbook portrayals of oppressed groups are often trivial or mechanical. The goal of helping young people achieve an equity perspective is not accomplished when publishers think only of satisfying the letter of the law and not the spirit of the law.

Perhaps the strongest argument for state-textbook-adoption policies is that in a few states, such as California, a statute mandates that all materials adopted must meet specific minimum criteria for including diverse points of view, multiple approaches, and so forth. For example, the California State Board of Education's (1984) list of instructional materials approved for legal compliance includes only those materials that fairly represent males and females, ethnic groups, the aged, and the disabled. However, many state-adoption guidelines do not include these criteria on their evaluation forms.

Advantages to State Adoption

Proponents of state-textbook-adoption policies cite three areas of strength: (1) efficiency, (2) comprehensive public review, and (3) dollars saved. Efficiency in terms of saving time and money for local school districts is often cited (through lower freight costs and publishers maintaining at least one depository in the state). Another advantage cited is the fact that the public has more input—because books under consideration must be displayed at several locations throughout the state.

State Adoption—Sequence of Events

Figure 23—State-Textbook-Adoption Process, outlines the process in flowchart form. The sequence of events may be considered typical and is based upon the common denominators in states having textbook-adoption policies.

Reviewers

Members of the State Curriculum Evaluation Committee are selected by the State Superintendent (Commissioner) and the State Board of Education. Usually, one person is

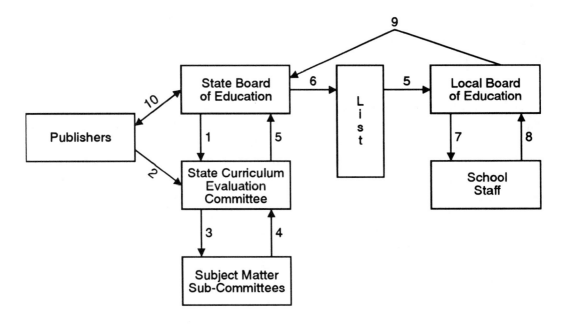

Figure 23. State-textbook-adoption process.

appointed from each congressional district in the state. In several states, the state board appoints a special textbook committee or commission which in turn appoints the actual reviewers. In local districts, reviewers may be appointed by the administration or school board or may represent constituent groups. In some cases, anyone who volunteers may serve on the committee. Members of committees are usually appointed on the basis of their roles (teacher, supervisor, principal, parent) or as mentioned above, on the basis of location—regions in the state.

Educators, especially teachers, make up most of the committee members at both the local and state levels. Eighteen of the adoption states and most of the localities about which there is information include lay citizens on the review committees. About 25 percent of the local districts that have negotiated contracts with teachers include teacher participation on selection committees in the contract (Cody, 1986). In nineteen adoption states, the final adoption is made by the State Board of Education; in four adoption states, the final decision is made by the board-appointed state textbook committee. In most local districts, the local school board is the official adopting body.

Is the Task Too Large and Too Difficult?

Committees in adoption states can be responsible for reviewing hundreds of books. For example, over 1,200 books were considered in Oklahoma in 1985, and 27 elementary reading series were considered in Texas (Cody, 1986). Adoption states reported that the amount of time allotted for the committee's work varied from a matter of days to an entire year. There is little data on the actual amount of time spent reading the books. Sixteen of the adoption states have some form of training program for committee members. Although most of the training has to do with legal requirements and logistics, committees are receiving more training in the application of criteria. About half of the local school districts reported that teachers on local committees are released from teaching to review books. In other locations, the time is contributed after school or during the summer. State committee members may receive some reimbursement for expenses; no states report that committee members are paid for their time.

Publishers are notified of hearing dates and are invited to submit their textbooks and instructional materials to the committee. During the review process, books are displayed at several locations throughout the state and public feedback is invited. Various subcommittees may be formed at the request of committee members, to aid in the evaluation of texts in assorted disciplines. All findings and evaluation forms are submitted to the committee members who then vote on each textbook. A two-thirds vote is commonly required for placement on the state-adoption list. In the past, some of the adoption states selected only one book for the entire state. Now, however, all adoption states allow districts greater latitude. State-approved-textbook lists may range from as few as three books in each subject and grade level to as many as 30 or 40.

The multiple listings are then finalized by the State Board of Education and sent to various local school boards. Texts are selected locally, but the contracts are usually made between the state and the publisher. All adoption states also have a procedure to allow districts to petition a state agency to use state funds to purchase a book not on the state list. In general, adoption states have established cycles for the adoption of books in the subject areas; for example, reading, literature, and language arts one year, mathematics the next year, science the following year. Adoption cycles are commonly 5 to 7 years long.

Funding

How does funding for textbooks influence the textbook market? It is important for those of us who are not accustomed to thinking about marketing to understand that the books published will be only those that publishers believe will be profitable. Since publishers must decide what books to develop and print years ahead of actual sales, any clues to a future market—earmarked funding or a concentrated market such as those that large adoption states (California and Texas) can promise—will influence their decisions. Such was the case in the Fall of 1985, when the California Board of Education rejected all high school biology textbooks that publishers submitted on the grounds that they contained watered-down science, including little or no mention of evolution. Again, in the Fall of 1986, California rejected all the mathematics textbooks submitted by the publishers because of the watered-down content.

Fourteen of the adoption states and two open states provide earmarked funds for textbooks, usually by statute, and most commonly on a per pupil basis. States vary from $15 to over $50 per student per year. Texas and California, the largest state markets, each spend over $100 million each year on textbooks. Few states provide full funding for textbook purchases; full funding means to provide enough funding to remove old books and buy new books for each subject in the year of the adoption. In most adoption states, local districts supplement state funds with local funds to give every student a new book. It is more common, however, for districts to use both state and local funds and still replace only some of the books used in the classrooms. This means that many books in use are older than the cycle would indicate. The costs of books are influenced by funding legislation. Requirements by adoption states and some local districts require that publishers post performance bonds, provide free samples, maintain depositories, conduct learner verification, maintain on-site sales representatives, provide cross indexing to curriculum frameworks, etc. This involves large publisher investments in the adoption process and often affects book costs. All adoption states have a provision stating that they will not pay more for a book than is paid in other states. Working under such "most-favored-nation" price controls, publishers find new ways to negotiate with large purchasers. Although publishers may not negotiate price, they may offer to provide free inservice, more manuals, workbooks or other ancillary materials to encourage larger sales. Not surprisingly, such criticism does not sit well with the publishers who are, in all fairness, caught between powerful interest groups and, in all honesty, trying to make a buck.

Publishers Respond

In response to growing external pressures, textbook companies have developed formal policies that reflect guidelines for authors and editors that are aimed at reducing bias and stereotyping in textbooks. Since the middle 1970s, over 170 groups, including publishing companies, educational organizations and associations, have responded by developing guidelines for their staffs. The growing consciousness of the industry is a result of both their concern with the current attitudes in the society and their awareness of the impact of instructional programs on young people's thinking.

The Association of American Publishers prepared a Statement on Bias-Free Materials (1979) in order to further the cause of fair and equitable treatment for all people. This position paper states that the publishing industry is responding today to the challenge of bias-free materials that reflect the contributions of all cultures and both sexes. What follows this stated commitment are general guidelines for achieving bias-free materials in the areas of: (1) content, (2) illustrations, and (3) language.

Content

Individuals of all ages and ethnic groups have much to gain from the elimination of stereotypes in content. Bias-free educational materials more accurately represent reality, encourage tolerance for individual differences, and allow more freedom for children to discover and express their needs, interests and abilities. Specifically, bias-free educational materials are those that:

▶ represent different groups of people in varied activities and vocations, including positions of leadership, and show children aspiring to a variety of careers.

▶ represent fairly and accurately the historic and current achievements of people, especially women and members of ethnic minority groups, and include a fair proportion of materials about, and written or executed by, women and minority people.

▶ use material that honestly conveys the exploitation of people and the real hardships imposed on people through such exploitation.

▶ depict all men and women as having the full range of human emotions and behavior, and finding for themselves attributes that lead to self-esteem and success.

▶ represent minority and majority groups in varied communities—urban, suburban, and rural; and all ranges of socioeconomic levels.

Illustrations

Illustrations in educational materials, by virtue of their visual immediacy, may carry an even stronger message than the text they illustrate. Pictures may leave a lasting impression about the tone of a book; the array of illustrations in a book is a strong projection of its intent. Specifically, bias-free illustrations should:

▶ reflect a fair and reasonable balance of representation with regard to race, religion, ethnic group, age, economic level, sex and national origin.

▶ provide positive role models for students of different ethnic and racial backgrounds and of both sexes.

▶ avoid stereotypes and caricatures of individuals and groups to offer a realistic and broad view of physical features.

▶ promote opportunities for placing women and minority group members in positions of prominence, leadership and centrality.

Language

Bias-free language is language that includes all people and treats them with equal dignity and respect, whatever their race, sex, age, religion or national and ethnic origin. Bias-free language deals with people as individuals, not as members of stereotyped groups. It minimizes the cultural differences on which prejudice is often based, avoids insults and derogatory connotations, and does not trivialize or patronize, slight or slander, mock or deride whole classes of people. It is language of equal opportunity. Specifically, bias-free language is language that:

▶ seeks to encompass members of both sexes by (1) avoiding the use of *man* and its derivatives to denote the average person or the human race; and (2) designating occupations by the work performed, not only by the gender of the worker.

▶ avoids excluding women by the use of the generic pronoun *he* by pluralizing, shifting to one, you, or we; rephrasing to eliminate gender pronouns altogether, or balancing he with she.

▶ understands generic terms such as doctor, lawyer, teacher, secretary, and poet, as applying to both sexes and to all races or ethnic groups.

▶ uses parallel language to give equal treatment to various persons and groups through the use of the equivalent terms and construction. Parallel style in name means that the style employed for one individual is used for all and does not vary depending on the sex, race, or social or marital status of the persons named. Parallelism in descriptions calls for an emphasis on pertinent information and an avoidance of role stereotypes.

▶ reflects our cultural diversity by including a variety of ethnic names as well as the more common Anglo-Saxon ones.

▶ avoids loaded words, biased connotations, and prejudiced assumptions. Particularly it expresses critical or negative judgments with words not associated with a particular race or sex, as, an evil heart rather than a black heart, affected mannerism rather than effeminate mannerisms. (Association of American Publishers, 1976).

Despite publishers' efforts, students continue to read many similar stories with little or no changes in series after series. When one considers that there is an average time lapse of approximately four years between textbook editions, and coupled with the fact that state laws may only require new textbooks every six or eight years, it may become apparent how an entire generation of students can pass through schools using biased textbooks even after it is evident to many that these texts limit the potential for many students. While the guidelines of textbook publishers for the promotion of fair policies have not been completely successful, publishers should not be considered solely responsible, either for the existence of bias in textbooks or for its elimination. It is important that other educational agencies and institutions take action on this issue.

Changing textbooks is a slow process. First of all, it is expensive, both to rewrite and to launch a new textbook series. A series is sometimes promoted as a new edition even though extensive changes have not been made. For a book or series to qualify as a new edition, copyright law only requires a 10 percent change, which may be made in the binding, by the addition of color plates or illustrations, by revising a teacher's guide, or by inserting a few new pages.

Local Strategies

The responsibility for selecting instructional materials is an important responsibility and one which needs to be addressed in a consistent and systematic fashion at the local level. Local communities are in the best position to assess and respond to the educational needs of their students.

Local authorities can take steps to make sure that instructional materials do not promote bias and stereotyping. If we are to improve textbooks and instructional materials, we must improve the review processes of each individual reviewer. That is, we must understand and help to improve the procedures that both individuals and committees utilize when they review textbooks. It is when a textbook is in the hands of a reviewer that the most important phase of the textbook evaluation process takes place. To improve that process, the following are suggestions:

▶ **Develop a philosophy of textbook use**. The criteria for evaluating a textbook needs to be stated so they are understood by everyone involved in the process, and these criteria should be determined with an understanding of what a textbook can and cannot do as an adjunct to an instructional program. We need to understand that textbooks are not total programs, nor do they establish curriculum; they are instructional aids to be used as part of a program.

▶ **Develop a set of review and selection criteria on local situations**. Check the comprehensiveness of the list by comparing it to other lists developed by other educators. Evaluation techniques for reviewing books need to be developed, reviewed, and revised. Textbook review committees need to have practice in using these procedures prior to the time that the books are actually reviewed.

▶ **Provide adequate training and release time for the evaluation process**. Those who review textbooks must receive a significant amount of training in how to review a textbook. It is not a task that one should learn while engaged in the process. Teachers should be provided with ample release time to carry out their reviews. When review times are squeezed between scheduled classes and added to after-school demands, the result is usually a cursory review rather than an in-depth review. If textbooks are an important part of the school's academic mission, then the process of evaluating materials must be valued.

▶ **Use sampling techniques**. Sampling techniques must be developed so that a smaller number of specific items can be reviewed in greater depth. There is no way that every topic in a particular text can be reviewed thoroughly. Research (Farr, 1986) has demonstrated that random selection procedures have adequate validity. These techniques can help textbook evaluation committees do a much more thorough evaluation.

▶ **Train textbook reviewers to provide specific information regarding each point that they review.** It not enough to say that something is good or bad or to provide general summaries. The evaluation evidence must be specific to each point that is reviewed.

▶ **Provide feedback to publishers**. Feedback from the results of textbook reviews must be specific and thorough. Publishers must learn what it is about their books that reviewers like and dislike. Publishers need to be convinced in very specific ways that books aren't adopted because they are not acceptable.

Biased and stereotyped instructional materials continue to find their way into our classrooms for a variety of reasons. It is important for us as teachers and administrators to develop criteria for accurately assessing bias in existing classroom textbooks and supplementary materials. In this way we can make a conscious effort to compensate for bias when it does occur. In addition, through constructive use of biased materials, we can teach students about bias in textbooks, and give them the skills and tools necessary to counteract the biased images they may confront daily in the society around them.

Textbook Evaluation

Farr and Tulley (1985) conducted a study which indicated that the number of criteria on any one selection sheet is overwhelming. The average number of items included on the criteria sheets they studied was 73. The longest sheet included 180 items and the shortest included 42 items.

Are the standards by which books are evaluated appropriate? There are many guides to textbook selection available; most provide a fairly standard list of the important features of textbooks, for example: (1) physical characteristics, (2) readability formulas, (3) pictures and graphics, (4) content—currency and accuracy, (5) content—difficulty, (6) curriculum and test alignment, (7) social issues, (8) instructional design—vocabulary, (9) instructional design—organizational features, (10) instructional design—questions, and (11) ancillary materials—teachers' manuals, software, and workbooks.

Certainly, when one begins to consider all of the identified areas that are important aspects of instructional materials, then one can understand the overwhelming number of criteria that can be generated for one text. As mentioned above, there is a need to generate "sampling techniques" in the review process so that a smaller number of specific items can be reviewed in greater depth.

A Sampling Technique for Equity

Specific items will be identified to analyze textbooks and instructional materials for equity. Although there are numerous guidelines for evaluating instructional materials for equity, Sadker and Sadker (1978) have identified six forms of bias that are useful to watch for when examining materials. The following identified areas are not to be used as a template for evaluating equity, but rather as a guide. These biases include: 1) invisibility, 2) stereotyping, 3) selectivity and imbalance, 4) unreality, 5) fragmentation and isolation, and 6) language.

Invisibility

Invisibility means that certain groups are under-represented in materials. This omission implies that these groups have less value, importance, and significance in our society. Invisibility in instructional materials occurs most frequently for women, ethnic minority groups, individuals with disabilities and older persons.

Materials can be examined for invisibility simply by counting the number of different groups represented in illustrations, in various roles, occupations, in biographies, or as main and secondary characters. Additional factors to consider with invisibility include:

▶ Do the materials include contributions and a variety of roles of our diverse population?
▶ Are a variety of socioeconomic levels and settings (urban, rural, suburban) included?
▶ Is diversity in terms of religion, cultures and family lifestyles included?

▶ It is important to remember that visual images (illustrations) should accurately depict physical images, lifestyles, cultural traditions and surroundings when portraying persons from diverse backgrounds. It is not enough to simply change skin color or names.

Stereotyping

The concept of stereotyping was mentioned in previous chapters, but since it is crucial to the expectations that we build up for our interactions with others, a closer examination will be provided.

The concept of stereotyping was first popularized by Lippman (1922). He defined a stereotype as "a factually incorrect simple description of a person or group resulting from illogical, rigidly held reasoning." Katz and Braly (1978) regard a stereotype as "a fixed impression which conforms very little to the facts it is supposed to represent and is the result of defining first and observing after."

Stereotypes are commonly believed to be associated with hostility towards certain categories of people. In their analysis of stereotyping, Seccord recognized three components of stereotyping. He said that we first identify a category of people, like students or police officers. Then we agree that the people in that category share certain traits, like being liberals or exercising an authoritarian personality. Finally, we attribute those traits to everyone in that category, however conservative or benign they may be. Several arguments are developed in the literature against the process of stereotyping:

▶ Categorizing people is unacceptable.
▶ Stereotyping is based on inaccurate data.
▶ Stereotyping implies that the categories of people are based on inborn, unchangeable characteristics.
▶ There is an implicit assumption that one's own cultural group represents the norm by which other groups should be judged.
▶ Categorizing people becomes a self-fulfilling prophecy.
▶ Stereotyping is often objectionable to individuals who are stereotyped.

The most powerful criticism of stereotyping is that there is a hidden assumption that most stereotypes are based on inborn characteristics which cannot be changed. This silent assumption is probably the strongest with respect to ethnic stereotypes. The hidden assumption is that "our" characteristics form the norm from which we judge all other groups, and the closer a group is to us in physical attributes, the greater our attraction to it in most respects and the more favorable the stereotype we hold for it [Seccord, Backman, Slavitt (1976), and Sadker & Sadker, (1978)].

By assigning traditional and rigid roles or attributes to a group, instructional materials stereotype and limit the abilities and potential of that group. Not only are careers stereotyped, but so are intellectual abilities, personality characteristics, physical appearance, social status and domestic roles. Stereotyping denies all students a knowledge of the diversity, complexity, and variation of any group of individuals. Additional factors to consider when examining materials for stereotypes and stereotyping include:

▶ Do men and women, boys and girls, show a wide variety of emotions?

▶ Are both sexes involved in active and passive activities, indoors and outdoors?

▶ Do visual depictions clearly make apparent the differences in appearance within a group as well as between groups?

▶ Does the plot or story line exaggerate the exoticism or mysticism of the various ethnic groups? For example: customs and festivals.

▶ Are older people shown in active as well as passive roles?

▶ Is old age and aging usually equated with death?

▶ Are disabled persons usually portrayed as members of problem-ridden families?

▶ Must representatives from previously excluded groups have super hero/heroine characteristics?

▶ Do members of the aforementioned categories fill both support and leadership roles?

Selectivity and Imbalance

Selectivity and imbalance occurs when issues and situations are interpreted from only one perspective, usually from the perspective of the majority group. Many issues, situations, and events described in textbooks are complex and can be viewed from a variety of viewpoints or perspectives. However, only one perspective is often presented. For example, the relationship between the U.S. government and the American Indian is usually examined only from the government's perspective in terms of treaties and protection. An American Indian's perspective also may examine broken treaties and the appropriation of native lands, but from a different perspective. This is an example of bias through selectivity and imbalance.

What can we do about this situation? As classroom teachers, we must be conscious of what textbooks and curriculum materials present. Although the materials we use may indeed be limited in their viewpoints, our sensitivity and understanding can then provide further research and discussion by our students to examine the issue or situation from another point of view. It is not necessary that each and every situation or event be examined with this in-depth scrutiny, but once students become aware and conditioned to looking at situations or issues from a variety of perspectives, then the role of the classroom teacher can become one of facilitator in discussing the various alternatives that present themselves.

Unreality

Textbooks frequently present an unrealistic portrayal of our history and contemporary life experiences. Controversial topics are glossed over or are not included in the textbook. As we saw earlier in the state-adoption-policy section, several "controversial" topics are being hotly debated between selection committees and textbook publishers. However, when sensitive and unpleasant issues such as racism, sexism, prejudice, discrimination, intergroup conflict(s), AIDS, drugs and alcohol abuse, religion(s), divorce and death are not included in instructional materials, students are then not provided any guidance or information in handling such complex and contemporary problems. Contemporary problems faced by the disabled or elderly are often disguised or simply avoided. American Indians, in discussions or illustrations, are often pictured in "historical" context rather than in a contemporary image. Most materials (where appropriate) do not consider sex bias and ethnic bias that do exist in employment practices and in salary schedules. These avoided issues do include those that many students may very well have to face in their lives. This unrealistic coverage denies or prohibits students the information needed to recognize, understand and perhaps someday conquer the problems that plague our society (Sadker & Sadker, 1978).

This unreality issue appears to be taking on a new added dimension. The two court decisions that were handed down in 1986 and 1987 are examples. The 1986 case, *Mozert v. Hawkins County Public Schools*, probed the issue of whether fundamentalist Christian students had a right to be free from exposure to concepts not compatible with their religious beliefs—concepts that may be as varied as idol worship, nontraditional sex roles, evolution and secular humanism.

The lawsuit focused on the Hawkins County school board's decision before the start of the 1983-84 school year to adopt as part of its curriculum for Grades 1 through 8—a reading series published by Holt, Reinhart and Winston. During the course of the academic year, several parents began scrutinizing their children's texts and found a host of stories and assignments that offended their fundamental Christian beliefs.

Eleven of the families filed suit against the district in December of 1983 after the school board denied their request to supply the children with alternative textbooks. Their suit sought unspecified monetary damages and a permanent injunction barring the Hawkins County Board from forcing the students to use the textbooks and from punishing them if they refused. U.S. District Judge dismissed all complaints against the Board in early 1984. But a Federal Appeals Court overturned the decision in June 1985 and instructed the lower court to schedule a trial to resolve the disputed fact in the case. In particular, the appeals panel directed the judge to decide whether the reading texts unconstitutionally impinged on the families' religious beliefs and, if so, whether "a compelling state interest" overrides the families' right to free exercise of religion.

In the fall of 1986, the judge ruled in favor of the parents. The landmark decision sent shock waves around the country. The decision sent a clear message—parents do have a right regarding what their children are taught in public schools. What was at stake is whether people who have religious objections to certain ideas can force their public school to provide their children with a curriculum tailored to their own particular beliefs. On appeal, the Supreme Court ruled against the parents in the fall of 1988.

In the spring of 1987, *Smith v. School Commissioners of Mobile County, Alabama*, a federal judge in Mobile, Alabama ordered 44 textbooks removed from the Alabama public schools because they unconstitutionally promoted the "religious belief system" of secular humanism. This latest ruling was viewed widely as a major victory for fundamentalist Christians, many of whom have long contended that secular humanism is a religion that places an individual's values above any divine authority, and that its tenets pervade the public schools' curricula. This decision marked the first time that a federal court had ruled that humanism is the equivalent of a religion for First Amendment purposes.

"Teaching that moral choices are purely personal and can only be based on some autonomous, as yet undiscovered and unfulfilled inner self is a sweeping fundamental belief that must not be promoted by the public schools," Judge Hand wrote. "With these books, the State of Alabama has overstepped its mark, and must withdraw to perform its proper non-religious functions."

The chairperson of the civil liberty group that aided the State Board of Education in its defense of the textbooks characterized this decision as "judicial book burning." Buchanan, chairperson of "People for the American Way"—a lobbying group that monitors civil liberty issues—described the decision nothing less than "government censorship of the school curriculum" (Goldberg, 1987).

As with the Tennessee case, this Alabama decision by the federal court is being appealed. It appears that the two decisions will not be isolated instances and that this particular issue will run through the judicial court systems of this country for years to come.

Fragmentation and Isolation

Fragmentation and isolation is a popular method in which many publishers include some of the ethnic groups, women, elderly and disabled, in their instructional materials. Issues, contributions, and information that we have discussed previously as being relevant are typically separated from the regular text and discussed in a section or chapter of its own. This "add-on" approach is easier to accomplish than trying to integrate the information throughout the text. There is nothing wrong with having some information separate from the regular text if it is not the only place students read about this added-on information. However, the isolation of particular information does often suggest negative connotations or mixed messages for students. This approach suggests that the experiences and contributions of these groups are merely an interesting diversion and not an integral part of historical and contemporary developments (Sadker & Sadker, 1978). The same analogy can be made with regard to our earlier discussion of single-group studies, comparative group approaches and the broader concept of equity. As discussed earlier, our society is very diverse and pluralistic, and it is important that instructional materials and textbooks reflect this diversity as a part of the total text rather than discussing particular groups in a separate section or as an add-on.

Language

Examples of linguistic bias in materials include the use of masculine pronouns or only Anglo names throughout the textbook. The lack of (1) Spanish, Polish, Filipino, African, and other non-Anglo names, and (2) feminine pronouns or names in materials will be evident to the sensitive teacher. When teachers are aware that linguistic bias blatantly omits female and many ethnic group references, they can develop strategies to correct the biases and ensure that these groups are an integral part of the curriculum (Sadker & Sadker, 1984). In examining curricular materials for language usage, several questions should be considered:

▶ Is the language and terminology used up-to-date?
▶ Is the language void of derogatory words or phrases?
▶ Are the terms used to refer to an individual or group so broad they are inaccurate or nondescript? For example: Indian vs. American Indian or Native American vs. Dakota.
▶ Ladies–gentlemen, boys–girls, rather than men—ladies, or men–girls.

Technology

School improvement is high on the national agenda, and while there is some disagreement about just what should be done to make schools better, the consensus is that computers and related technologies are critically important to building and maintaining a strong education system.

There is general agreement among researchers that people have short-term retention of about 20 percent of what they hear; 40 percent of what they see and hear; and 75 percent of what they hear, see and do. By employing video, sound and interaction, multimedia instruction provides the best chance for superior retention.

A Department of Defense study on interactive video instruction has found that over all instructional settings and applications, interactive video instruction improves achievement by an average of 38 percent over more conventional instruction, while reducing time to competency by 31 percent. Significantly, interactive video was most effective in higher education, with achievement a full 50 percent over conventional instruction (T.H.E. Journal, 1991). Such conclusions provide formal confirmation of news heard everywhere from pre-school to post-graduate education: multimedia instruction is real, proven and working. The role technology can play in our teaching provides a quantum leap in education—by personalizing the information revolution. By using technology as a teaching tool, we give our students the chance to become excited by learning; once engaged, their natural curiosity will propel them further.

Multimedia

Multimedia is like a toolbox. Classroom teachers can use it to build a total learning environment, or they can use certain multimedia elements for simple but effective enhancement of teaching. Multimedia technology can simply be defined as the combination of video, sound, text, animation and graphics with a computer to tie these components together. The teacher-driven paradigm can be extended considerably. Educators can build a highly sophisticated hypermedia system (interlinking of related information through instantaneous connections) complete with audio and full-motion video, then use the system themselves to direct class learning. With the tools (i.e.,CD-ROM, Laserdisc, Liquid Crystal Display-LCD, desktop publishing, spreadsheets, word processors, databases), educators can react in "real time" to the ebb and flow of class discussion, responding to each student inquiry as it arises by branching between segments from a rich multimedia format. The current explosion of instructional software is remarkable. Resources that were traditionally only found in printed form are now available in a variety of formats. Many states and school districts are adopting instructional software instead of purchasing the standard textbook as the resource for their curriculum. Within the next ten years, instructional software will take a greater place in the adoption of instructional materials for classrooms at all levels. Technology can impel, even lead, school reform in the next decade. American education needs to make the connection between technology and curriculum to achieve systemic, lasting change.

Teacher Training

Teacher training programs can no longer avoid being part of the information age. Why don't teacher educators use the technology in their classroom instruction? Why have we failed to "get up to speed" with the technology? Are we responsible for holding back the computer revolution in education? Before placing blame, we need to remember that the majority of teacher educators developed teaching practices well before the advent of the microcomputer. Computers weren't part of their experiences as learners, either in their K-12 schooling or in their collegiate pre-service education.

In the mid '90s, there are more than two million computers in K-12 education. We are still faced with a huge problem. If we want teachers to feel comfortable using these tools in the classroom, if we hope to give educational technology the chance to fulfill its potential, teacher educators need to begin modeling and preparing our future teacher with these essential skills.

First, teacher educators must move beyond using the computer as simply a word-processing tool. Secondly, we must stop isolating educational technology as a separate discipline. In fact, most teacher education programs have set up a separate course called Technology in Education, and the "technology person" teaches it. This is one reason that teachers graduating from Schools of Education are arriving in public school classrooms not prepared or ready to use the technology. As students, they did not see the integrated use of technology in other disciplines within their training program. As a result, public schools are continually playing catch-up with in-service training for their new and experienced teachers. Teacher training programs must take a different approach.

Breaking Old Habits

For many years, the emphasis within educational computing was to put computers into labs or computing centers. The then-current wisdom was that computers would eventually find their way into the curriculum—if only enough of them could be brought together in one place. But, too often, labs were underused or, worse, became a haven for computer-game playing. In addition, several schools are using their computer labs for dumping or tracking their slower students into remedial instructional learning settings. The problem that came to be seen was that no one had instructed teachers about how computers can be used to teach the curriculum and, perhaps more importantly, the teachers themselves did not have access to a computer.

The emphasis has changed. Now the idea is to put computers into classrooms and onto teacher's desks. This evolution that is occurring in many school districts will require classroom teachers to think of the computer as an instructional tool that can enhance the teaching and learning process. Classroom teachers must be willing to incorporate technology into their curriculum and to break the old habits that have stereotyped the profession of what the "art of teaching" is.

Creating Good Uses for Technology

Can classroom computer technology enhance learning rather than disempower teachers and students? As mentioned with the multimedia section above, these are only tools; strategies for their use must come from the teacher's themselves.

The process of devising those strategies must begin by focusing on *purpose* rather than *technique*—by asking what one wants a program for, rather than how to use what currently exists. It requires teachers to consider the important curricular questions of what is worth knowing and why, of what learning is appropriate and for whom. It demands the primacy of teachers and students, and the community of the classroom. Above all, it avoids letting the technological tail wag the pedagogical dog.

If teachers are prepared to use technological tools to meet needs that arise from their comprehensive classroom planning and practice, and if software developers focus on creating ever more flexible tools, the future of technology in the classroom can be productive and positive.

Strategies to Counter Biased Material

Individual awareness of bias and stereotyping in instructional materials is an important *first* step in changing materials and their impact on all of us. Each of us has a responsibility for using our awareness to bring about some changes and support others who are working in this area.

▶ Look for and learn to recognize bias that may be found in textbooks, curriculum materials, software, supplementary materials, library books, television programs, magazines, etc.

▶ Level with the students in your classroom. Point out bias and stereotyping in books and materials. Help them learn to identify sources of bias and important omissions in the materials.

▶ Develop classroom instruction and activities around identifying bias and stereotyping found in television, textbooks, movies, video-discs, CD-ROM, library books, magazines, etc.

▶ Identify or develop supplementary materials which can help "correct" some of the bias found in materials or their identification of supplementary materials.

▶ Assign student research projects. These might include a study of their own textbook materials or their identification of supplementary materials.

▶ Ask students to rewrite materials, write their own materials on subjects omitted from the textbook, or rewrite the material from other persons' points of view.

▶ Use bulletin boards, posters, pictures, magazines and other materials to expose students to information commonly excluded from traditional materials.

▶ Develop a collection of nonbiased reading materials for students. Identify books that students may be encouraged to seek out in their personal reading.

▶ Request and use funds available for instructional materials to build supplementary materials resources for your classroom(s) or school(s).

▶ Conduct a study and periodic review of the bias found in the textbooks and materials used in your course(s) or school program(s).

▶ Meet with the librarian or media specialist and ask him/her to assist faculty in the identification (nonbiased) of equity books and materials. Urge him/her to order and provide resources for supplementary materials.

▶ Organize a central file in your department or school that will have supplementary materials, curriculum outlines, or other resources for identifying bias and supplementing the curriculum.

▶ Develop a "Yellow Pages" of resources for equity education which would be helpful to faculty; this might include a list of speakers, resource persons, organizations and places for good out-of-class learning experiences within the community (field experiences).

▶ Identify nontraditional publishing firms, alternative presses and other groups developing materials in this area. Distribute this information to all faculty members.

▶ Publicize studies, workshops, and other efforts to improve instructional materials or reduce the impact of biased materials.

Summary

The role models presented in textbooks are very important in helping students identify with and learn from the curriculum. The influence of materials on a student's sense of self-worth depends on the extent to which the student identifies with the characters and situations presented as he or she becomes emotionally involved with them.. Besides transmitting knowledge about the world around him/her, curriculum materials may also affect a student's career interests and expectations, especially through the role models presented. Interest and expectations, in turn, may influence a student's level of achievement and career choice in later years.

By inference, the content of textbooks has the institutional stamp of approval. Moreover, as mentioned earlier, textbooks often determine curriculum, since what is covered in a text is usually what ends up being taught, and what is left out of a text is usually not considered important to course content. Because, as we have seen, textbooks and other instructional materials are critically important, they must be designed to avoid the perpetuation of bias and stereotyping. They should foster for all people, regardless of their diverse backgrounds, a sense of personal worth and dignity and a respect for their abilities and rights.

There is little argument that school texts and supplementary materials help students identify possible future lifestyles, careers, and goals and provide learners with role models. However, numerous studies have indicated that despite an increasing social awareness of bias and stereotyping, publishers are still producing books that portray a number of groups in a limited number of roles, a very limited number of skills, or not at all.

Whatever paradigms may be used to understand and describe the role of the information age, it seems certain that there will be more and more machines in the classroom. Technology will prevail. The problem that lies ahead will be—as it always has been—direction and control: direction of education in terms of its goals and purposes and control of technology in terms of its application.

Will technology be used to continue, with greater speed and efficiency, what has always been done in school? Or will technology make possible new ways of learning that only it can provide?

While deeply ingrained societal attitudes and habits cannot be changed overnight, policymakers must work toward eliminating bias and stereotyping in future instructional materials. An effective step is for all those involved at local and state levels to take responsibility for what students read and work with in school. For the benefit of individuals as well as society, it is necessary to eliminate inequities in educational material.

 END NOTES

Bernstein, Harriet T. "The New Politics of Textbook Adoption." *Phi Delta Kappan*, Vol. 66, 1985.

Bowler, Mike "Textbook Publishers Try to Please All, but First They Woo the Heart of Texas." *Reading Teacher*, February, 1978.

California State Department of Education. *Instructional Materials Approved for Legal Compliance*, Sacramento, CA, 1984.

Cody, Caroline B. *A Policymaker's Guide to Textbook Selection*. National Association of State Boards of Education. Alexandria, VA, 1986.

Educational Products Information Institute (EPII). *Report of the Nature and the Quality of Instructional Materials Most Used by Teachers and Learners*. New York, NY, 1977.

Farr, Roger. "Do Our Textbook Selection Process Work?" In a *Policymaker's Guide to Textbook Selection,* by Caroline B. Cody. National Association of State Boards of Education. Alexandria, VA, 1986.

Goldberg, Kirsten. "Federal Court Finds Secular Humanism a Religion." *Education Week*, March 11, 1987.

Lippman, W. *Public Opinion*. Harcourt Brace, New York, NY, 1922.

Mozert v. Hawkins County Public Schools, 1986.

Sadker, M. & Sadker, D. "The Teacher Educator's Role." In S. McCune and M. Matthews, eds. *Implementing Title IX and Attaining Sexual Equality: A Workshop Package for Post-Secondary Educators*. Washington, D.C. 1978.

Sadker, M. & Sadker, D. *Year III: Final Report, Promoting Effectiveness in Classroom Instruction*, NIE Contract No. 400-80-0033, Washington, D.C., 1984.

School Division—Association of American Publishers. *Statement on Bias-Free Materials*, New York, NY, 1976.

Seccord, P.F., Backman, C.W. & Slavitt, D.R. *Understanding Social Life.* McGraw Hill Publishing Co: New York, NY, 1976.

Smith v. School Commissioners of Mobile County, Alabama, 1987.

Technology in Higher Education Journal, September, 1991.

Tulley, Michael A. & Farr Roger. "Do Adoption Committees Perpetuate Mediocre Textbooks?" *Phi Delta Kappan*, Vol. 66, 1985.

 ## SUGGESTIONS FOR FURTHER READING

Apple, Michael W. "The Political Economy of Text Publishing." *Educational Theory*, Vol. 34, 1984.

Bernstein, Harriett. "The New Politics of Textbook Adoption." *Phi Delta Kappan*, March 1985.

Blaunstein, P. "An Overview of State Textbook Selection Procedures." In *Brunelle, R., Eds. How Can We Improve Both the Quality of Textbooks and the Process for Selecting Them?* National Forum on Excellence in Education Conference Papers, Washington, D.C., 1983.

Comas, J. "Review of Seventy Textbook Adoption Criteria Sheets from both Adoption and Non-Adoption States." Unpublished paper, Indiana University, 1982.

Komoski, K. "Instructional Materials Will Not Improve Until We Change the System." *Educational Leadership*, Vol. 42, 1985.

Muther, C. "What Every Textbook Evaluator Should Know." *Educational Leadership*, Vol. 42, 1985.

Osburn, J., Jones, B. & Stein, M. "The Case for Improving Textbooks." *Educational Leadership*, Vol. 42, 1985.

Phi Delta Kappan, "Technology in the Schools." December, 1992.

Tulley, M. A Descriptive Study of the Intents of State-Level Textbook Adoption Processes. *Educational Evaluation and Policy Analysis*, Fall, 1985.

Name _____ Date _____

✔ DISCUSSION QUESTIONS

1. Are classroom teachers, in your opinion, as dependent upon textbooks as the research indicated in this chapter?

   _____

   _____

   _____

   _____

   _____

   _____

2. How much influence do instructional materials have on the curriculum?

   _____

   _____

   _____

   _____

   _____

3. If publishers have gone on record against bias and stereotyping, why do we still have bias and stereotyping in current textbooks and instructional materials?

_____

_____

_____

_____

_____

4. What is an adoption state?

_____

_____

_____

_____

An open state?

_____

_____

_____

_____

What are the advantages and disadvantages of each process of adoption?

_____

_____

_____

_____

_____

5. What suggestions were cited in this chapter that would improve the process of textbook evaluation at the local level?

_____

_____

_____

_____

_____

6. What are the implications for classroom teachers with regard to the two recent court cases involving fundamental Christians (Tennessee) and the teaching of secular humanism (Alabama) in textbooks?

_____

_____

_____

_____

7. How can classroom teachers counter stereotyping and bias that exist in textbooks and instructional materials that they are presently using?

_____

_____

_____

_____

8. What role can technology play in the area of instruction? Explain.

_____

_____

_____

_____

_____

_____

_____

SMALL GROUP WORK

Evaluating Instructional Materials

Objectives

To demonstrate the complexity of instructional material adoption and selection.

To experience a variety of perspectives in the process of adoption.

To develop a list of criteria for evaluating instructional materials.

Task

Divide into eight subgroups (3-4 to a group is ideal).

Each group will *randomly* select one of the represented groups which they will then represent in the activity.

To evaluate a series of instructional materials i.e., elementary reading series. (Should include—teacher's manual, teacher's guide, student workbooks and reading book.)

To prepare a summary of the instructional materials to be presented to the class.

Represented Groups

1. Fundamental Christians for a Better Life
2. Black Caucus for Improving Schools
3. Local P.T.O.
4. Women for the American Way
5. West Side Parents for a Better School
6. The Foundation for the Back to the Basics in Schools
7. Elementary Classroom Teachers
8. The Coalition for Students with Disabilities

FUNDAMENTAL CHRISTIANS FOR A BETTER LIFE

(Founded 1991)

General Objectives and Beliefs

About 10 percent of the community favors your position.

You strongly believe that curriculum materials in public schools should not perpetuate anti-Christian beliefs.

You believe in creationism.

You believe that evolution should not be evident nor endorsed in public schools.

You favor the role of women in "traditional" roles.

You strongly favor a "tuition-tax credit" system for public education.

You believe that schools should accommodate your children with special curriculum materials that are not offensive to your religious convictions.

Task

Identify two (2) criteria that must be considered in the evaluation of curriculum materials (from your group's perspective):

_____

_____

_____

_____

Summary of Evaluation

_____ Recommended
_____ Not Recommended

Comments that will be made to the class supporting the above decision.

BLACK CAUCUS FOR IMPROVING SCHOOLS

(Founded 1974)

General Objectives and Beliefs

About 21 percent of the community is African American.

You believe that curriculum materials either perpetuate stereotypes (negative) or omit the contributions of African Americans.

You believe that the school district has been extremely negligent in correcting these curriculum practices.

You are also sensitive to the lack of any "ethnic authenticity" in the district's curriculum materials (Hispanic, Asian and American Indian perspectives).

The role of African American women is highly suspect in curriculum materials.

The diversity of African American people is nonexistent in curricular materials.

Task

Identify two (2) criteria that must be considered in evaluating curriculum materials (from your group's perspective):

_____

_____

_____

_____

Summary of Evaluation

_____ Recommended
_____ Not Recommended

Comments that will be made to the class supporting the above decision.

LOCAL P.T.O.

(Founded 1967)

General Objectives and Beliefs

About 34 percent of the parents in the district are active in the P.T.O.

You strongly believe that "competency" in subject areas should be a high priority.

You are concerned that today's textbooks are "watered down" in content and validity.

You are cautiously concerned that textbooks have gone "overboard" in their attempt to portray America's diversity.

You are very concerned about the "readability" levels textbooks that are being published today.

You believe that too many "special interest" groups have taken control of the textbook adoption/selection process.

Task

Identify two (2) criteria that must be considered in evaluating curriculum materials (from your group's perspective):

_____

_____

_____

_____

Summary of Evaluation

_____ Recommended
_____ Not Recommended

Comments that will be made to the class supporting the above decision.

WOMEN FOR THE AMERICAN WAY

(Founded in 1988)

General Objectives and Beliefs

A recent survey indicates that about 28 percent of the households in the community support your objectives and beliefs.

You believe the balance between males and females in curriculum materials is slanted toward the males.

You strongly believe that the role of females is very stereotypical.

You contend that most of the "content" concerning the role of women is superficial.

You would like to see a district policy that states no textbooks will be considered or adopted that contain sexist images, language and roles.

The roles of ethnic minority women are almost nonexistent.

The lack of female authors is also disturbing to your organization.

Task

Identify two (2) criteria that must be considered in evaluating curriculum materials (from your group's perspective):

_____

_____

_____

_____

Summary of Evaluation

_____ Recommended
_____ Not Recommended

Comments that will be made to the class supporting the above decision.

WEST SIDE PARENTS FOR A BETTER SCHOOL

(Founded in 1979)

General Objectives and Beliefs

About 45 percent of the community is low income.

You believe that curriculum materials totally neglect any "real-life" experiences for your children.

You believe that curriculum materials are geared toward middle-class students.

You believe that your libraries are less adequate than other schools in the district.

You believe that many materials neglect the one-parent family.

You believe that materials neglect the extended family.

You are concerned about the high drop-out rate of your children: currently 58 percent are not finishing school.

Task

Identify two (2) criteria that must be considered in evaluating curriculum materials (from your group's perspective):

_____

_____

_____

_____

Summary of Evaluation

_____ Recommended
_____ Not Recommended

Comments that will be made to the class supporting the above decision.

ELEMENTARY CLASSROOM TEACHERS

(Founded in 1957)

General Objectives and Beliefs

You are concerned with textbooks that are "readable" with the age group you are working with.

You are concerned that the textbooks have a good format.

You are concerned with "content difficulty."

You want textbooks that have good instructional design: vocabulary, questions, workbooks.

You want good teacher manuals.

You want materials that have been classroom tested.

You want materials that are outcomes-based.

You are considering a whole-language approach in the curriculum—thus eliminating the purchase of textbooks in the "series" approach.

Task

Identify two (2) criteria that must be considered in evaluating curriculum materials (from your group's perspective):

_____

_____

_____

Summary of Evaluation

_____ Recommended
_____ Not Recommended

Comments that will be made to the class supporting the above decision.

THE FOUNDATION FOR THE BACK TO THE BASICS IN SCHOOLS

(Founded 1985)

General Objectives and Beliefs

You are strongly in favor of a sound "basic" education (reading, writing and arithmetic).

You believe that all students must pass a competency level before moving on to the next grade level.

You strongly believe that there are too many "frills" in today's textbooks that get away from the basics.

About 70 percent of the community is in favor of your objectives and beliefs.

You believe that subjects other than math, reading, arithmetic and writing are not appropriate for elementary children.

You strongly believe that students should have homework.

You believe that constant drilling and repetition is the most effective way to get competency in basic skills.

You are strongly opposed to the whole-language approach.

Task

Identify two (2) criteria that must be considered in evaluating curriculum materials (from your group's perspective):

_____

_____

_____

Summary of Evaluation

_____ Recommended
_____ Not Recommended

Comments that will be made to the class supporting the above decision.

THE COALITION FOR STUDENTS WITH DISABILITIES

(Founded 1976)

General Objectives and Beliefs

About 16 percent of the students in the district are in special education.

You believe that curriculum materials are negligent in their fair and unbiased portrayal of disabled populations.

The portrayal of any disability is very narrow (usually a child in a wheelchair).

Curriculum materials are unfavorable for the truly gifted student. Materials are geared for the "average" student.

You are concerned that textbooks have responded more favorably to women and ethnic minorities than to disabled populations.

You wish the enthusiasm for the "Special Olympics" would be as great for textbook selection and adoption for disabled populations in instructional materials.

Task

Identify two (2) criteria that must be considered in evaluating curriculum materials (from your group's perspective):

_____

_____

_____

_____

Summary of Evaluation

_____ Recommended
_____ Not Recommended

Comments that will be made to the class supporting the above decision.

INDIVIDUAL WORK

Introduction

As discussed in this chapter, there are numerous guidelines, charts and forms that could be used to evaluate instructional materials in the field of education. Every educational organization, school district, publisher, and scholarly journal has at one time or another, proposed guidelines and suggestions for evaluating materials. In other words, the problem hasn't been one of the lack of an information base, but one of how to go about it systematically. Instructional material analysis is neither a quick nor an easy task.

As you will learn along the way, there are many instructional materials that are very well done, but at the same time there are many materials that fall far short of an equitable perspective. If we can imagine the different levels of equity displayed in Figure 24— Rating the Level of Equity Input, this, in fact, is the diversity of equity within textbooks and instructional materials found today. The following exercise will provide you with a first-hand experience in: 1) evaluating materials for equity, and 2) acquainting you with how your specific area or level has responded to equity from two distinct periods of time.

Task

You are to locate *two* resources (i.e., textbooks, software, workbooks, curriculum materials) in your specific field or level. One source must have been published before 1975, and the second source must have been published after 1990. Based upon the evaluation forms provided on the following pages, you are to analyze the two resources.

Level 4
- · **Overall Integration**
- · **In-Depth Development of Concepts**
- · **Alternatives Provided**
- · **Challenges and Sensitivities**

Level 3
- · **Some Integration**
- · **Development of Examples Provided**
- · **Some Sensitizing to Issues and Concepts**

Level 2
- · **Brief Mention of Equity Concepts**
- · **Minimal Sensitizing**
- · **Add-On Sections**

Level 1
- · **No Equity Input Offered**

Figure 24. Rating the level of equity input.

EVALUATING INSTRUCTIONAL MATERIALS
IN <u>YOUR</u> AREA OR LEVEL

Name of Evaluator: _____

Title: _____

Publisher: _____

Date of Publication: Before 1975: _____

Level: (Circle One)   **Subject Area**

Elementary _____

Middle Level _____

Secondary _____

Post-Secondary _____

Level of Equity

1	2	3	4	Criteria for Evaluation
				Diversity of Representation
				Positive Portrayal of Individuals or Groups
				Variety of Perspectives
				Realistic in Approach
				Integrated Material (No Add On Sections)
				Terminology Is Fair and Unbiased
				Total Number of Points (24 possible)

1. Why did you rate the material as you did? Explain your score.

_____

_____

_____

_____

2. Identify specific examples to support your evaluation (page numbers, sample statements, illustrations).

_____

_____

_____

_____

3. Would you recommend the use of this particular material? Why or why not?

_____

_____

_____

_____

EVALUATING INSTRUCTIONAL MATERIALS
IN <u>YOUR</u> AREA OR LEVEL

Name of Evaluator: _____

Title: _____

Publisher: _____

Date of Publication: After 1990: _____

Level: (Circle One)   **Subject Area**

Elementary _____

Middle Level _____

Secondary _____

Post-Secondary _____

Level of Equity

1	2	3	4	Criteria for Evaluation
				Diversity of Representation
				Positive Portrayal of Individuals or Groups
				Variety of Perspectives
				Realistic in Approach
				Integrated Material (No Add On Sections)
				Terminology Is Fair and Unbiased
				Total Number of Points (24 possible)

1. Why did you rate the material as you did? Explain your score.

_____

_____

_____

_____

2. Identify specific examples to support your evaluation (page numbers, sample statements, illustrations).

_____

_____

_____

_____

3. Would you recommend the use of this particular material? Why or why not?

_____

_____

_____

_____

Part 3

Affirming Equity:
Strategies for Schools and Teachers

Understanding Change: Redefining Staff Development  9

Training for teachers ought to be more like sex education. Would you want your son or daughter to take a sex training course or would you want them to take a sex education course? Okay, assuming you got this one right, why do you think we treat so much of staff development as training and not as education?

(November, 1993)

Introduction

Although the above analogy is humorous, much of what we do in the area of staff development is not. If we really want to educate teachers to think about and apply knowledge to improve education, we will inevitably challenge the basis of our current system. Obviously it is easier to stay in the training business. Education is much more of a risky business.

Part of the reason staff development too often stops with training and never moves on to the important education/thinking level is a lack of respect in the professional culture for the teacher as learner. Unlike many corporations that place a high premium on their professionals' capacity to learn and apply new skills, education has no tradition for valuing the teacher as a lifetime learner. Case in point: It is not unheard of for an engineer to be paid up to 100 days a year to learn, yet the average teacher in the U.S. gets one to three days.

The words in-service, staff development and professional development generally produce images of workshops, conferences, seminars or classes. Each and every fall schools jump to thoughts of mobilizing to meet the in-service priority at hand: finding the right consultant or speaker, room arrangements, audio-visual needs, handouts, and maybe even snacks.

Faced with a multitude of survey-induced staff wants, schools frequently choose to meet as many of the needs as possible: filling the mostly inadequate in-service time slots with a smorgasbord of short-term, one-shot awareness sessions. We trade quality for quantity; skill attainment for idea generation, and a flurry of activity for a job well done.

We tend to judge our successes in terms of number of participants, satisfaction ratings regarding the speaker's skills, hours of training, or numbers of recertification hours generated. We seldom ask the critical question: "Has staff development resulted in improved student learning?"

Chapter Nine—**Understanding Change: Redefining Staff Development** is intended to (1) briefly examine the process that schools generally use in educating (training) staff, (2) identify those approaches that seem to be more effective than others, (3) understand the isolation of the teaching profession, (4) outline what it means to collaborate as professionals, (5) examine efficacy and its impact on school improvement, (6) identify characteristics of the change process, and (7) identify a continuum for changing current practice and priorities that can better position schools engaged in staff development initiatives.

A Matter of Priority

We've all heard it said, or said it ourselves at one time: "I can't leave my classroom to attend training. My students need me, and it will take days to recover from having a sub in class." On the contrary, are we saying that, if we can't leave students for a few days or even a week without the process becoming totally disrupted, maybe there is something wrong with the model that perpetuates students' overdependence on a teacher for learning.

Improvement cannot flourish in a school where there is no shared vision of how much more students can achieve. From my experience as a consultant, there are probably more good ideas within the schools that I have worked with, than I could ever provide as a presenter. But, too often, these ideas are useless unless they are shared among colleagues at the school level. Yet, research indicates that teachers typically spend less than five minutes a day talking to each other about ideas. How can we possibly apply systemic change in our system if the professionals responsible do not feel comfortable about sharing ideas all the time? Limited idea sharing, in turn, limits the scope and effectiveness of school improvement.

Effective Staff Development

The research base on change and effective staff development is extensive, often quoted, but seldom seriously followed or put into practice. An effective staff development approach clearly emphasizes what educators must do in order to bring about the changes in teacher and administrator behavior that will lead to improvements in student performance. The following summaries provide an overview of the critical research necessary to drive an effective approach to staff development (KSBE, 1992).

▶ **Adult learning theory tells us that the participants in the training must be involved in planning and developing the training**. The most common translation of this practice is to survey teachers about their staff development needs and plan in-service activities based on the most common responses. Their involvement is mainly responding to a survey instrument and not to the planning and development of the training. Many staff development initiatives take the form of something that is done to teachers rather than with them, still less by them.

▶ **Research on effective staff development espouses that the training must be sequentially structured and supported over time, linked to individual participants competence and relevant to their work**. Current staff development practices primarily involve one-shot workshops, little or no follow-up, and almost no application training. Murphy (1992) states that less than 10% of teachers are able to use the knowledge and skills gained in a one-time workshop in their classroom settings. Staff development research (Joyce & Mckibbin, 1983; Wood, 1981) have presented models of training that, if followed, provide a high degree of transfer from the workshop to the worksite. With the requisite follow-up training, on-site practice, and maintenance of staff; 80% of in-service participants will be able to successfully apply the interventions during the teacher-learning process in the classroom.

▶ **Individual schools are not the unit of change, but the center of change**. Research clearly shows the most effective staff development programs are designed for school improvement rather than for staff personal professional improvement. Past efforts have focused on the desires of individual teachers (separate from their buildings) or district-wide thrusts. For staff development to result in increased student success, individuals must focus on the learning needs of their building's students, and plan individual and faculty staff development to resolve these real needs. Staff development focused at the building site, with follow-up in the classroom, offers the greatest power for staff development results.

▶ **Expectations of staff need to be clearly articulated and individuals need to be held accountable for learning and changing**. Most current staff development efforts are designed to increase staff knowledge, not staff competence. Planning and accountability focus almost entirely on "seat time." Since myriad individual actions are the predominate focus, attempts at assessing the vast diversity of growth or change is seldom feasible. Effective staff development, especially activities supporting common building needs, includes expectations of change by all staff in a building and lends accountability to individuals and staff as a whole.

▶ **Staff development must be an integral component of organizational development**. Current in-service planning frequently occurs in isolation from curriculum development, school improvement, external accreditation efforts, or other district level planning. A district focus integrating the various on-going efforts, integrating the staff development needs and actions of each committee and providing coordination and prioritization of resources is a must. Staff development which integrates district, school and individual needs by focusing on improved student learning, offers the greatest power for results.

▶ **School leaders face an equally pressing slate of "new workforce skills."** Instructional leadership has changed. Managing a school and its programs is important, but leading a restructured school requires a restructured slate of skills. Facilitating groups, building teams, decision making, building consensus, empowering staff, etc. are foundational skills for the 21st century educational leader.

▶ **Effective staff development must accommodate the change process**. Many staff development efforts assume that all participants are at the same level of readiness for change. However, if the intent of staff development is to produce change in practices, beliefs and attitudes of teachers, then the success or failure of staff development is tied to the ways in which individual participants experience the change process. A variety of research over the years by Hall, Drucker, Fullan, et al. has provided testimony to our experiences with change. Change is a private matter, experienced differently by every participant. Stress, confusion, and uncertainty accompany every stage of change, even when that change is gradual and self-selected. Failure to consider the dynamics of the change process has serious and negative implications for staff development initiatives.

When considering the change process in staff development, the stages of innovation must be explored. Within each stage of the innovation careful attention must be paid to the characteristics of the change itself, as well as to characteristics of individual innovators. Does this innovation hold promise for meeting demonstrated student needs? How will this innovation be received by prospective implementers (teachers, administrators)? Does this innovation enjoy empirical validation with students whose characteristics are similar to the students *we* serve? How efficient is implementation likely to be? What will be the needs and concerns of participants?

▶ **Effective staff development requires unequivocal and on-going support from district-level and building-level administrators**. Research has shown that cues received from the organizational environment influence individual behavior toward congruence with organizational goals and objectives. Such cues might include specific work assignments, physical resources available to facilitate that work, physical structure within which that work must be accomplished, or expectations held for individuals by work groups existing within the organization. When administrators' support of an innovation is perceived as equivocal, inadequate , or short-term, teachers often decide to "wait this one out," assuming the commitment to the innovation is not in their own best interest.

► **Staff development for student improvement means all staff are responsible for the learning needs of all students**. Especially in building-based school improvement initiatives, the data on every student must drive the needs assessment process. Moreover, every staff member who affects students must be seen as collaborative partners in the solutions. Excusing coaches, special staff, or others from the staff development program weakens the intervention and the success of the program. All staff can include secretaries, custodians, board members, substitutes, para-professionals, parents, etc.

The single distinguishing characteristic of the best professionals in any field is that they consistently strive for better results, and are always learning to become more effective, from whatever source they can find. As Block (1987) stated: "One of the fastest ways to get out of a bureaucratic cycle is to have as your goal to learn as much as you can about what you're doing. Learning and performance are intimately related; the high performers are those who learn most quickly."

The Problem of Isolation

Teaching has long been called " a lonely profession." The professional isolation of teachers limits access to new ideas and better solutions, drives stress inward and accumulates over time, fails to recognize and praise success, and permits incompetence to exist and persist to the detriment of students, colleagues and the teachers themselves. Isolation allows, even if it does not always produce, conservatism and resistance to innovation in teaching (Lortie, 1975).

Isolation has many causes. Often they can be perceived as a personality weakness revealed in competitiveness, defensiveness about criticism, and a tendency to gather all of the resources. But people are creatures of circumstance, and when isolation is widespread, we have to ask what it is about our schools that creates so much of it.

Partly, isolation is a matter of habit. It is historically ingrained in our working routines. In research studies conducted by Fullan (1991), many teachers could not imagine and never really thought of any working arrangement other than teaching alone. The alternatives had never been experienced. Sometimes, physical isolation is unavoidable because of the structure and organization of buildings. Portables in particular can isolate teachers from their colleagues, making them overly protective and possessive about their own classes. This physical isolation is also revealed in the segregated classroom of so many of our schools—what Lortie (1975) called the traditional "egg-crate structure of schooling." Classrooms tend to isolate teachers. This is no accident. As educational historians have pointed out, the 19th century "batch-system of production," where isolated teachers taught fixed programs to age-segregated groups of children, was designed as a way of disciplining and controlling the masses. This outdated tradition of isolation has unfortunately come to be regarded as the "normal" way to teach in many schools.

As Fullan (1991) states, "the problem of isolation is a deep-seated one. Architecture often supports it. The timetable reinforces it. Overload sustains it. History legitimizes it." There is simply not enough opportunity and not enough encouragement for teachers to work together, learn from each other, and improve their expertise as a school community.

Collaboration

We seem to be caught in a real bind. On the one hand, the demands for school reform continue strong; on the other hand, financial cutbacks grow more extensive and more severe. At the same time, the past decade taught us that teachers must have a strong voice and hand in reform implementation, or it is unlikely to succeed (Berman & McLaughlin, 1978; Louis & Miles, 1990). We also have learned that on-going teacher collaboration is important if we are to have better schools and teaching.

Collaboration is a style for direct interaction between at least two co-equal parties voluntarily engaged in shared decision making as they work toward a common goal (Cook & Friend, 1991). Characteristics of collaboration are:

▶ **Collaboration is voluntary**. Schools have to choose collaboration, not have it imposed upon them.

▶ **Individuals who collaborate share a common goal**. The common goals must be stated very specifically in such a manner that they can be operationalized and evaluated.

▶ **Collaboration requires parity among participants**. Professionals involved in collaboration must believe they have something valuable to contribute; and they must feel their contribution is valued by others.

▶ **Collaboration includes shared responsibility for decisions**. Once parity is created, there is a basis for shared responsibility for decisions.

▶ **Individuals who collaborate share accountability for outcomes**. When responsibility is shared among participants, successful and unsuccessful outcomes are also shared, and jointly owned.

▶ **Collaboration includes sharing resources**. It is necessary that participants in the process have a sense of ownership. One way to develop ownership is through the contribution of resources, i.e., time, money, and/or materials.

Several research studies conclude that if teaching is going to get better and education is to become more effective, then we've got to reconfigure schools along with the roles and relationships within them. It doesn't work to have "experts" making the decisions and showing teachers how to carry them out. It doesn't work to have teachers—even the strongest and the best of teachers—operating independently and as solo performers in their classrooms.

Efficacy

Most effective educational practices seem to be driven by combinations of people thinking effectively. Many educators are beginning to understand the process of change in a more concrete manner. The success many schools are beginning to see in their schools has been due in large part, to a change in attitudes of everyone in the system.

Efficacy, the belief in our ability to execute certain courses of action, is partly a result of our perception of our locus of control. As efficacy relates to our beliefs about being able to make things happen or not happen, locus of control relates to our perception of what we can and cannot control.

For example, good coaches help their players take control of the situation, the play, the game. Good coaches help their players perceive that each player individually has control of his or her position and what happens in it. Locus of control concerns our perceived ability to take responsibility for our own actions—to control and be responsible for our own destiny—rather than seeing control of our lives residing elsewhere. Like good coaches, good educators help other educators shift more of their locus of control from external to internal so we become more efficacious.

If athletes believe they have little control over their positions, their teammates, or the game, they have little internal locus of control and their efficacy to win is reduced. Educators think the same way. If educators believe they can effect control of the causes or results of education problems, they then have a strong internal locus of control—that is, they believe they are in charge. Their efficacy about problem solving will be high and they will solve those problems. The relationship between locus of control and efficacy is summed up as follows: no internal locus of control, no efficacy—no efficacy, no performance (Fields, 1993).

Locus of Control

Locus of control is not fixed. It can be changed. Since locus of control resides in individuals, and organizations are teams or groups of individuals, then organizations have a collective locus of control—a collective perception of their ability to solve problems.

Educators who have a strong belief in their capabilities think, feel, and behave differently from those who doubt their capabilities. Educators who doubt their capabilities shy away from difficult tasks. When educators don't judge themselves able to do something, they may not even try to do it, regardless of how well they could actually do it.

Efficacy has four major effects on educator behavior. They are:

▶ **set high, clear goals for themselves**. If we believe that we will succeed at a task, then we involve ourselves in it. When we believe we will perform poorly at something, we refrain from involvement in that task.

▶ **orchestrate more effort to succeed**. If people believe they can solve a problem or they can influence others to solve it, they work harder to succeed.

▶ **perservere regardless of negative situations or obstacles**. They are resilient. They bounce back, seeing setbacks as temporary. They expect setbacks and learn from them. They know if continual improvement is to occur, they must persist in seeking solutions.

▶ **be "possibility thinkers."** In attacking the problem, they believe that they will solve it. They just don't know when. They even invent ways to solve problems. Schools will improve depending on the degree of educator efficacy in the school. School staffs with high collective efficacy will make continual improvements by attacking any problems that restrain educational progress.

Checking on the Schools' Locus of Control

The following five statements can serve as a barometer to determine the level of locus of control in a school. "Yes" answers indicate an internal locus of control in your school; "no" answers suggest an external locus of control.

▶ We can do something about most of the problems relative to education at my school.
▶ Few outside events continually control education performance at my school.
▶ We have a positive attitude about solving any education problem.
▶ Educators I work with are involved in solving education problems at all levels.
▶ We can control most of the elements of education in my school environment.

Checking on the School's Efficacy

The following five statements can serve as a barometer to determine the level of efficacy in a school. "Yes" answers indicate high efficacy in your school; "no" answers indicate low efficacy.

▶ We have collective evidence this is a school that learns by inquiry and experience.
▶ We have evidence we deal with root causes of social problems restraining educational improvement.
▶ Once we decide to solve a problem, we will solve this problem.
▶ We think "possibilities" evidenced by "can-do" attitudes.

▶ We express individually and collectively that we may be part of the problem and we are confronting that issue.

Establishing the Right Frame of Mind

One of the first steps in addressing equity in our schools is the change in attitude. From the previous chapters that were devoted to framing the equity perspective; we are aware of the host of diverse backgrounds students arrive at school with and some of the policies and practices that create an inequitable environment. To simply write off a significant number of these students because we can't control the conditions they come from is educational malpractice. If we think we can, or we think we can't, either way we are right. We know thinking we can't is wrong. We know thinking we can't is an excuse that results from old experiences, of being tired of trying, tired of losing, tired of confrontation, conflict, criticism, and confusion. And so it's soothing to say to ourselves, there is nothing we can do about that. It's beyond our control.

Educators must realize that perceptions, beliefs, and attitudes are the greatest obstacle to school improvement—which translates to student success. When educators change their perceptions, beliefs, and attitudes to a positive direction about what can be, schools will improve significantly.

A Philosophical Framework

Whenever the schools' faculty and administration consider a strategy for improvement, a philosophical framework will help guide the initiatives to a more focused and effective outcome.

▶ Someone should always ask, "what impact will this program or activity have on student achievement?" If a clear and plausible answer is not forthcoming, it would be most prudent to drop further consideration of the proposed innovation.
▶ Someone should be prepared to cite research or other evidence from the field indicating that the strategy under consideration has had an impact on valued student achievement—somewhere, at some time. If these connections cannot be made, drop further considerations.
▶ Do not seriously consider an improvement strategy until such time as teachers and administrators generally can agree on the outcome evidence they will look for and accept as evidence of improvement.
▶ Encourage teachers, administrators, and other staff to formulate their individual theories of cause regarding the nature of the problem itself. For example, they are not likely to attribute low math scores to the teachers' distrust of the principal—or each

other. The resulting discussion is likely to produce better ideas about what could and should be done to make a positive impact on the problem.

▶ An improved school is a school that can, in outcome terms, reflect its learning-for-all mission, demonstrate the increasing presence of quality-with-equity. If your goals for school improvement meet this basic vision of school improvement, then the likelihood of success will be realized. Always begin school improvement with the end clearly in mind.

Understanding Change

Fullan (1990) who has written and conducted numerous presentations on "change" offers some assumptions about seeking change in the process of schooling.

▶ Do not assume that your version of what the change should be is the one that should be implemented.

▶ Assume that any significant innovation, if it is to result in change, requires individual implementers to work out their own meaning.

▶ Assume that conflict and disagreement are not only inevitable, but fundamental to successful change.

▶ Assume that people need pressure to change (even in directions that they desire). But, it will only be effective under conditions that allow them to react, to form their own position, to interact with other implementers, to obtain technical assistance, etc.

▶ Assume that effective change takes time; 3-5 years for specific innovations, greater than 5 years for institutional reform.

▶ Do not assume that the reason for lack of implementation is outright rejection of the values embodied in the change, or hard core resistance to all change. There are a number of possible reasons: value rejection, inadequate resources to support implementation, insufficient time elapsed.

▶ Do not expect all or even most people or groups to change. Progress occurs when we take steps that increase the number of people. Our reach should not exceed our grasp...but by such a margin that we fall flat on our face.

▶ Assume that you will need a plan that is based on the above assumptions.

▶ Assume that no amount of knowledge will ever make it totally clear what action should be taken.

▶ Assume that changing the culture of institutions is the real agenda, not implementing single innovations.

As we have discovered throughout the text, there are systemic changes that have to be addressed in our schools in our quest for quality-with-equity schools. We also have become aware that reform (change) is difficult for many reasons. Fullan (1990) identifies some reasons for resistance to change that may be helpful in understanding the difficulty some schools have in "changing" current practice or policy; or to better understand many of the "false starts" schools end-up with in their initiatives. Some of the reasons for resistance may be:

▶ The purpose is not made clear.
▶ The participants are not involved in the planning.
▶ The appeal is based on personal reasons.
▶ The habit patterns of the work group are ignored.
▶ There is poor communication regarding change.
▶ There is fear of failure.
▶ Excessive work pressure is involved.
▶ The cost is too high, or the reward for making the change is seen as inadequate.
▶ The present situation seems satisfactory.
▶ There is a lack of respect and trust in the change initiator.

Classroom and School Improvement

How does staff development reflect upon the improvement of classroom practices and eventually result in to school improvement? As discussed earlier in the chapter, attitudes, beliefs and behaviors must be addressed (efficacy) and the locus of control needs to be addressed internally. Educators grow professionally as learners by (Fullan, Bennett & Rolheiser-Bennett, 1991):

▶ reflecting upon their work with students so that they can better understand what they do.
▶ exploring their classroom experiences to research and develop new practices.
▶ sharing their professional learning about their students with other colleagues.
▶ refining and expanding their repertoire of skills and strategies in response to the needs of their students.

Educators influence classroom improvement by:

▶ focusing on content that reflects educational goals and the needs of the learner.
▶ managing the classroom to prevent and respond to student behavior in ways that create environments that encourage students to learn.
▶ employing a variety of instructional strategies that increase the chances of more appropriately meeting student needs.

▶ employing specific instructional skills that more meaningfully engage learners to be actively involved in learning.

Educators influence school improvement as colleagues by:

▶ establishing norms of continuous improvement and experimentation in their schools.
▶ practicing collegiality that reflects those norms.
▶ supporting change through appropriate structural changes in scheduling and budget, etc.
▶ helping to create a shared purpose and vision.

A Matter of Time

It has even begun to appear that in order for schools to accomplish the improvement now expected of them, the most important single resource may be *time* for teachers involved to meet and talk together on a frequent, regular, and continuing basis (Louis, 1992).

A now-classic study of a decade ago revealed that it is possible to separate successful schools from those that are less so on the basis of the frequency and extent to which teaching practice is discussed, to which teachers design and prepare teaching materials together, to which they in effect teach and critique one another (Little, 1982). Such interaction appears an essential ingredient if teachers are to improve their own practice and if schools are to be good schools. In collegial schools, as another major study confirmed, teacher quality is higher, their commitment stronger, and their rewards greater (Rosenholtz, 1989).

What these findings suggest is that collaboration time for teachers is necessary not just to *change* schools but simply to *maintain* them as good schools. The case for regular, frequent and sustained collegial interaction time for teachers is being made from several different research perspectives, and such time is being asserted as important to the accomplishment of several different purposes: successful school change and improvement; sustaining a good school and facilitating the professional growth of individual teachers; and enabling schools to remain capable of self-renewal.

Several factors will need to be used as criteria for allocating and scheduling the time found for collaboration among teachers (Raywid, 1992).

▶ If we expect teachers to undertake serious collective examination of their programs—and the design of new programs—we can't just add such concerns onto the end of the school day.
▶ The collaborative time must not only come from the "prime time" contained within the school day, but it must represent a sustained slice.

► While some of the time needed can be left for concentrated periods when students are away from school (summer), not all collaborative opportunities can be left to such periods. To capture collaboration this way would deny the opportunity for reflection on daily events which both teacher growth and on-going school renewal require.

► Teachers should not be asked to deduct all the time needed from their personal lives (weekends and holidays), even with compensation.

► There needs to be an on-going, carefully planned program for classroom coverage — as opposed to the more casual arrangements for substitutes.

What ultimately must occur is a change in both public and professional conceptions about teacher productivity. It has long been assumed that teacher's productive time consists of contact time spent with students. Time spent otherwise has been seen as either a bureaucratic necessity or an individual professional obligation or a job benefit. What must change is the idea that for a teacher it is only in the classroom with students that one is productive.

A Continuum of Staff Development

In large measure, changes in staff development have been spurred by a shift in governance to site-based decision making. In moving away from a centralized system, staff development initiatives have the opportunity to move from the current practice of staff development to a more effective model. Below are shifts in the staff development approaches facing schools (KSBE, 1992):

Moving From	Building Toward
► Individual focus	► Equal focus on the individual, building (School Improvement), and the district (Organizational Development)
► Input orientation	► Outcomes orientation
► Staff wishes	► Student needs
► TYNT (This year's new thing)	► Staff development as expansion, refinement, or replacement for current practice
► Focus on good things to do (multiple wants)	► Prioritization based on the needs of students

Moving From	Building Toward
▶ Many ideas, superficially addressed	▶ Doing one thing right before moving on to the next
▶ Current & popular decisions	▶ Research-based decisions
▶ Staff development as going to a workshop or conference (primarily)	▶ Staff development beginning at a workshop, conference, or school site—but follow-up leading to implementation at the school site
▶ Awareness (motivation, inspiration & gains in knowledge)	▶ Skill attainment (Implementation leading to student success)
▶ Resource allocation based on how little or much we want to spend	▶ Resource allocation based on what needs to happen
▶ Expectations: you might want to grow; primarily an opportunity	▶ Expectations: It is your professional responsibility to grow (an obligation)
▶ Decisions based on "gut-level" feelings	▶ Decisions based on student data, school profiles, school improvement plan goals
▶ Reactive to change	▶ Proactive
▶ An activity	▶ A process
▶ Opportunities	▶ Responsibilities
▶ Gaining information	▶ Gaining skills that will impact student success
▶ Rewarding inputs	▶ Rewarding results
▶ Evaluation based on: attendance and satisfaction with the workshop	▶ Assessment based on: What difference does it make for students?
▶ Using evaluation at the end of an activity as a signal that it's over	▶ Using evaluation as a feedback activity loop (assess progress toward goal completion), in order to make decisions whether to re-train, stop training, or move on to a new goal

Moving From	**Building Toward**
▶ Expertise exists primarily outside our school	▶ Building expertise among our staff
▶ Accountability: individuals elect	▶ Accountability: individuals may (if they feel like it, voluntary) elect for themselves, but individuals cannot opt out of school improvement plan goals or district development efforts
▶ Passive participants in the learning	▶ Active partners in the staff development process; I am shaping the intervention

Results-Oriented Staff Development

Effective staff development has a strong research base in what is the most effective approach and strategy to implement. Figure 25 is a summary of the research—Effective Staff Development—by Joyce & Showers (1988) that indicates which combination of strategies are most effective. Figure 26—Results-Oriented Staff Development—indicates which strategy in isolation is least effective in transferring to the worksite (classroom). As you read the chart, do not be concerned about the columns adding up to 100. The question that is posed is reflective to the actual number under each heading that will be able to perform the desired behavior (based on the training strategies incorporated).

Based on our knowledge base of staff development approaches used by schools, most schools engage in the "presentation" strategy. That is, conducting a one-day, one-shot workshop/seminar to share an educational concept or theory based on what the school staff has requested. What has historically taken place in many school settings is a mindset that workshops have done little for changing classroom practices. They have been effective for getting colleagues excited, interested and reinforced about certain theories and concepts; but little has transferred to the classroom application process. It is not uncommon for educators to remark, "this is wonderful, but I don't see any practical application for my classroom." Quite frankly, they are correct. Our knowledge base with regard to getting results from staff development is that the approach taken must not only include presentation, but must also include the following components: demonstration, practice with feedback, coaching and follow-up. Staff development cannot be a one-shot approach; if schools choose this approach, then they should not be surprised if little transfer is evident. As you recall, the Teacher Expectations and Student Achievement (TESA) model was

> · **Knowledge & Theory**
> · **Demonstration**
> · **Practice**
> · **Feedback & Coaching**
> · **Follow-up Training**
>
> Joyce & Showers (1988) Student
> Achievement Through Staff Development

Figure 25. Effective staff development.

briefly explained as an excellent model for addressing the interaction patterns of classroom teachers with their students. The primary reason for TESA's effectiveness is that it follows the training strategies mentioned above. It is a six-month training program, not a one-shot presentation. The approach that schools choose in making staff-development decisions must be based on the research findings about what strategies are most effective and plan accordingly.

OUTCOMES Out of 100 participants, the number that will be able to:			
Training Strategies	**Demonstrate Concept Knowledge**	**Demonstrate a New Behavior**	**Transfer to the Worksite**
Presentation of Concepts & Theory	85	15	10
Provides Demonstration of Behavior	85	18	10
Low-Risk Practice with Feedback	85	80	15
Coaching in Work Setting Regarding Behavior and Decisions	90	90	80

Figure 26. Results-Oriented Staff Development.

Basic Beliefs or Assumptions on Staff Development

▶ All school personnel need staff development throughout their careers.

▶ Significant improvement in educational practice takes considerable time and long-term staff-development programs.

▶ Staff development should focus on improving the quality of school programs.

▶ Educators are motivated to learn new things when they have some control over their learning and are free from threat.

▶ Educators vary widely in their competencies and readiness to learn.

▶ Professional growth requires commitment to new performance norms.

▶ The school is the most appropriate unit or target of change in education.

▶ School districts have the primary responsibility for providing the resources for professional development.

Summary

Faced with a multitude of survey-induced staff wants, schools frequently choose to meet as many of the needs as possible—filling the mostly inadequate staff-development time slots with a smorgasbord of short-term, one-shot awareness sessions. We trade quality for quantity; skill attainment for idea generation; and a flurry of activity for a job well done.

We tend to judge our successes in terms of number of participants, satisfaction ratings regarding the speaker's skills, hours of training, or numbers of recertification hours generated. We seldom ask the critical question: "Has staff development resulted in improved student learning?"

To achieve systemic change schools must focus on the quality of the work or teaching process that allow people to succeed. Moreover, many leading researchers seem to be convinced that a focus on how to achieve "quality-with-equity" in teaching, learning, managing, supervising, communicating, and performing is a key to enhanced individual and team performance.

If we want quality-with-equity, then we need different operating structures and procedures than those we have inherited from the old leadership model of top-down, hierarchical, segmented structures of modern school management. The most promising structure that applies at the classroom level, and the school building level, is a framework that permits common team planning and learning, site-based management, and self-directed teams.

Leaders of corporations, schools, communities, colleges and universities speak about problems associated with the increasingly diverse populations. As we have learned, this can mean anything from ethnicity, gender, socioeconomic status, language, etc. Diversity in learning, however, is not ethnic. Research confirms each individual performs significantly higher when learning in his or her own best way. Regardless of our particular view of diversity, learning organizations—whether school, workplace, or neighborhood center—no longer can emphasize or impose uniformity or the one best way of teaching, training and learning. Today diversity must be understood as an asset, not as a deficit in need of remediation.

Getting people to learn more in less time with fewer resources at higher levels of achievement is a common hope. New performance criteria require changes in what people know, how they learn, and the mechanisms or technologies through which they learn. For example, the curriculum in schools is changing in ways similar to the shift in industry to learning about work processes and system linkages rather than learning short-term or dated skills.

All organizations want to and must create cultures of positive self-esteem with environments free of mockery, put-downs, abusive treatment, stereotypes, demeaning character judgments and violence. We must begin discussing what it means to create a culture in the school that expresses the expectation that people are constantly searching for ways to do their jobs more effectively.

As we become more aware of how change happens, particularly organizational change, then it becomes important to use that knowledge and to look at things from a systemic approach.

Making an impact on student achievement requires that classroom teachers learn and use more appropriate instructional techniques. That will require sustained and focused staff-development programs. Teachers must be assisted as they strive to acquire new skills. Further, their work in the classroom must be supported by ancillary programs such as those that strengthen parent involvement or that increase the number of adults working directly with students.

As more and more emphasis is being placed on the "culturally different" student and the implications for teaching and learning— we must plan, develop and implement staff development initiatives that will generate the results we all strive for— that is, student success. If we continue to offer and accept staff-development initiatives as they have been implemented in the past, the net effect will be minimal.

We already know effective approaches to staff development; what remains to be seen is whether schools are willing to redefine staff development as we know it.

 END NOTES

Bennett, B., and Rolheiser-Bennett, C. "Cooperative Learning: Where Heart Meets Mind," *Education Connections*, Toronto: 1991.

Block, P. *The Empowered Manager.* Jossey-Bass Publishers, San Francisco: CA, 1987.

Cook, L and Friend, M. "Principles for the Practice of Collaboration in Schools," *Preventing School Failure,* 1991.

Fields, Joseph C. "Unlocking the Paralysis of Will." *The School Administrator,* Arlington, VA June 1993.

Fullan, Michael. "What's Worth Fighting For," Commissioned by the Ontario Public School Teacher's Federation. Toronto: 1991.

Fullan, M., Bennett, B., & Rolheiser-Bennett, C. "Linking Classroom and School Improvement." *Educational Leadership,* 1990.

Fullan, M., & Miles, M. "Getting Reform Right: What Works and What Doesn't," *Phi Delta Kappan,* October, 1992.

Joyce, B, and Showers, B. *Student Achievement Through Staff Development.* Longman Publishing Co, Inc., New York, NY 1988.

Kansas State Board of Education. "Outcomes Based Staff Development." Paper developed by Boyer, Crowther, Fast, Kasselman, Nolte, and Wilson. August, 1992.

Little, Judith W. "Norms of Collegiality and Experimentation: Workplace Conditions of School Success," *American Educational Research Journal,* Fall 1982.

Lortie, D. *School Teacher: A Sociological Study.* University of Chicago Press, Chicago, IL, 1975.

Louis, K. & Miles, M. "Improving the Urban High School." Teachers College Press. New York, NY, 1990.

Murphy, J. "Restructuring the Workplace: School Renewal as Cultural Change." In B. Joyce (Ed.) *Changing School Culture Through Staff Development.* Virginia: ASCD, 1990.

November, Alan. "Risky Business," *Electronic Learning,* February, 1993.

Raywid, Mary A. "Making Time to Do Reform." Paper was prepared for the Center on Organization and Restructuring Schools. University of Wisconsin, Madison, Wisconsin, 1992.

Rosenholtz, S. *Teacher's Workplace: The Social Organization of Schools.* Longman Publishers, Inc. New York, NY, 1989.

 ## SUGGESTIONS FOR FURTHER READING

Barth, Roland *Improving Schools from Within.* Jossey-Bass Publishers, Inc. San Francisco, CA, 1990.

Hargreaves, A., & Fullan, M. "Understanding Teacher Development," Teachers College Press. New York, NY, 1992.

Louis, K. & Miles, M. "Improving the Urban High School." Teachers College Press. New York, NY, 1990.

Rosenholtz, S. *Teacher's Workplace: The Social Organization of Schools.* Longman Publishers, Inc. New York, NY, 1989.

Name _____   **Date** _____

DISCUSSION QUESTIONS

1. What is the most common approach for staff development that schools incorporate?

_____

_____

_____

_____

_____

_____

Is it effective? Why or Why Not?

_____

_____

_____

_____

_____

_____

_____

What is a more effective approach? Explain.

_____

_____

_____

_____

_____

_____

_____

2. Do you agree that the teaching profession is one of "isolation"? Explain your response.

_____

_____

_____

_____

_____

_____

_____

3. What is collaboration?

_____

_____

_____

_____

_____

_____

_____

Why aren't schools using this method more frequently? Explain.

_____

_____

_____

_____

_____

_____

_____

4. What is efficacy? How important do you think efficacy is within the organization of a school? Explain.

_____

_____

_____

_____

_____

_____

_____

_____

5. What is "locus of control"? Can schools control their locus of control? Explain.

_____

_____

_____

_____

_____

_____

_____

6. What do we know about "change"?

_____

_____

_____

_____

_____

_____

_____

_____

7. Why is it so difficult to "change" our schools? Explain.

_____

_____

_____

_____

_____

_____

_____

7. Identify five factors from the continuum presented in the chapter that you believe to be paramount in addressing the equity concept in schools. Explain.

_____

_____

_____

_____

_____

_____

_____

_____

_____

_____

_____

_____

_____

INDIVIDUAL AND SMALL GROUP WORK

Characteristics I Value in a Colleague

The chapter discussed the importance of collaboration. We do have to work with others often in many work environments, including the schools. Below is a list of qualities or characteristics that might describe someone you work with (or could work with). Read through the list and select the three most desirable or important characteristics and the three least important or desirable.

Each group member should take two minutes to explain their choices and the reasons for them. After that, the group as a whole should make an attempt to arrive at group consensus on the three most important or desirable and the three least important or desirable. *It may be difficult for you to select the three most and least desirable dispositions, but force yourself to make the necessary adjustment.* (Record your responses on the following page)

1. Listens carefully and communicates effectively
2. Friendly and sociable
3. Orderly and efficient
4. Good sense of humor
5. Admits errors openly and honestly
6. Is creative and has new ideas
7. Shows respect and consideration for others
8. Uses praise frequently
9. Does what you want them to
10. Is willing to compromise
11. Never becomes angry, stays calm and cool
12. Follows rules and procedures
13. Says what he/she thinks; is frank
14. Honest and trustworthy
15. Helpful and supportive of others
16. Independent and self-reliant
17. Punctual and responsible
18. Strives to do her/his best

Most Important or Desirable (individual):

1. _____

2. _____

3. _____

Most Important or Desirable (group):

1. _____

2. _____

3. _____

Least Important or Desirable (individual):

1. _____

2. _____

3. _____

Least Important or Desirable (group):

1. _____

2. _____

3. _____

INDIVIDUAL AND SMALL GROUP WORK

Promoting Ownership

Listed below you will find recommendations that have been made by teachers, administrators and university personnel for promoting ownership of school improvement initiatives. Review the list and identify the three things which are most likely to promote ownership and the three that are least likely to promote ownership. **Force yourself to make these choices.**

Once you've made your choices, each person in your group should take approximately two minutes to indicate which were their top and bottom three choices and why. *After everyone* has shared their choices, *try to reach consensus* on the top three you all believe will most likely result in faculty ownership of your initiative. (Record your responses on the page following the choices)

Selecting Ways of Promoting Ownership

1. Involve school faculty (teachers and administrators) in the development of improvement goals for the school.
2. Relate the improvement goals more directly to the day-to-day problems and concerns of the faculty.
3. Involve teachers in planning the who, what, where and how of the staff development to achieve the improvement goals.
4. Use peers whenever possible to conduct staff development.
5. Make participation in staff development mandatory, but involvement in specific goals and activities a matter of choice.
6. Involve school faculty in the selection of projects and programs to achieve improvement goals.
7. Provide opportunities for peer coaching after training.
8. Increase the funds in the district budget to support local school improvement activities.
9. Provide recognition and rewards for those who actually learn and implement school improvement plans.
10. Provide more faculty time (during school hours) to work together on planning and implementing school improvement initiatives.
11. Increase the central office support for school-by-school rather than district-wide improvement.

Most Likely to Promote (individual):

1. _____

2. _____

3. _____

Most Likely to Promote (group):

1. _____

2. _____

3. _____

Least Likely to Promote (individual):

1. _____

2. _____

3. _____

Least Likely to Promote (group):

1. _____

2. _____

3. _____

INDIVIDUAL AND SMALL GROUP WORK

Purposes of Staff Development

Below is a breakdown of five areas that staff development may fulfill. Individually assign a percentage of the role staff development should play in any or all of the five areas. After you have placed a percentage of purpose; share the information with your group. Then, your group is to come to a consensus on the percentages that should be assigned.

Individual	**Group**
Inspiration:	Inspiration:
_____ %	_____ %
Enrichment:	Enrichment:
_____ %	_____ %
Cadre Training:	Cadre Training:
_____ %	_____ %
School Improvement:	School Improvement:
_____ %	_____ %
Organizational Development:	Organizational Development:
_____ %	_____ %

Moving Forward  10

Introduction

The mid-1990s are alive with the spirit of change in our system of education. The future of education will be affected by the recommendations of the various commissions, studies and task forces cited throughout this book. To what extent change takes place remains to be seen. It would appear that the tidal wave of reforms will produce basic changes in how teachers are educated, in how their career opportunities will be structured, and in how elementary and secondary schools will be organized. The future is bright and challenging as well.

It is easy to criticize America's educational system because, as we have seen throughout this text, discrepancies between the *ideals* (as embodied in the slogan of quality-with-equity) and *reality* (as documented by our inequities) are plainly visible. The search for solutions to those problems has never been an easy one.

Over the past several years, extensive research and numerous studies have been conducted pertaining to schools and the issues of race, ethnicity, culture, language, laws, religion, sex, age, economic status and the varying abilities of students. These past and present efforts have created inroads in establishing the meaning, value and virtue of equity. However, like other educational doctrines, any evidence of a uniform acceptance and incorporation are the exception, rather than the rule. Where quality-with-equity is evident, the research indicates that the intended outcomes are learned by *all* students, regardless of the issues cited above.

There is a gap between the recommendations or suggestions presented throughout the previous chapters and the specific information that schools and school districts need in order to begin an equity-improvement process. Chapter 10—**Moving Forward** attempts to provide some direction for filling this void. This chapter is intended to assist school personnel and planning groups in identifying the various links and present the vast array of possibilities for improving equity. Those who administer or coordinate these changes will need to have information on questions such as: What would a strategic plan look like? What area(s) is involved in the equity-improvement process? What factors need to be in identified at the beginning? This chapter is designed to address these questions and assist individuals involved in the school improvement process. The chapter is designed to further build upon the concept of quality-with-equity; with the notion that as educators we must take a personal role and responsibility. We need to choose to be involved, to lend our efforts and to possess an eagerness to make a difference.

As we have learned, equity is not a course, subject area, nor is it restricted to simply infusing one's own curriculum. Equity (a multidimensional concept) does have a link to every facet of the educational system. This multifaceted concept will require a detailed process and strategic plan, but is essentially based on four simple statements. Approaching equity from the viewpoint of an individual educator; as a department; or as a total school staff—these four statements could serve as the foundation for improving equity.

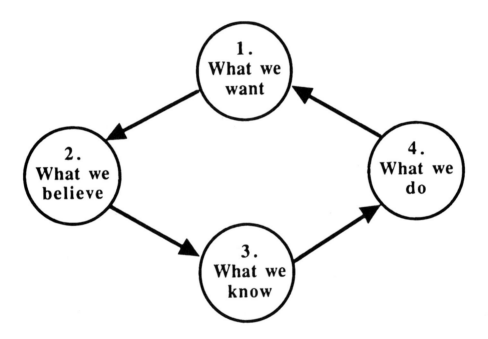

What do we want? From our students: Do we have a common understanding of the goals, objectives and outcomes that we expect our students to achieve? What do we want for ourselves? Do we have a common mission in our school? Do we have a vision of what we would like our school to become? What is it? And, more importantly, what does it mean to us?

What do we believe? Do we believe that all students can be successful learners? Do we believe that we can teach *all* students? Do we believe the research evidence concerning the teaching and learning processes? Do we believe that our schools must continually strive to improve?

What do we know? What is the evidence to support equity? What does the research literature suggest about teaching and learning? What is the knowledge base that guides our thinking and planning? What do we know about the process of change? What do we know that works? What do we know that doesn't work?

What do we do? How do we plan? Where do we start? Who makes the decisions? How do we know if we make a difference? Are we willing to take a risk? Do we allow for flexibility (trial & error)? How do we assess our progress?

These four statements could be the foundation for a total school-improvement process. Although the statements are simple, the process needed to answer each is more complex. This chapter is organized to provide a designed strategic planning process with specific examples on how to approach improvement. The process of improvement will be addressed from three different levels:

I. Equity Action Plans
Individual Lesson Plans or Activities

II. Classroom Applications
Analysis of Policies and Practices

III. School-Wide Applications
Analysis of Policies and Practices

First, at the individual level, **Equity Action Plans** are outlined to assist and guide you in the development of specific plans, lessons or activities that can be incorporated within your teaching level(s) or area(s). Second, policies and practices within the classroom is an extension of the individual lesson plan or activity which analyzes **Classroom Applications;** for example, this may involve examining your policies with grouping students, instructional materials, teaching styles, learning styles, classroom climate or an evaluation of the curriculum. The third link is the **School-Wide Applications** which may examine: administrative support, school mission, on-going assessment of school programs, course scope and sequence, outcomes, enrollment patterns in courses (upper and lower division courses), support services, drop-outs, suspensions, and remedial programs.

This linkage from the individual classroom teacher to school-wide application is a necessary stages that will address the four fundamental statements of: what we want, what we believe, what we know and what we do.

Developing a Capacity for Change

The first stage toward equity improvement is that of assessing current beliefs, attitudes, policies and practices that are prevalent in the school. The second stage is the design and implementation of a plan that will ensure the concept of equity within the total school improvement process.

Research studies (Clayton, 1985) that focus on the school improvement process do so because they believe the way a change is instituted determines how effective and long lasting the change will be. Several studies, cited in the previous chapter, in fact, suggest that one of the most important improvements a school can make is to develop a permanent capacity for change, a capacity that would allow the school to continually improve itself and to respond to the changing needs of both its students and the outside world. This capacity consists of the development of a strategic planning team on an agreed-upon process for articulating needs, then designing and implementing changes to meet them.

Developing a Strategic Plan

Most leading educators agree that strategic planning is the key to reforming American education. But what exactly is strategic planning? How do we do it? And what does it have to do with equity?

Basically, strategic planning means skillful planning. It means integrating short-term plans with long-term objectives. It means putting yourself in the most advantageous position for achieving desired results. Strategic planning is a process for answering three basic questions: Where do we want to go? How are we going to get there? and How will you know when you've arrived? (Kinnaman, 1991)

Where does equity fit in this scenario? To begin with, equity, perhaps more than any other single factor, has created the need for strategic planning. In a single generation, thousands upon thousands of students are failing within our system of education. As the previous chapters have suggested, without a systemic change in the delivery of educational services as we currently know them, the cycle of educational failure will continue. There is a disproportionate number of educational failures among ethnic minority groups, low-income groups and limited English proficient groups. That is not to suggest that only those students are failing in our system of education; but their numbers are exceedingly high as compared to the rest of the student population.

As the previous chapters have suggested, for the most part K-12 education has failed to make the transition from the industrial age paradigm policies and practices to the information age demands of today's society. Ironically, although the diversity of our student population is a primary cause of much of the current crisis in education, it (diversity) can also be a key ingredient in its solution.

This strategic plan is based on two fundamental concerns. First, it is an appeal to consider carefully, at all levels of planning, how the equity concept can be applied to improve education. Second, it is an appeal to avoid isolating equity planning from planning for other school-improvement initiatives.

Building the Strategic Planning Team

The first step in strategic planning is to put together a planning team to determine the overall direction in which the district will move with regard to everything from curriculum to school organization. Most strategic models emphasize the need for a strong planning team, but they differ considerably with regard to the makeup and function of the group. A synthesis of several strategic planning models designed for education reveal several key factors to consider in building a strategic planning team.

Scope of the Plan. Strategic planning needs to occur at a variety of levels (i.e., society/community, school district, individual school). Generally, planning should begin at the highest or broadest level. For example, planning should occur with regard to the overall needs and goals of the community before a specific strategic plan is developed for an individual school. This is not to suggest that planning shouldn't occur concurrently at more than one level, but that the specific goals at lower levels should be consistent with the broader goals at higher levels.

Makeup of the Team. For the team to have the power to effect systemic change in the district or school, it needs to include representatives of every group that has a stake in the plan. It is important to have the "decision makers," involved, but equally important are those individuals who wield less official power, but who can clearly articulate the needs and interest of major constituent groups. Parents, teachers, students, social service providers and religious leaders generally can fill this role.

In all likelihood, there will be teams already in place in most districts to focus on specific high-priority areas (i.e., outcomes-based education, gang activity, drug and alcohol education, authentic assessment), it is essential to include leadership from each of these teams, as well as from each level of schooling. This ensures that the efforts of these groups will be united around a common vision which will encourage them to plan and grow collaboratively rather than in isolation.

Team Size. Strategic planning groups can number anywhere from about a dozen members to well over 70. Proponents of some planning models advocate large teams to ensure that every constituent group is adequately represented. The equity issue is no different, but there are inherent problems with large teams. They are harder to manage and they tend to operate more slowly and inefficiently than smaller teams. A large team, simply by virtue of its size, tends to generate more motion than movement.

Ideally, the strategic planning team should be kept as small as possible while still including representation from every group that the plan will affect. One way to control team size is to include a number of team members who can effectively represent multiple constituent groups (i.e., a business representative who is also a school board member or a city official who is also a parent).

Methods of Selection. There are three basic options for selecting members of the strategic planning team: Ask for volunteers, have the superintendent or others in a leadership role recruit representatives from the different constituent groups, or ask the groups themselves to select individuals to represent them on the team. While volunteers should rarely be turned away, a combination of the other two approaches is generally more effective. With some of the larger constituent groups (i.e., teachers and parents) a formal election process might be appropriate. With other groups (i.e., city government or the teacher's union) there already will be official leaders who can be approached to participate or to appoint others who can represent them.

A recruited team or elected team is more likely than a team of volunteers to enter the planning process with a sense of mission and to be perceived with respect and cooperation by the community at large. The result is that such a team is better positioned to accomplish more in less time.

Laying the Groundwork. Before setting out to answer the questions, "Where are we going?" and "How will we get there?" the strategic planning team must focus on preliminary tasks: conducting a needs assessment to determine specific areas and issues that are most important to address; and articulating an underlying philosophy of education that will guide its actions and recommendations (Kinnaman, 1991).

Needs Assessment: Using a variety of methods, both formal and informal, the strategic planning team should gather data about the following: the district problem areas (i.e., gaps between where it is and where it wants to be); its successes (including on-going needs that are currently being met but that might be jeopardized by changes in school structures or functions); and built-in barriers to the types of changes that might be necessary to address the problems.

Large numbers of people from each key constituent groups should be polled with regard to their perceptions in each of these three areas. Not only does this provide the team with valuable information, it also provides the community with a sense of ownership in the process of change. A university faculty member or state department of education consultant might be recruited to oversee this portion of the needs assessment process.

A Guiding Philosophy: The central task of the strategic planning team is to respond to the needs identified by the community with a clear vision of the future it proposes to construct. An important first step is to identify the underlying philosophy that will shape this vision. With a team made up of highly qualified professionals, each team member is likely to begin with a set of strong beliefs about effective education. The challenge is for the team members to reach consensus on the central beliefs that will guide them and to articulate these to the general public. Here are examples of fundamental belief statements (found in various commission reports, school district mission statements and current policy statements) that might result from this process:

▶ Basic skills for all students in the information age include the ability to solve problems, to think critically and to communicate effectively.

▶ More effective teaching and increased student achievement are not likely to occur without better and more versatile methods of teaching and learning.

▶ Learning at all levels should be meaningful and should involve students actively in acquiring and applying academic skills.

Formulating Strategic Goals

With the results of a needs assessment to narrow their focus and a basic philosophy to guide them, the members of the strategic planning team are ready to turn their vision into a set of outcome-based strategic goals. Each broad goal the team sets generally needs to be supported by more specific goals, as well as strategies for meeting the goal.

For example, given the belief statement above and a needs assessment that identified lack of student motivation and inadequate preparation for real-world jobs as key problems, one strategic goal might be: All students will participate regularly in interdisciplinary units and in projects that involve solving real-life problems. Specific subgoals or strategies might include a requirement that all teachers at the secondary level meet together in multidisciplinary planning teams; a suggestion that students at all grade levels have the opportunity to participate in apprenticeships (to parents, local businesses, or staff members within the school who can help them apply academic skills in a real-world setting); and compiling a list of recommended computer-based programs that emphasize real-world problems.

This phase of the planning process is extremely challenging because it means rethinking the entire organization and operation of the typical American school. To formulate effective goals, the planning team must focus on desired outcomes, not current practices; on possibilities, not constraints; on impact, not cost. Here are some guidelines that can assist with this difficult process:

▶ There are no sacred cows. The parameters of strategic planning have to be wide enough so that no program and no structure is immune from review and change. You can't, for example, support systemic change but say that changes to the system can't affect the way in which the Chapter 1 program is run, or that the fourth-grade curriculum is untouchable, or that the daily bell schedule at the high school can't be changed. After re-examination, you might very well decide that certain existing programs and structures are successful and need not be changed. However, no program or structure should be treated as "hands-off" from the start.

▶ Listen to the experts. Given its extremely broad mandate, there's a real danger that a strategic planning team can get bogged down in details such as "What types of instructional materials should we buy?" There is no way that a team of 10-20 members can jointly arrive at every specific goal and strategy to be included in the plan. Instead, subcommittees or separate groups with appropriate expertise should be called upon to propose goals and strategies to the entire team. By delegating such details to experts and then working together as an entire group to support and possibly modify the experts' recommendations, the team manages to remain efficient while still putting its official stamp on a strategic plan to which every team member is committed.

▶ Build community support as the work progresses. The strategic planning team needs to communicate its vision and strategic goals to taxpayers and other decision makers. If the planning team can successfully build consensus regarding the need for change and the likelihood that its plans will lead to outcomes valued by the community, it will be far more likely to receive cooperation once the implementation phase begins.

▶ Set an appropriate timeline. This perhaps the biggest obstacle to successful strategic planning. The tendency is to get "stuck" in the initial planning phase. The statement "you can't steer a parked car" is a good description of the challenge faced by planning teams. There is no one best timeline for the initial phase of strategic planning, but it is probably best to avoid strategic planning models in which planning can occur for a year or more without any actions being taken. In fact, it is a safe bet that if you plan for even just a few months without taking any action, you will begin to lose momentum. One way of speeding up the process without cutting corners is to drop the idea that a strategic plan must be complete before it can be approved and acted upon. An alternate approach is to focus on one or two high-priority areas first and then, once goals and strategies have been set in these areas and the implementation process has begun, move on to other portions of the plan (Kinnaman, 1991).

Implementing the Plan

A forward-looking strategic plan is not only difficult to formulate, it is also likely to meet with some serious resistance when it comes time for implementation. After all, an effective plan will demand changes in school structure and function, and such systemic change is always difficult to attain. Following are some general strategies that are likely to assist with the process:

▶ **Build Frameworks.** One of the most effective ways of implementing system-wide change is for the planning team to define a basic framework for achieving a particular strategic goal and then to allow the school(s) implementing the plan considerable latitude to build the framework.

▶ **Use an incremental approach.** Considering the fiscal realities and resistance to change inherent in most school districts, another key to success is an incremental approach. Leaders within each building might decide to begin with a specific grade level in year one and then, once those teachers are fully "trained" and feel comfortable with the new strategy, move on to other grade levels. Even when a new structure or strategy has been implemented officially, the institutionalization of the innovation might require further incremental steps. Understanding the importance of transitional time is crucial to the successful implementation of change. If the new system is superior to the old one, and if those who are expected to use it are adequately supported in making the transition, almost everyone, including those who were reluctant initially, will get on board willingly.

▶ **Integrate initiatives.** Strategic goals that require systemic change are more likely to be accomplished if they are integrated among several important school improvement initiatives. Throughout the implementation process the strategic planning team needs to continue to foster interdisciplinary cooperation and ownership to attain its desired outcomes.

▶ **Build support.** No matter what the strategic goal is, the primary role of the planning team during the implementation phase is to create a climate of support—especially among the teachers and administrators most affected (and potentially most threatened) by the proposed changes. While it is important for the planning team to step back and leave day-to-day decisions about implementation in the hands of the practitioners, it is also important for the team to be available when questions or problems arise—and be prepared to re-think a particular goal or strategy if feedback warrants it.

Assessing Where You Are

By its nature, strategic planning is both cyclical and on-going. In developing a three-year or five-year strategic plan, it's important not to assume that there is a clear end-point to the process. In a sense, you never really do "arrive," but it's important to stop and look around at both predetermined and random points along the way you've chosen to take.

What you're looking for can be expressed in two questions: To what extent has the plan been successful in achieving each of the strategic goals? and How happy are you with the progress?

There are a variety of methods for answering these questions. The most formal way to look around is to measure student achievement through standardized testing. However, before you make decisions about the merit of your strategic plan on the basis of standardized testing, you need to be sure you understand what the test is measuring. If your strategic plan is focused on different types of achievement than the test measures, you need to select a different instrument. Furthermore, even if the test is compatible with your goals, it is important for the strategic planning team to gauge the time needed before the strategic plan can be expected to yield its intended results. A strategic plan that requires dramatic changes in school structures or functions is most likely to yield level, or even lower, achievement scores during its initial implementation. It is also highly recommended that at least two different forms of assessment be conducted. To totally rely on the "standardized" test is to rely on outside sources to conduct an assessment that has local perspectives to be measured (Kinnaman, 1991).

Assessing student attitudes provides another important look around. Has the strategic plan increased student motivation, effort or enthusiasm for learning? Student attitudes can be measured using formal instruments, but it is equally helpful to build a less formal "portfolio" of student attitudes through such techniques as interviews and teacher observations. Additionally, valuable inferences about student attitudes can be made from such data as truancy rates. Other variables that should be measured include the impact of the strategic plan on interaction between students, transfer of learning, teacher attitudes and behaviors and student/teacher communication.

Adjustments and modifications are an expected part of the planning process, and the flexibility to make changes based on the results of on-going evaluation should be built into any strategic plan. Just as older programs should not be protected from change, no strategic goal should be viewed as not being able to be refined or retained if a new direction would be preferable.

Developing the "Can-Do" Approach

The following describes a common expression when discussing change at any level—how many times have we heard the comment "I will believe it when I see it." I suspect that this is a fairly common reaction, which supports my claim that if we don't believe in what it is that we want changed, any real systemic change will not occur.

```
┌─────────────────────────────────────────┐
│  ┌───────────────────────────────────┐  │
│  │                                   │  │
│  │        A Vision for Change        │  │
│  │                                   │  │
│  │  "I will see it when I believe it" │  │
│  │                                   │  │
│  │               vs.                 │  │
│  │                                   │  │
│  │  "I will believe it when I see it" │  │
│  │                                   │  │
│  └───────────────────────────────────┘  │
└─────────────────────────────────────────┘
```

General assumptions for accomplishing change in our schools with regard to equity are based on the following:

▶ Planning for equity improvement is a process, not a prescription.

▶ Planners should start with a long-term view based on their vision of quality-with-equity, not with a single problem.

▶ There is no one vision of quality-with-equity, each school must develop an individual vision.

▶ Basic to the equity-improvement planning process is the establishment of a strategic planning group that represents all who will be involved in making the improvements.

▶ The plan of action developed by the planning team should specify clear objectives for equity-improvement activities, anticipated costs of the activities, personnel responsible for carrying out each activity, and how and when each action will be evaluated.

▶ Equity improvement plans should be flexible enough to change as obstacles arise.

Assessing Equity: An Individual Equity-Action Plan

As the previous chapters suggested, one can become overwhelmed with the vast amount of information that should be considered with the concept of equity. With this acknowledgment comes a sense of not knowing where to begin. The strategic planning team can address this real concern by its very existence. However, there are factors that individuals also can be involved with that may net some needed results at the personal level. One such method can be an individual equity-action plan. It may indeed require a period of time to organize, plan, and develop the necessary strategies for an individual equity-action plan.

The first step is to identify one area, issue, group or topic under the large umbrella of equity to incorporate within your instructional area. One very important decision that should be made at the beginning is to limit yourself to one specific area, issue, group or topic. This strategy will force you to focus more specifically, which will produce a greater likelihood of success. Certainly, the ideal is first to understand the process of designing an action plan and becoming comfortable with it, and then, to begin the process of adding and modifying other areas, issues, groups or topics to your overall instruction—a total integration is the ultimate goal. This process is not intended to give the impression that teachers need only to integrate and diversify their curricular offerings to be equitable, but rather it provides a strategy for evaluating and improving our own classroom(s) or subject area(s).

Levels of Equity Understanding

The analysis of one's curriculum or teaching area should also examine the levels of equity understanding that teachers and students need to move through to gain the desired competence and outcomes. Working definitions of these levels are:

▶ **Awareness—Consciousness Level**. What should students feel or believe? Example: Research clearly shows that teachers can make a difference; regardless of the background of the student(s).
▶ **Knowledge—Content Level**. What should students know? Example: Examination and study of different learning styles and classroom arrangements could capitalize on students needs.
▶ **Skill—Implementation Level**. What should students be able to do? Example: Design a unit which allows students to utilize different learning styles to arrive at the unit objectives and outcomes.

What are the outcomes that you expect from your plan? Is it intended to provide your students with a level of awareness, specific content information, or teach a skill? Using these levels, a detailed and specific plan can be designed. Too often, we design lesson plans or activities in our classrooms that are too general and the proposed outcomes are unclear. On the following pages is an outline of a process that may assist you in organizing an individual equity-action plan.

EQUITY ACTION PLAN FORM

Name: _____

Level: _____ Elementary _____ Middle _____ Secondary

_____ Postsecondary _____ Special populations

Subject Area: _____

Area of Concern: _____

Method for change I will use: _____

Level of plan: _____ Awareness _____ Knowledge _____ Skill

Desired outcome of your plan: _____

_____

_____

What are your objectives? (Write them in measurable terms)

Objective 1: _____

_____

_____

Objective 2: _____

_____

_____

Objective 3: _____

_____

_____

Objective 4: _____

_____

_____

Instructional Materials (titles, year of publication, type of material(s) that you will use with your plan):

_____

_____

_____

Additional Resources (displays, hands-on materials, worksheets, software, activities, teacher-made materials, speakers, consultants):

_____

_____

_____

Assessment Procedures: (outcomes)

How will you know if and when your objectives have been met?
Method:_____

_____

_____

Stumbling Blocks:

What constraints might hinder the implementation of your plan?

_____

_____

_____

Personal Reflection (Individual Analysis)	Instructional Materials	Allowing for Differences
• Mission of the School vs. Teaching Philosophy • Beliefs about Teaching & Learning • Expectations for Students • Management Style • Discipline Policies	• Analysis of Curriculum • Use of Supplementary Materials • Teacher-made Materials • Use of Informal Curriculum • Scope and Sequence • Outcomes Based • Mastery Learning • Field-Based Experiences • Community Resources	• Classroom Climate • Learning Styles • Teaching Styles • Grouping Placement Policies • Interaction or Patterns with Students (Perceived highs & lows) • Assessment

Figure 27. Classroom Applications.

Assessing Equity: Classroom Applications

The second stage in the equity-improvement process is to examine and analyze classrooms, specific levels, subject areas or departments. This stage is designed to answer two questions: (1) what are we currently doing? and, (2) what area(s) could we improve upon? Figure 27—**Classroom Applications** is a *sample* of the levels of analysis that could be addressed:

▶ *personal reflection*—beliefs on teaching and learning, expectations, management style, discipline policies, understanding organizational change and assessment methods.

▶ *instructional materials*—analysis of the curriculum for equity perspectives, criteria for evaluation, supplementary materials, teacher-made materials, technology and software and use of the informal curriculum as a teaching tool.

▶ *allowance for differences*—classroom climate, learning styles, instructional skills, teaching styles, analysis of classroom interaction patterns with students, pull-out policies and grouping of students.

Each classroom teacher should be visited to determine what equity concerns he/she considers most relevant for their particular area and, in general, for the school. The communication between an individual strategic-planning team member and the classroom teacher also may serve to sensitize faculty to the greater range of issues and reinforce the importance of their role and responsibility. Also, many times individual faculty members are hesitant to speak out in larger settings. Finally, this process allows the individual faculty member to clarify and amplify any information they provided.

A list of questions that are to be considered should be prepared before visiting with individual classroom teachers. (Disseminating the questions prior to the visit is recommended.) Some sample questions are shown below:

▶ What students are most likely to enroll in your classes (middle and secondary levels)?

▶ Are there any prerequisites that prohibit certain students from being in your classroom?

▶ Does the equity concept relate to your grade level, course or subject area? If so, how? If not, why not?

▶ What is your policy or practice in sorting students within your classroom for certain activities or instructional methods?

▶ Do your instructional materials reflect an equity perspective?

▶ With regard to equity, in what strategies or methods do you believe your course or subject area is strong?

▶ Do you believe quality-with-equity is evident in your department or subject area? In the school? Why or why not?

▶ Are there any special instructional skills or methods used to address the needs of low-achieving students? What are they?

▶ What method(s) is/are used for the evaluation, promotion and placement of students? Are they consistent between teachers and departments?

▶ Generally, who are the students who do well in your classroom?

▶ Generally, who are the students that don't do as well? Can you explain this?

▶ What forms of assessment do you use?

Grade Levels/Subject Areas or Departmental Analysis

Figure 28—**Analyzing Your Department** outlines the process for improving specific grade levels/subject areas or departments. This model can easily be adapted to fit any educational level (elementary, middle, secondary and postsecondary). As mentioned earlier, there is no blueprint that exists for equity improvement that will work for every school, nor should there be one. The differences among schools would preclude the package deal from working for everyone, but direction and guidance is essential.

Assessing Equity: School-Wide Applications

It is important to avoid presenting the equity concept in airtight compartments; it should instead be integrated into all content areas and policies and practices of the school—the

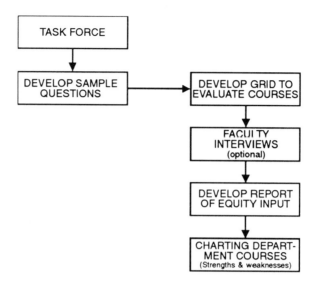

Figure 28. Analyzing your department.

multidimensional linkage. The areas, issues, questions, problems, knowledge level(s) and skill level(s) which are a part of any concept can be most effectively understood when all faculty are involved. Too many times, schools attempt to incorporate or improve concepts and often they fail—primarily because a designed plan and purpose was not organized well enough. The following proposed model hopefully will allow you and your colleagues to have at the very least a direction, a guide and a focus to the equity-improvement process. (See Figure 29—**School-Wide Applications**).

Guiding Principles

In order for any concept to succeed, the administration and the faculty must express enthusiasm and support for it; the equity-improvement process is no different. The concept should be initiated by the school or department before support can be generated from school policymakers. If the outcomes are understood and supported by the school policymakers, support from the school board is likely to follow, enhancing the probability of greater support.

There are many critical issues and decision points in the improvement process—decision points such as adopting a vision, identifying goals, determining priorities, establishing timelines, etc. (as mentioned in the strategic planning team section of this chapter). In each instance, commitment and consensus should be attained.

Administrative (District and Building Level)	Assessment	Faculty and Staff
• Level of Support • Priority Level • On-going Process • Contact Person • On-going Evaluation	• Disaggregation of Student Data • Course Offerings • Enrollment Trends • Grouping Patterns or Policies • Retentions, Suspensions, Referrals, Drop-outs. • Special Populations • Support Services • Scope and Sequence • Assessment Practices • Grading Policies	• Needs & Priorities • Staff Development • Teacher Assessment • Teaching Loads • Teaching Rotations • Diversity of Staff • Master Teachers

Figure 29. School-Wide Applications.

The faculty is the backbone of the improvement process. The faculty, the students and the community must function well together. Failure to have a high percentage of faculty support likely will lead to less than satisfactory results.

The school or department must have the flexibility to move as slowly or as rapidly as the conditions warrant. To try and force a new concept on everyone at the same time is not in the best interest of the faculty, students or the basic tenets upon which the equity-improvement process is built.

Individuals must not only be allowed to be different, but differences must be appreciated, supported and encouraged. Assuming common goals, individuals can make unique contributions by utilizing their own expertise, personality and content.

If the faculty members are informed about and involved with the concept and improvement process, it becomes a part of them and they begin to own it. Ownership immediately makes them concerned about the success of the improvement process.

If school-wide equity improvement is to be successful, the diverse perspectives of the school community must be incorporated. While it would be impossible to reach consensus on each and every item, faculty and staff rapport may assist the planning team in drafting and implementing a well-rounded, meaningful set of goals. The diversity of opinions also serves as an example of what equity is all about—different people working together for a common purpose. The faculty and staff are a rich resource and the basis upon which equity for school improvement is built. Failure to make significant use of the faculty and staff will result in a much less effective school improvement plan. Even the smallest schools are diverse and complex and from them meaningful learning can emerge if planning is careful and thoughtful. However, a word of caution is provided: Focus on the *best* interest for all, versus, the *special* interest of some.

The issues, questions, problems, knowledge and skills which are all a link to equity, can be most effectively understood when all faculty and disciplines are utilized. Thus, interdisciplinary teaching, collaboration and learning gives all teachers the opportunity to contribute uniquely to the equity-improvement process.

The greatest gains can be made when the faculty is involved in establishing, monitoring and assessing the equity-improvement process. Since the concept is not curricular in the sense that instructional materials are provided, the success of the plan depends heavily upon the staff's understanding of the equity vision, goals and outcomes and their willingness to develop and improve all students' learning experiences. Faculty and staff members must be willing to define their own professional growth needs. While external assessment may be used to assist the staff in evaluating school improvement effectiveness, some monitoring of the plan should be a staff responsibility.

Gauging Progress

As discussed earlier, the process of equity improvement many times will have to be incremental. To see lasting systemic change in our schools that benefits *all* students takes a tremendous amount of time and energy. As I have often said, "No one will remember how quick you did it, they will remember how well you did it." The process of equity improvement at the individual, classroom, and school-wide level is no different. A *sample* of questions to determine progress are briefly outlined:

▶ Disaggregate student data—what students are enrolled in these specific grade levels, subject areas or departments? (ethnicity, gender, income levels, disabilities).

▶ Are course outcomes reflective of equity?

▶ What are the policies and practices for sorting students into various classes?

▶ Are supplementary materials used? If so, are they equitable in their perspective?

▶ Are there gaps or overlapping of content within grade levels, subject areas or courses?

▶ Are instructional materials evaluated for equity perspectives? How often? By whom?

▶ Are there prerequisites for course placements? If so, what impact does that have on perceived low-achieving students? On the perceived high-achieving student?

▶ Is equity-related "content" integrated throughout the course, in instructional materials and in subject areas? On what criteria is this based?

▶ What professional staff development initiatives are in place? What is the research base with regard to the initiatives planned?

▶ What different method(s) are used for assessment, promotion and placement of students?

▶ What students are successful? What students are not as successful?

▶ What evidence do you have? Is the data disaggregated? If so, how?

Summary

During this century, perhaps no concept has given educators more difficulty than that of equality. As teachers and administrators, we have gradually come to realize the inequities that have existed in our educational systems for so long. Segregated schools invariably penalized Asians, African Americans, American Indians and Hispanics. Although boys and girls attend school together, too frequently we educate them by traditional images of male and female roles. We are still far from genuine educational equity. Our human responses have seemed to function much like a pendulum. Where once we educated only the few and ignored many, we now attempt to educate all, but from a single and traditional perspective. By doing so, we mistake uniformity for equality. Equity is a positive response in that it broadens perspectives and provides a more meaningful and effective education for all.

Implementation of a concept to accommodate the necessary competencies for an equity perspective will require significant changes in policies, practices and academic content than currently are provided. These changes will affect all facets of the educational program and will require the cooperation of a large segment of the academic community. Internally, the faculty of each school must become aware, sensitive and committed to the concept of equity with school improvement. Anything less than a concentrated, committed and cooperative effort will result in mere tinkering with the existing program(s).

When changes are small or when only a few people are involved, our procedures for monitoring, assessing and revising plans can be informal. Implementing changes at a classroom, department, or school-wide level requires more systematic procedures. We need to learn continually from our experiences and the experiences of others.

Improving schools has become a national goal. National commissions, governors, corporation executives and educators are determined that education must change. Some of us contend that schools are more successful than the public seems to think, but we also want them to be even better.

There is much less agreement, however, about the kinds of changes that are needed—and about how those changes should be made. Much has been written already about what schools should do: i.e., raise standards, ensure quality-with-equity, identify and better serve at-risk students, examine teacher training programs/teacher expectations and ensure purposeful outcomes for all students.

Some of those who advocate these changes have suggestions for how to implement them, but most have little to say on the subject. It is a matter of either convincing educators to try something new or having some authority outline the plan. This chapter has identified the necessary stages for assessing and improving upon equity; and has offered specific strategies for the initial stages.

One of my beliefs is that it takes the energy of a lot of people, over a fairly long period of time, to improve a school. Primarily, this chapter is written for educators responsible for an improvement effort in their own community: for all educators engaged in school reform, for the classroom teacher, for the department head trying to change the emphasis of the department, and for the administrator responsible for the new staff evaluation process.

The contents of this chapter also have important implications for those who train teachers and administrators, for those who provide expertise and support to schools from the outside, and for those who make decisions that schools have to implement. Schooling and its improvement is everyone's business. It is critical that those who are involved both directly and indirectly know how to make things happen.

 ## END NOTES

Clayton-Felt, Marilyn. *Improving Our Schools.* Education Development Center, Inc., Washington, D.C., 1985.

Kinnaman, Daniel E. "Strategic Planning for a New Generation of American Schools," *Technology and Learning*, September, 1991.

 ## SUGGESTIONS FOR FURTHER READING

Fullan, Michael & Miles, Matthew. "Getting Reform Right: What Works and What Doesn't," *Phi Delta Kappan,* June, 1992.

Louis, Karen Seashore, "Restructuring and the Problem of Teachers' Work," in *Changing Contexts of Teaching*, edited by Ann Liberman. 91st Yearbook of the National Society for the Study of Education, Vol. 1. Chicago, IL, 1992.

Louis, Karen Seashore & Simsek, H. "Paradigm Shifts and Organizations Learning: Some Theoretical Lessons for Restructuring Schools." Unpublished paper, 1991.

Louis, Karen Seashore & Miles, Matthew. *Improving the Urban High School: What Works and Why.* Teachers College Press, New York, NY, 1990.

Name _____ Date _____

✔ DISCUSSION QUESTIONS

1. What do each of the following statements mean? (a) What we want. (b) What we believe. (c) What we know. and (d) What we do.

_____

_____

_____

_____

_____

_____

_____

_____

_____

_____

_____

_____

_____

_____

_____

In your opinion, which of the four statements is most important? Why?

_____

_____

_____

_____

_____

2. Why is it essential to analyze and review the grade levels, subject area(s) and department(s) for equity?

_____

_____

_____

_____

_____

3. What is the difference between the awareness level, the knowledge level and the skill level?

_____

_____

_____

_____

_____

4. Identify specific areas or issues that classroom teachers should examine for equity.

_____

_____

_____

_____

_____

5. Identify specific areas or issues that schools should examine for equity (school-wide).

_____

_____

_____

_____

_____

6. What is meant by, "I will see it when I believe it."

_____

_____

_____

_____

_____

7. What is a strategic plan? Why is it needed? Isn't it just another layer of a bureaucracy? Explain.

_____

_____

_____

_____

_____

_____

_____

_____

_____

8. What is meant by the statement, "No one will ever remember how quick you did it, but how well you did it."

_____

_____

_____

_____

_____

_____

SMALL GROUP WORK

Task

Each group (3-4 persons) will randomly select a school. You will be provided with some very limited but specific information about a particular school. You and your group should read the information about your school. Given this information and what your group has learned about the concept of equity; address the following questions. Be as specific in your responses as possible. Your group will need to identify a recorder and a presenter.

1. Your school is interested in addressing equity in their school improvement plan. What factors should this particular school take into consideration in the development of such a plan? Be specific in your suggestions or recommendations.

2. What additional information would be helpful to know about this particular school that is not currently available to your group? Why do you need this information? Be specific.

_____

_____

_____

_____

_____

3. What educational initiatives (i.e., programs, innovations, strategies, policies, practices) should this school actively pursue? Why should they pursue this initiative? Explain.

_____

_____

_____

_____

_____

_____

_____

_____

4. Where would you rate this school on the "continuum of equitable competence?" Why?

_____

_____

_____

_____

_____

5. What professional staff-development plan would you recommend for this school? Be specific and explain your recommendation(s).

_____

_____

_____

_____

_____

6. What does the future hold for this school? Explain your group's response.

_____

_____

_____

_____

_____

MOSBY ELEMENTARY SCHOOL
K-5

Community: 12,745

Suburban community (metropolitan area is 20 miles north)

Community breakdown: 4% ethnic minority population

Total School Enrollment: 312

Mosby is one of three elementary schools in the district; along with one middle school and one high school.

Breakdown of the district: 7% ethnic minority population

Per pupil expenditure: $6,389

Student Breakdown

Less than 1% ethnic minority students (African American)

3% of the students are in Special Education (LD and BD)

6% are receiving free or reduced lunches (based on socioeconomic status)

98% of the students attend school on a daily basis

Staff Breakdown

Full-time principal (female, white)

Full-time teachers (20, female, white)

Part-time paraprofessionals (4, female, white)

Background Information

Mosby is located in a rapidly growing school district, where bond issues have been presented and passed by the community on an every other year basis for the past 6 years. Mosby is located in a strong corporate area (Sprint, Apple Computer, Xerox, State Farm Insurance).

Mosby is a progressive elementary school. They have incorporated whole-language, portfolio assessment and computer technology in the past three years. Each classroom teacher has a computer on their desk. They have a computer lab of 15 stations that are networked and have the capability of communicating with other schools across the country. They have a dynamic principal who came to Mosby when the school opened four years ago. The staff is a mixture of new and veteran teachers. They are now focusing on interdisciplinary teaching, beginning to explore the multi-aged, nongraded school for levels K-3, and introducing a foreign language within three years. There are no pull-out programs at Mosby, all students are integrated into the regular classroom setting. There is a strong parent teacher organization (PTO) with many successful fund-raising initiatives.

Mosby students (91%) score above the State minimum competency assessments in math, reading and writing.

GRADY ELEMENTARY SCHOOL
K-6

Community: 75,000

Industry-based economy

Breakdown of community: 19% ethnic minority population

Total School Enrollment: 356

Grady is one of 18 elementary schools; along with 5 middle schools and 3 high schools in the district.

Breakdown of the district: 21% ethnic minority population

Per pupil expenditure: $2,457

Student Breakdown

64% ethnic minority students (African American, Hispanic and Laotian)

21% of the students are in Special Education (LD, EMH, BD)

53% are receiving free or reduced lunches, based on socioeconomic status—Chapter 1 school

23% of the students are absent each day from school

39% of the students are bused to school

Staff Breakdown

Full-time principal (male, white)

Full-time teachers (32 female-white, 4 male-white, 2 Female-African American and 1 Female-Hispanic)

Part-time paraprofessionals (including 2 Chapter 1 teachers, 1 Special Ed Resource Teacher)

Background Information

Grady is located in the heart of the community, two blocks off of the "main street," nestled between the plastics plant and the fertilizer factory. Grady is an old, established school that was built in 1937. Many of the workers in the two plants attended Grady as youngsters. There is a tremendous amount of pride from the community about Grady elementary school—as they say, "there is a lot of history in those bricks."

Grady is maintaining the instructional focus of strong basic skills, with several remedial programs in place. There are 3 computers in Grady, one of which is in the principal's office. The principal has been at Grady for 17 years and has a reputation as a strong manager. The staff has a relatively high turnover rate (approx. 20% per year); with the major complaints of being burned-out and not enough resources to get the job done. The school has been exploring the year-round schedule for the past two years. Approximately 28% of the resources for Grady come from grants and remedial programs from federal and state levels. Grady is departmentalized by grade level and students rotate to a given teacher for a particular subject. On the average, 15-18% of the students are "pulled-out" for special programs on a regular basis. The Grady staff is now faced with the "inclusion" of special education students this coming year. They feel overwhelmed at the task that this holds for them.

There is a strong community appreciation for Grady; but little involvement can be generated with parent conferences or fund-raising activities. Grady students (47%) score above the State minimum competency assessments in math, reading and writing.

JEFFERSON HIGH SCHOOL
10-12

Community: 28,000

Industry-based economy

Breakdown of community: 9% ethnic minority population

One Community College in the community

Total School Enrollment: 1,175

Jefferson High is the only high school; along with 2 middle schools and 9 elementary schools in the district

Breakdown of the district: 18% ethnic minority population

Per pupil expenditure: $2,890

Student Breakdown

15% ethnic minority students (African American, Hispanic and Asian)

8% of the students are in Special Education (LD, EMH, BD)

21% students are in English as a Second Language (2 days per week)

12% are low-income

8% drop out of school (predominately male)

31% attend a post-secondary school after graduation

13% of the students are absent each day from school

Staff Breakdown

Full-time principal (male, white)

Full-time assistant principals (1 white, 1 African American—both male)

Counselors (2 white males, 1 white female)

Ethnic minority teachers (4 African American females, 1 African American male)

Full-time teachers (32 female-white, 4 male-white, 2 Female-African American and 1 Female-Hispanic)

Part-time paraprofessionals (including 2 Chapter 1 teachers, 1 Special Ed Teacher)

Background Information

Jefferson High is the pride and joy of the community. A tradition-rich school, with many athletic accomplishments and successful graduates having walked the hallways over the past 58 years. Jefferson was once located in the center of the community, but now finds itself more toward the Eastern edge of the city. There have been discussions about the need for another high school; as the enrollments in the elementary schools are at capacity. It is projected by the year 2,000, Jefferson's enrollment will be 2,285 students. The student population is growing at a faster rate than the economy of the community. Dollars are tight, job security is now being threatened more with the advanced technologies that will replace much of the labor force in the community. The city is actively pursuing businesses to locate in the community. There is a growing sense of uneasiness by the community, but a real sense of urgency by the school community.

   The principal of Jefferson is a former graduate of Jefferson High School—albeit 27 years ago. Prior to the principalship, he was a coach and assistant principal at Jefferson for seven years. He has been described as a "traditionalist" in his capacity as principal. The staff is very experienced; with the average years of teaching 17.5 years. The staff is comfortable with the school's current policies and practices — and really do not believe they need to improve much of what takes place at Jefferson. Through surveys, it is apparent that the staff believes that they do a good job, teach well and for those students who happen to academically fail; it is the student's fault because the assistance is there if they choose it.

   Jefferson has one computer lab of 12 stations, but it is used for remediation part-time and serves as the writing lab the other part of the time. Some of the faculty are concerned that too much attention is being placed on the low-achieving student at the expense of the college-bound student. The school has been involved with the effective schools research and have a mission statement that was adopted by the faculty last year. The school is exploring the option of going to a seven-period day (currently a six period day), but scheduling of classes is the main stumbling block. Other initiatives being considered by the faculty and staff are: the six-trait writing system, portfolio assessment, creating a school-within-a-school approach and an advisor-based system. Not all of the faculty are interested in any of these initiatives—clearly one-third of the staff are opposed to any structural or functional changes in the programs currently operating.

There is strong community support for Jefferson High. Athletic events are the activities that hold the community together. A major controversy erupted three years ago with the new policy of "no pass, no play." Little involvement can be generated with parents in other school activities. Jefferson students (77%) score above the State minimum competency assessments in math, reading and writing.

PINE VALLEY HIGH SCHOOL
9-12

Community: 11,500

Agriculture Based Community

Community breakdown: 2% ethnic minority population

Vocational Technical College (20 miles west)

Total School Enrollment: 413

Pine Valley is the only high school; along with 1 middle school and 1 elementary school.

Breakdown of the district: 3% ethnic minority population

Per pupil expenditure: $3,167

Student Breakdown

5% ethnic minority students (Hispanic)

2% of the students are in Special Education (BD)

34% are low-income

19% drop out of school (predominately male)

8% attend a post-secondary school after graduation

9% of the students are absent each day from school

Alcohol is a major concern in the past three years (surveys indicate that over 60 percent of the student body consumes alcohol regularly).

Staff Breakdown

Full-time principal (male, white)

Full-time assistant principal (male, white)

Counselor (female, white)

Full-time teachers (18 male-white, 6 female-white)

Part-time paraprofessionals (special ed, gifted, social worker, school psychologist)

Background Information

Pine Valley is a two-story brick structure that was built in 1928. It has stairways on both ends of the building and is not air conditioned. Several renovations have taken place over the years: new windows, suspended ceilings, new lighting and several coats of paint. At the north end of the building sets the football field, circled by the track. The high school sets in the center of the community. Almost all of the residents attended Pine Valley High at one time or another. The community seems to let the school run itself; almost taking the operation of the school for granted. The statement, "no news is good news" is appropriate when it comes to the community interest in the instructional focus of the school. However, "everyone knows everyone."

The principal has been at Pine Valley for two years, having arrived from a near-by state. This recent development sparked an interest in the community for a brief period, but curiosity has diminished. The principal has been relatively subtle about some of the initiatives that he believes need to be taken at Pine Valley. His philosophy at this point is to develop a rapport with his faculty and staff and not disrupt the current direction of the school. The staff at Pine Valley is experienced and have on the average 15.8 years of experience behind them. The instructional focus is on providing a sound basic education. There are very few "advanced" courses offered in the sciences and mathematics areas. Some of the past initiatives have been seeking accreditation from the state; which required a self-study and committee work to piece together a portrait of their school in report form. In terms of staff development four days are allotted each academic year. In the past, these four days were coordinated with a neighboring school—which eased the cost of a speaker/ or consultant. The faculty can be described as doing a good job without seeing the "possibilities" that could happen in a school like Pine Valley. There is a tendency to see what lies in front of them; rather than what may lie ahead. There are several good teachers in the school, but several have become complacent and comfortable with the way things are. The staff has been discussing the notion of outcomes-based education; but are not convinced that this is needed at Pine Valley. There is a concern by the faculty over the number (19%) of students who drop out. They are seeking assistance on approaches or strategies that should be considered. They also have been trained in the areas of substance abuse. The curriculum that is offered has been very consistent over the past several years; with little change or modification. Pine Valley students (78%) score above the State minimum competency assessments in math, reading and writing.

INDEX

A

A Nation At-Risk 30, 32, 39, 189
AACTE 118
Action Plan for Equity 68
Accelerated School Model 115
Adler, Mortimer 102
Amalgamation 159
Anglo-Conformity Theory 161
Arreola v. Board of Education 238
Assessing Equity: Classroom Application 359
Assessing Equity: School-Wide Application 360
Assessing Intelligence and Ability 107
Assessing the School's Perspective in Bilingual
    Education 234
Assimilation 158
Association of American Publishers 267
At-Risk Students 192
    Academic Performance 199
    Attitudes Toward School 200
    Drug and Alcohol Abusers 195
    Identification Strategies 208
    Involvement with Justice System 201
    Involvement with School Activities 199
    Nature of Family Support 201
    Need for Employment 200
    School Attendance 199
    Student Behavior 200
    Teenage Parents 194
    Youth Unemployment 195
    Prevention Strategies 206

B

Baca, Leonard 232, 237
Banks, James 6,156,166
Bennett, Barrie 323
Bernstein, Harriet 263

Bilingual Education 231
Bilingual Education Act 230
Bills, David 197
Block, P. 317
Borus, Michael 202
Bowler, Mike 262
Boyer, Ernest 40, 102, 110, 112
Brandt, Ron 74
Brown v. Board of Education 38
Business Roundtable 32

C

California State Board of Education 263
Care Team Approach 205
Carlos, J. 237
Carpenter, Susan 202
Castaneda, Alfred 166
Castellanos, Diego 226, 228
Catterall, James 195, 196, 203
Cervantez, Leonard 232, 237
Chapter 1 202, 228
Charter Schools 41
Civil Rights Act of 1964 229, 240
Classroom and School Improvement 323
Classroom Interactions 105
Clayton, Felt-Marilyn 348
Cody, Caroline 260, 264
Coleman, James 58
Collaboration 68, 318
Collier, Virginia 237
Comparative-Group Approach 7
Compensatory Education 202
Conant, James 112
Conklin, Nancy 225
Continuum of Equitable Competence 75
Continuum of Staff Development 325
Continuous Progress Programs 113

Cook, L. 318
Cooperative Learning 114
COPA 117
Correlates for an Effective School 61
Crawford, James 227, 231, 241
Cuban, Larry 197
Cubberly, Ellwood 160
Cultural Pluralism 162
Cummins, James 234, 236

D

Developing a Strategic Plan 348
Devos, G. 156
Diana v. State Board of Education 238
Diversity–A Five Level Approach 167
Dunn, Kenneth, 167
Dunn, Rita 167

E

Edmonds, Ron 57
Education Commission of the States 108
Educational Products Information Institute 260
Effective Schools 42, 59
Effective Staff Development 314
Effective Teachers 99
Efficacy 319
English as a Second Language 231, 237
English-Only Movement 241
English-Plus Movement 242
ESEA 202, 228
Ethnic Minority Groups 157
Ethnic Minority Teachers 118
Ethnic Studies 6
Ethnicity 156
Equality of Educational Opportunity 58
Equity: A Working Definition 10
Equity Action Plan Form 357
Equity and Reform 40
Equity in Education 11

F

Farr, Roger 262, 270
Fields, Joseph 319
Finn, Chester 80
Fisher, Richard 165
Fishman, Joshua 241
Fiske, Edward 31
Fitzpatrick, Kathleen 70
Formulating Strategic Goals 351
Friend, M. 318
Fullan, Michael 316, 322

G

Garcia, Ricardo 238
Gardner, Howard 165
Glasser, William 165
Glazer, Nathan 162
Goldberg, Kirsten 275
Goodlad, John 102, 110
Gonzales, Josue 228
Gordon, Milton 161
Government Accounting Office 192
Grouping and Tracking Practices 109
Growth of At-Risk Population 190
Guttmacher, Alan 203

H

Hayakawa, S.I. 241
High School Graduation Rates 193
Higher Order Thinking Skills 41
Higher Standards and Equity 39
Hilliard, Asa 166
Hodgkinson, Harold 4, 155
Humphrey, Hubert 203

I

Immersion Bilingual Approach 234
Increased Requirements and Equity 74
Increasing the School Day/Year 205
Individual Equity Action Plan 355
Industrial Age & Information Age 35
Instructional Focus 63
Issues of Culture and Ethnicity 166

J

Jacobsen, L. 104
Joyce, Bruce 315, 327

K

Kansas State Board of Education 315, 325
Kinnaman, Daniel 348
Kolstad, Andrew 192
Korentz, Daniel 190

L

Lau v. Nichols 239
Lazotte, Lawrence 59
Learning Styles 164
Legal Implications in Bilingual Education 238
Leibowitz, Ann 230
Lessons Learned 14
Levels of Equity Understanding 356
Levin, Henry 115, 189, 191, 192
Limited English Proficient 230
Lipton, Martin 110
Lippman, W. 272
Local Strategies for Instructional Materials 269
Locus of Control 319
Lortie, D. 317
Louis, K. 318
Lourie, Margaret 225
Love, Ruth 32
Lykes, Bob 193

M

Maintenance Bilingual Approach 233
Making the Grade 32
Mann, Hoarce 5
McCune, Shirley 167
McDill, Edward 202
Melting Pot 158
Meyers v. Nebraska 227
Miles, Mathew 318
Minimum Competency Testing 203
Minority 153
Moynihan, Patrick 162
Mozert v. Hawkins County Public Schools 274
Multi-Age Grouping 113
Multicultural Education 8
Multidimensional Concept of Equity 12
Multimedia 277
Murphy, Joseph 31

N

Nation of Immigrants 157
National Center for Educational Statistics 190
National Center for Health Statistics 195
National Commission on Excellence 116
National Education Goals Report 33, 41
Nativism 162
Nature of the Reports in the 1980s 32
NCATE 117
NEA 238
Nieto, Sonja 154, 166
Non-English Mother Tongues by State 229
Novak, Michael 162
November, Alan 313

O

Oakes, Jeannie 39, 109, 110, 112
One School at a Time 61
Oski, Frank 58
Outcomes Based Approach 41, 69, 70
Owings, Jeffery 192

P

Past Responses to At-Risk Students 197
Percent of U.S. Population by
    Race & Ethnicity 152
Planning Teams 67
Plessy v. Ferguson 75
Policy Information Center of the
    Educational Testing Service 31
Pollas, Aaron 199, 205
PPST 121
Price, Gary 167
Professional Development Schools 121
Purkey, S.C. 60

Q

Quality-with-Equity 64, 70

R

Raising Teacher Expectations 106
Ramirez, Manual 166
Ravitch, Diane 163
Raywid, Mary 324
Reform: Criteria for Progress 43
Reform Cycle of Excellence and Equity 37
Reich, Robert 34
Research About Teacher Education 116
Resnick, Lauren 164
Results Oriented Staff Development 327
Robles, Eugene 195
Rolheiser-Bennett, Carol 323
Rosenholtz, S. 324
Rosenthal, R. 104

S

Sadker, David 271, 274
Sadker, Myra 271, 274
SCANs Report 33
School (site) Based Management 41

School Choice 41
School Dropouts 192
School Improvement 62
Seccord, P.F. 272
Self-Fulfilling Prophecy 104
Shifts in Diversity 155
Shifts in Society 34
Showers, Beverly 327
Single-Group Approach 6
Slavin, Robert 113, 114
Smith, M.S. 60
Smith, G.P. 121
*Smith v. School Commissioner of
    Mobile County Alabama* 275
Spady, Bill 69
State Textbook Adoption Policies 261
State Textbook Adoption Process 264
Strategies to Counter Biased Materials 279
Stereotyping 272
Success for All Program 114
Systemic Reform 33

T

Teacher Centered Instruction 100
Teacher Education Programs 115
Teacher Expectations 103
Teacher Isolation 317
Teacher Testing and Certification 119
Teachers for the 21st Century 32
Technology 276
TESA 107, 327
Textbook Adoption Policies and Equity 262
Textbook Evaluation 270
The Holmes Group 121
The Many Names of Reform 41
The Matter of Time 324
Total Quality Management 42
Tracking 111
Transitional Bilingual Approach 233
Troike, Rudolph 235
Tulley, Michael 262, 270
Two-Way Bilingual Approach 234
Tyack, David 197

U

Understanding Change 322
Unresolved Issues in Bilingual Education 235
U.S. Bureau of Census 151
U.S. Change in Total Population by
    Race & Ethnicity 151
U.S. Crime Statistics Report 193
U.S. Department of Education 33, 40, 191, 196
U.S. General Accounting Office 235
U.S. Total Population by Race & Ethnicity 152

V

Ventresca, Marc 190
Verdugo, Richard 199, 205

W

WASP 160
Wilbur, Gretchen 167

Y

Youth Offenders 193

Z

Zangwill, Israel 158